The Meaning of Lives

The Meaning of Lives

Biography, Autobiography, and the Spiritual Quest

Richard A. Hutch

CASSELL

London and Washington

Cassell
Wellington House, 125 Strand, London WC2R 0BB, England
PO Box 605, Herndon, VA 20172, USA

First published 1997

British Library Cataloguing-in-Publication Data
A catalogue record for this book is available from the British Library.

ISBN 0-304-33917-2

Library of Congress Cataloging-in-Publication Data
Hutch, Richard A.
    The meaning of lives: biography, autobiography, and the spiritual
quest / Richard A. Hutch.
        p.   cm.
    Includes bibliographical references and index.
    ISBN 0-304-33917-2 (hardcover)
    1. Biography as a literary form.   2. Autobiography—Authorship.
3. Spiritual life.   4. Self-realization—Religious aspects.
I. Title.
CT21.H87   1997
808'.06692—dc21   96-52894
                                                                        CIP

Typeset by BookEns Ltd, Nr. Royston, Herts.
Printed and bound in Great Britain by Biddles Ltd, Guildford and King's Lynn

Contents

Preface

Reading and writing lives has the capacity to change the life of the investigator. This book suggests that a spiritual quest is involved in the process of coming to grips with biography and autobiography in particular. Such a spiritual quest takes place along a *trajectory of personal realization*, a course of reckoning with the lives of others from a number of different but related angles of vision at the same time. The trajectory travels across three terrains, or has three major phases. First, it begins by constituting individuals as 'texts,' or unfamiliar accounts of lives that are taken to be basically foreign or different from one's own life story. The text of such remains 'Other': the last thing one assumes it to bear is any possible impact, moral or otherwise, on the life of the investigator. Most professional life-writing and reading of lives has been of this sort, with only several noteworthy exceptions. Simply put, the question is raised of how biography and, to a lesser extent, autobiography are written within the structure of conventional genre requisites that regulate the presentation of individual lives.

Two major requisites for which account must be taken are based upon such life texts understood in the first instance to be foreign or different from one's own personal story, and in the book they are called a record of 'coherent character' and a countervailing account of 'fateful irony.' Biography and autobiography can be easily recognized as stories about the sameness and continuity of a person's abiding character, itself often referred to by modern readers and writers of lives as the 'personality' of an individual, along with ironic twists of fate, or the unplanned or unexpected design of circumstances that would subvert one's best intentions and conscious lifestyle choices. These dimensions of the genre of life 'texts' in general are taken up in the first three chapters of the book. The two dimensions, or genre requisites for the presentation of individual lives, have been traditional canons of interpretation in professional literary biography and autobiography for at least the past three hundred years, but in this book these are given a psychobiographical twist in order to reflect a more modern idiom of presenting lives as 'texts.'

The second terrain or phase of the trajectory of personal realization of lives assumes a different angle of vision. It takes the texts of individuals that have been constructed by the reader and writer of lives and, instead of assuming them to be foreign or different from one's own life story, interrogates them along lines of similarity, even sameness to oneself: 'How is *that* story like *my own*?' Simple things like possible shared nationalities, migrations, vocational interests, family commitments, number of spouses and children, political involvements, class, race, hobbies, gender, and the like may serve to link together the reader and writer of lives to a subject in a personal way, one that presses the edge of familiarity. While differences will remain between the life-writer/reader and the person studied, ties that bind will be likely to appear to the mind's eye that is truly open to see. The question that arises is, How are these connections to be discerned? Interrogating a life about how it might be similar to one's own life is one thing, but a capacity to take this on board, so to speak, and to embrace affirmatively the life of another requires an additional tactic.

Knees may weaken at the risk of being presumptuous but, none the less, some degree of gusto is required to maintain the trajectory of personal realization. The tactic called for is empathy, this being based on cultivating a bodily sense of perceptual relatedness to one's subject. Empathy is an imaginative capacity to place oneself 'in someone else's shoes,' so to speak. In the first phase of managing a life as a 'text,' such a capacity usually is uncalled for, but in the second phase the *body* of the reader and writer of lives is itself the critical factor in the equation. An empathic response to a life requires of the reader and writer of lives experience in the meditational art of introspection, or examining oneself with a view to knowing who one actually is 'in the depths,' at least as much as possible. As empathy conveys the 'Other' to oneself, introspection will resound with an inner voice of solidarity, 'There go I.' Exactly how this can occur is suggested in Chapters 4 and 5, and the project of thinking bodily, even biologically in a broad sense, about lives is carried forward in the remainder of the book. A model of how one reader and writer of lives, namely, Erik Erikson, exemplifies this second phase of the trajectory of personal realization in the course of his study of lives along psychobiographical lines is offered in those two chapters.

The third and final phase of reckoning with lives aims the trajectory of personal realization at matters that are poignantly personal indeed, dare I say, dreadfully existential. The trajectory ends in interrogation of a sort different from the kind of questioning about the 'difference' (phase one) or the 'sameness' (phase two) of lives when compared and contrasted with the life of the investigator. The final interrogatives are about how a life may offer lessons on how to live, how to live more fully each day and have a 'full life.' However, the kind of lessons sought do not pertain merely to the ordinary, daily round of living as conventional wisdom would have it. The lessons do not teach such things as, perhaps, how to get rich, how to stay out of jail, how to raise a good family, how to stop drinking, how to ensure longevity, how to plan for retirement, and the like. The reader and writer of lives who gets this far along the trajectory of personal realization is not concerned about using lives as technical manuals about how to master the world so as to serve one's practical ends in living just in order to 'keep body and soul together,' so to speak. Rather, the point in questioning a life here is to ascertain the relationship that has been engendered between an individual's self-understanding and his or her body, especially those bodily-based existential forces over which little mastery or control is possible. Being born is a force in the face of which a person is powerless, as is dying, and its midwife, aging; and sexuality, as perhaps the most self-evident force (one also as thoroughly biological as the others), cannot be said to be easily contained during the time between birth and death.

Most people take no deliberate lessons from the subtle teachings of these deep currents beneath the surface swirls of daily living. None the less, together, these forces are clearly evident and loudly orchestrated in the lived experience of the body, with telltale signs, like a child's new teeth and an adult's first gray hair here, a positive test for a pregnancy or HIV/AIDS there. Such things mark the score of time. Together, they represent a power that may serve as a point of reference for living. The reference point is outside the self − virtually a transcendent religious object, but at the same time one that is embodied within a person's bodily sense in a real way. Autobiographical reflection becomes incarnational; 'spirit' and 'flesh' become one, so to speak. Such a point of reference, not only being beyond the self but also constituting the body of flesh and blood over time, can focus human awareness on the actual inherent *otherness* of the body. Without a recognition of such an actuality, life, at least for the insightful, could not be meaningfully lived. A sense of personal empowerment would be beyond one's grasp. A person is never quite certain about the extent to which control can be exercized in living, or whether it is oneself alone or fateful existential forces beyond the self's reach, that contribute most to one's identity.

The degree to which any particular subject of life-writing and reading lives draws together such an awareness, however tenuous, represents the cultivation of religious self-understanding, but a worldview that does not necessarily follow from traditional theistic or doctrinal theological or philosophical premises as such. The degree itself to which a reader and writer of lives inquires about this in a subject's life enjoins the investigator in a study of religious life in general. Moreover, insofar as the reader and writer of lives empathizes with such a self-understanding during the process of study, then the processes of life-writing and reading lives themselves become reckonings not only with human limitations and finitude, but also with destructive/malevolent and constructive/benevolent forces in living, and all the variations on the range of existential, dare I say god-like, 'powers' in between. A call to a nontheistic, nondoctrinal theological and nonphilosophical reckoning with an embodied 'Other' is what is at stake. This, then, is what a 'spiritual quest' of one's own is all about. One writer points directly to the presence of such a spiritual quest as an operation of the soul which is evident in reading and writing about lives.

In *The Art of Biography*, Paul Murray Kendall offers a schema of types of biographical writing: 'life-writing' stands midway between the 'scientific' chronicle biography and the 'literary' critical biography.[1] The biographical chronicle is based on the historical factuality of a life – date of birth, name of spouse, vocation, and so forth – while the critical biography emphasizes the actuality of the biographer's attitude or ideological stance towards a subject. Dangers lurk within each of these two types of biography. In the first instance, a life may get lost or buried under the weight of a plethora of historical facts. The individual life becomes but an excuse for writing history. In the second instance, a life may pale in the bright light of a biographer's critical argument. Here the individual life becomes little more than a foil against which the biographer projects his or her own views. For Kendall, however, the major aim of contemporary life-writing should be neither of these two options, but a third, namely, *life simulation*, itself soulful and essentially a spiritual operation:

> The simulation of a life attained by our best biographers grows from the conjunction of heightened perception, the dowry of psychology, and the realization of that perception in the literary projection of experience, the dramatic unfolding of personality-in-action. But the spiritual operation, if I may call it so, which makes heightened perception possible, even more essentially characterizes this mode of modern life-writing. The simulation of the life grows out of a liaison with the subject self-consciously cultivated by the biographer as the *primum mobile* of his enterprise. This liaison I have awkwardly named a simulated life-relationship.[2]

Thus, we may ask, how does a life, any life, measure up to Kendall's standard of life simulation? To what extent do the lives we may study engage in the 'spiritual operation' of life simulation? Furthermore, do they offer to a reader some sort of humane moral and spiritual force by which to live, one that results from their varying degrees of success as biographers?

The possibility of answers to the so-called 'big questions' is offered in this book. It arises from an interrogation of lived experience that is based not on running away from things beyond our control, but facing them squarely with no illusions about the bodily basis of existence, however grim. Grappling seriously with and finally acceding to the natal, sexual, and mortal body can be a source of spiritual awareness that is as close as a heartbeat, one to be felt deeply, and essentially, and strengthened. Reading and writing lives, as a biographical enterprise, finally becomes an endeavor of autobiographical reflection. One comes face-to-face with oneself and sees a body growing older in which dying is foreshadowed and palpable, but a body alive and somehow charged with a mission to live even more fully in the face of the facts. The final chapters of the book, Chapters 6 through 10 (with Chapter 10 being the most speculative and theological one), undertake this specific project, the third and final phase of technique and reflection along the trajectory of personal realization that is available to any reader and writer of lives. Reading and writing lives will change one's life, but mostly those lives for whom lessening the gap between what a life is and what it could become, moving in both directions at once, propels the experiment of living out the only life we have.

This book owes a debt of gratitude to colleagues and friends who have kept at me to bring it to completion, and who themselves have offered collaboration and inspiration along the way. First, I thank Donald Capps who provided much of the thought behind Chapter 1 and for saying not only that the book was a good idea, but also for his confidence in suggesting that it was a book that only I could write. My student, James Freeman, pointed me toward the material in Chapter 9, and he confirmed for me the importance of writing, as he put it, 'body biography,' and linking this to personal and spiritual change. I also thank my overseas colleagues in the history of religions who met in Mexico City in 1995 and those in the clinical psychology of religion who met in The Hague in 1996, and together discussed with me the illustrative materials presented in Chapter 9 and aspects of Chapter 10. Chapters 2 through 8 have gestated for almost a decade. They have come about not only for reasons of scholarly interest, but also because of religious interests related to the body that have for me cropped up, of course, in middle life and which as a result have concentrated and compelled my attention.

This longer standing, more personal aspect of the book owes considerable gratitude since 1990 to members of the Amherst Biography Group, especially to William Kimbrel for conversations on biography and autobiography. The academic hospitality provided to me by the Chairman and other members of the History Department of the University of Massachusetts, Amherst during 1990 enlivened my project. Most of the book fell finally into place during a study leave in Princeton in 1994–95, and special thanks for his encouragement then go to Father Daniel Skvir, a chaplain at Princeton University, and to Bert Keller of Princeton Theological Seminary. My gratitude also extends to the University of Queensland for such study leaves and for other support granted to me for research, and for support from my colleagues in the Department of Studies in Religion and from Peter Fenner of Deakin University.

I also thank my good friend and colleague, Dale Bengtson, who has so far culminated the lineage of my intellectual and spiritual mentors from an older generation. Those guides in my formation who preceded him include Arnold Holgerson, John Vannorsdall, Louis Hammann, and Alan Mermann, all personal chaplains of a sort. For his recent willingness to revive a friendship that had lapsed for for almost thirty years, I thank Thomas Merluzzi, who, it turns out, continues to provide me with personal, intellectual, and professional challenges as time turns our beards increasingly gray. Ongoing thanks also extend to fellow pilgrim and priest, Father John Jillions, especially, and to Deacon John Cryssavgis for nurturing my understanding of the interests pressed in this book since 1986, for drinking beer together with me at Oxford University in 1996, and for introducing me to others who are engaged as well in a similar effort of reading and writing lives in order to live more fully. I offer no apology for the distinctly masculine cast of my intellectual and spiritual lineage.

Brisbane, Australia
January 1997

Acknowledgments

Some parts of the book have appeared previously in scholarly publications, which I gratefully acknowledge here. Portions of Chapter 1 appeared in 'Biography, individuality and the study of religion,' *Religious Studies*, **23** (1987), 509–22 (reprinted with the permission of Cambridge University Press). Portions of Chapters 2, 3 and 6 appeared respectively in 'Explorations in character: Gamaliel Bradford and Henry Murray as psychobiographers,' *Biography: An Interdisciplinary Quarterly*, **4** (4) (1981): 312–25 (© copyright 1981 by the Biographical Research Center); 'Strategic irony and Lytton Strachey's contribution to biography,' *Biography: An Interdisciplinary Quarterly*, **11** (2) (1988): 1–15 (© copyright 1988 by the Biographical Research Center); and 'Reading lives to live: Mortality, introspection, and the soteriological impulse', *Biography: An Interdisciplinary Quarterly*, **17** (2) (1994): 125–43 (© copyright 1994 by the Biographical Research Center). With only minor revisions, Chapter 7 appeared as 'Biography as a reliquary,' *Soundings: An Interdisciplinary Journal*, **76** (4) (1993): 467–85. Even though what my book presents is substantially new material in a revised overall form, I thank the editors of these publications for granting me permission to use portions of my articles, themselves stepping-stones to the book.

It is often said that the only way to get to know other people is to put yourself 'in *their* shoes,' so to speak. This book not only asks readers to put themselves in the shoes of other people. They are also invited to turn the experience of doing so back on to themselves. Great importance is placed on finding a comparative angle of vision for viewing ourselves, and then to using such mirrored insight as a basis for growing beyond the present. Such is the spiritual quest. Thus, I thank R.M. Williams Pty Ltd, Frost Road, Salisbury, South Australia 5108, Australia for the photograph of their well-thought-of locally made boots. The pair pictured was made for Mr Colin Oliver in 1949, and they are still going strong today. May those boots remain an icon of a call to know other people by putting ourselves 'in *their* shoes' (or well-wrinkled enduring boots, as the case may be). And, perhaps, then walking at least a country mile in them.

To Glenda, Jemima and Annabel in Gratitude and Love

1 Biography and religious life

During June 1836 Søren Kierkegaard attended a soirée in Copenhagen where the wine flowed, witty conversation bubbled from every corner, and he himself was at the center of merriment − sparkling, acerbic, enormously entertaining. After the party he returned home and penned the following lines in his journal:

> I have just now come from a party where I was its life and soul; witticisms streamed from my lips, everyone laughed and admired me, but I went away − yes, the dash would be as long as the radius of the earth's orbit ... and wanted to shoot myself.[1]

The most important part of the story of Kierkegaard's life is not conveyed by the parties that he attended, the jokes he knew, or the unquenchable thirst he had for good red wine. Such superficialities were mainly marginal to his life or, as he himself put it, 'in the proper sense of the word I had not lived.'[2] What, we wonder, was central to Kierkegaard's life? How, we ask, might he otherwise have lived? The literary genre of biography, and its sub-genre, autobiography, we shall see, present such issues. In doing so, such writing points in directions that have spiritual bearing (as Kierkegaard insisted all life had), and also in directions useful to scholars of religion and the human sciences, and to practitioners of various religious traditions who reflect upon the nature of their personal commitments to the truths by which they have come to live.

It is this feeling of life unlived, of experience muted by reflection and volatized in imagination, that lay not only at the center of Kierkegaard's life. The feeling is transferable through the experiential idioms of empathy and introspection. It can also be said to describe many scholarly discussions in the interdisciplinary field of religion and the human sciences, discussions in which self-transformation, or 'spiritual formation,' is considered to be central. The problem is how to make such discussions concrete and meaningful, perhaps even devotional or, at least, akin to the depth of thought that was characteristic of the likes of Søren Kierkegaard. How might scholarship go beyond comparative scientific study and have an impact on contemporary human affairs? Short of enacting literally Kierkegaard's journal entry, and going home to shoot themselves, scholars in religion and the human sciences may find this nineteenth-century thinker's stark words an occasion to rethink their own project within the humanities, and in regard to life-writing and reading stories of lives in particular.

The particular discussion offered has to do with a distinction between what can be called 'implicit religion' and 'explicit religion.' Implicit religion is the core or set of personal beliefs and value orientations that sustain an individual and provide guidance, a sense of direction, and/or a sense of belonging in contemporary postmodern times, which is difficult indeed. In popular jargon, implicit religion is often referred to as 'spirituality,' as in 'she is a very "spiritual" person.' Explicit religion is the corroboration of implicit religion by means of interpersonal interaction and collective life. Simply put, and again in popular phrasing, this is a 'community of faith' in action together, giving (usually) institutionalized vent to their shared implicit religion. A people's longing for the sacred, or implicit religion, remains constant, while its institutionalized forms, or explicit religion, come and go with time and place. Once the distinction between explicit and implicit religion is recognized, readers and writers of lives may begin to broaden their understanding of the nature and dynamics of religion in the individual life. This books emphasizes implicit religion, or a person's capacity for spiritual awareness.

This means rethinking the concept of individuality, and those individuals who are engaged in explicit and/or implicit religious life as an idiom of lived experience. It means paying serious attention to the individual as a category of analysis, and how the self undergoes a process of construction and interpretation in biographical and autobiographical texts.[3] Clearly, these genres are major forms of life-writing that specifically draw attention to the individual as a proper focus for scholarly reflection. Indeed, interest in life-writing as a literary genre has recently been reinvigorated by religious studies scholars.[4] The general suggestion to be put here is that the use of writing and reading about individual lives in recent scholarship in religion and the human sciences, not to mention in the field of literary biography, has not only revived interest in the personal, concrete, meaningful side of the study of the world's great religions. It also sets terms of reference for discussions about the nature and dynamics of life-writing and reading lives themselves. Here the 'narrative' of the self is considered, and whether such narrations 'come alive' as spiritual operations for readers and writers of lives, as biographer Paul Murray Kendall suggests they should.[5] The recent popularity of biography and autobiography points to new historical and psychological possibilities for scholarship and personal religious growth.[6] This is particularly evident in the academic study of explicit historical religions and personal narratives of experiences of implicit spiritual transformation.

Another way to put it is to say that scholars who work at the interface between literature and religion are concerned about texts, and about how texts present, express, and shape the experience of individuals. A broad spectrum of types of different texts can be sketched. On the one hand, there are specific sacred texts from the many diverse religions of the world. Included, of course, are autobiographical testimonies, sacred biographies, and hagiographies, each being of interest to contemporary scholars of life-writing and reading. While many of these texts from the world's religions can be linguistic and philological nightmares for textual scholars, they are usually studied in terms of the worldview, or depiction of the cosmos and the place of the human within it, presented by the text, and also in terms of literary quality. Things like the identity and date of the authorship of the text, translations and word meanings, overall coherence, and the logic of any truth-claims made by texts, are some of the scholarly concerns brought to the major documents of world religions. Examples of such texts are the various books of the Old Testament, the Upanishads of Hinduism, the Buddhist edicts of Emperor Aśoka, and the Koran of Islam. All of these texts may, of course, undergo new interpretations, thus fuelling interests in the scholarly pursuit of 'hermeneutics,' or the science of textual interpretation. However, texts of this type remain fixed, and generally do not undergo major structural change through time. They usually represent religions of complex societies, where knowledge about religion is mainly a matter of interpreting a distinct written tradition that is handed down from generation to generation.

On the other hand, there are texts that are more devotional and existential in nature, even without sacrificing their intellectual bearing. The scholarly management of these sorts of texts is different from how the previous types are handled. Fewer scholarly questions are raised (or very different questions are put) about the logical certainty of the claims of these texts, and more emphasis is put on the impact that the text has within networks of personal relationships, including the relationship between the scholar and/or the religious practitioner and his or her personal response to texts. In fact, the literary critical theory called 'reader response criticism' has recently interested scholars in this regard.[7] Examples of such texts may not at first seem to be texts at all, but each functions as a text in conveying the meaning of worldviews of others. One example is Australian aboriginal rock drawings, and another is the liturgical enactments of the passion of Christ by Eastern Orthodox Christians at Easter when the moon is full. These sorts of texts deal with religion less as an historical and institutionalized form, and more as a psychological and personal idiom of spiritual potency. In this case, religion is understood as a timeless phenomenon in life, one that is conveyed more by the direct idiom of lived experience and word-of-mouth than by a written tradition of discourse. In the past, this emphasis has been given expression by the literary genre of the novel (along with the short story and poetry). The writings of Dostoevsky, Camus, Wiesel, O'Connor, and others, who are generally recognized as writers of fiction that has religious bearing, are examples of texts that reach beyond discrete and separate religious traditions. They point to the enduring human character of religious belief and practice in actual operation in a life, and this includes the personal challenge that these texts pose for the scholar who studies them. Not only do these sorts of texts undergo rapid change in actual usage; their immediate impact is not without power to transform a person's worldview. Thus, scholars work within a wide range of types of texts when they study the interface between religion and the human sciences with an aim of wresting meaning out of living. The range itself turns on whether texts are studied in themselves, or whether they are considered as being functionally efficacious to individuals and groups, including the working scholar as well as the religious practitioner.

The specific thesis to be pressed here is that the combination of life-writing and reading is an important 'bridge' between the outer limits represented by the range of texts in religion and the human sciences portrayed above. Together, life-writing and reading are a bridge, because they capitalize on the analytical category of individuality as a focus for study. Kierkegaard points with his surprising final words to the possibility of such a bridge, one that not only maintains scholarly decorum, but also actively sets the stage for the possibility of a life lived amidst a world of unperturbed preoccupation with the self, and with the existential process of recovering individuality. Life-writing and reading, and the comparison of people's stories, can be a vicarious means of sustaining encounters with oneself. Others' stories can serve as 'mirrors' that reflect oneself, characteristics shared, even peculiarities, of a 'common humanity.' As the scholar presses deeper and deeper in search of the facts and feelings of a life, a vicarious adventure into self-exploration beckons. In the proper sense of it, stories of lives – researched and written, or just simply read – can help us to live, and to live more fully. Shared human interests are concentrated in the individual life in biography and autobiography. To work within the genre of life-writing and reading is to challenge the scholar to make the foreign familiar in terms of the abiding touchstone of the full-bodied individual life, which itself can be said to span time and space and cultural differences. The challenge is directed to the heart in silence (*hesychia*), according to the care required in using one's own self as an indispensable tool for investigating another person's life.[8]

In his marvelous book, *Footsteps: Adventures of a Romantic Biographer*

(1985), Richard Holmes describes how, after weeks of imitative effort, he was suddenly struck by the impossibility of ever learning enough about Robert Louis Stevenson, in order to write a biography of him, by walking in the exact footsteps of Stevenson through the French countryside, following the itinerary in Stevenson's diary. Holmes had a dream which he took as a warning not to be so childish and 'literal-minded' in his pursuit of Stevenson.[9] One could not cross literally into the past. Even in the biographer's imagination the gap between past and present was there. It had to be recognized; it was no good pretending. Thus, the biographer 'could not play-act into the past,' he could not turn his work into 'a game of make-believe.'[10] Holmes' introspection produced the insight that 'there had to be another way. Somehow you had to produce the living effect, while remaining true to the dead fact. The adult distance – the critical distance, the historical distance – had to be maintained.'[11] Holmes had never thought about biography before, but tried to engage in it by making it 'a kind of pursuit,' a 'tracking of the physical trail of someone's path through the past, a following of footsteps.'[12] The insight that this could not be done was linked to whom Holmes understood himself to be:

> Have I explained myself at all? It is the simplicity of the idea, the realization, that I am after. It was important for me because it was probably the first time that I caught an inkling of what a process (indeed an entire vocation) called 'biography' really means.[13]

Instead of pursuing another person's footsteps, life-writing and reading bring alive a life by other sorts of skills and crafts and sensible magic. One can never catch the footsteps of another; no, never quite catch them. 'But,' says Holmes, 'maybe, if you were lucky, you might write about the pursuit of that fleeting figure in such a way as to bring it alive in the present.'[14] Our job now is to try to specify such luck, the luck cherished by Holmes' methodological insight, his empathy with his subject and introspection into himself.

The history of reading and writing lives, in which biography in particular predominates, has precedents for the emphasis on individuality and a deepening self-understanding. With the publication of James Boswell's *The Life of Samuel Johnson* in 1791, a debate about the nature of biography was initiated. The debate included the view of James Stanfield, whose only written work on the genre of biography, *An Essay on the Study and Composition of Biography* (1813) took a stance opposite to that of Boswell. We shall continue to appreciate the 'bridge' that is constituted by biography (and autobiography) if the existential nature of individuality is first recognized, albeit faintly, in the work of these two thinkers.

Boswell stressed the importance of historically accurate facts as the source and major criterion of true biography. His book about Johnson illustrated this stance. Said Boswell of his own method, 'I cannot conceive a more perfect mode of writing any man's life than not only relating all the most important events of it in their order, but interweaving what he [i.e., Johnson] privately wrote, and said, and thought.'[15] Through such a mode of writing, Boswell believed that he was enabling humankind to see Johnson 'live, and to "live over each scene" with him, as he actually advanced through the several stages of his life,' and thus to see him 'as he really was.'[16] Biography was not, wrote Boswell, merely to write Johnson's 'panegyric, which must be all praise, but his life; which, great and good as it was, must not be supposed to be entirely perfect.'[17] While Boswell introduced into life-writing a concern for historical-critical accuracy, he also aimed to recover vicariously a sense of Johnson's lived experience and to share it with his readership. Ideal biography was to be 'authentic history,' not the gloss of 'panegyrics,' let alone popular hagiography. Insofar as biography was what Boswell wanted it to be, the genre would be a bridge that linked the individual to the first of our two types of texts, namely, the text that is approached in itself, perhaps typified by the fact-filled 'scientific' chronicle biography.[18] Boswell was less interested in texts as 'simulations' of lives that could impact personally on individuals and groups than he was in making biography good historiography. Any personal meaning that he received from working on the life of Johnson was merely a curious but unpursued aside.

A different view of life-writing and reading lives is that of James Stanfield. He argued that the pursuit of accurate facts, strung along a chronology of life events, is less important than it was, perhaps, for Boswell. Stanfield's view was that biography originated in the mind of the biographer, usually in a way conducive to devotion and personal uplift. He pressed the edge of the 'literary' critical biography, one that approximated hagiography.[19] The true criterion of biography, argued Stanfield, is its didactic value, or its capacity to teach moral improvement. A biographer uses a life in order to offer a lesson to the public. In effect, while Boswell can be said to have countered the religio-literary trend of the panegyrics of his previous century, when laudatory descriptions of lives, usually those who were 'martyred' during the English revolution, were required, Stanfield resurrected the power of the ideals displayed by outstanding men and women of Britain. For Stanfield, people's characters were conditioned by the ideals of character with which they associated:

> The constitutional and moral circumstances of early youth have the chief influence in the formation of character. ... The impressions they received do, by situation, incline or strengthen the disposition to be peculiarly excited by circumstances of a similar nature ... in the continuance of this process of action

and reaction, a cast of permanency is given to the character, modified by the strength and duration of the impression, the susceptibility of the disposition, and the power of resisting the influence of contravening influences.[20]

Because one can be influenced by another person, biographies had to accentuate themes that were conducive to building good characters, especially in youth. Thus, writes Stanfield, it is the job of the biographer 'not only to describe, but connect, not only to narrate, but philosophize.'[21]

Therefore, biography 'bridges' Boswellian verisimilitude, with its stress on the authentic facts of a life ('chronicle'), and possible Stanfieldian lessons about the personal moral meaning of a life ('critical biography'), thereby itself laying emphasis on what biographer and literary scholar, Leon Edel, calls the biographer's 'commemorative emotion.'[22] The world's religions, including contemporary new religions, have usually been founded by individuals who push given limits and whose lives thus make headlines and good stories. Religion itself is also a response by both the living and the once alive to the limitations and possibilities of our shared human existence, and to the possibility of achieving a sense of immortality amidst life, in spite of a lack of certainty about the metaphysical underpinning of such a conviction. Our emotions, as Edel implies, are stirred by commemorating exemplary individuals. Insofar as Boswell and Stanfield pointed in the direction of the existential nature of individuality, or the lived experience of the self, they were both major biographical thinkers. Each portended further work in linking together life-writing and reading lives, biography in particular, with a preoccupation about reading and writing lives oneself as a spiritual quest.

Comparative biography: in quest of *homo religiosus*

Not many scholars of religion work with biography, but those who do often have dual interests in psychology and history.[23] Psychology and history are taken as avenues into the study of cultures, which include religious beliefs and practices. In the past, if such scholars were to assign themselves a professional label, then most would have been fairly comfortable with the hybrid and maverick-like term, 'psychohistorian' or, of less pretension, 'psychobiographer.'[24] This particular professional label has become generally accepted by those who are engaged in using psychological methods for studying historical phenomena. Scholars in religion and the human sciences generalize the designation, and demonstrate interests in the history and psychology of religions, without abandoning psychohistorical or psychobiographical preoccupations.[25] The major focus of their work is primarily on the study of individual leaders of religions.[26] Thus, while scholars like E.R. Dodds and Zevedei Barbu have directed their attention to the psychological styles of selected historical epochs (i.e., the first centuries of the Christian era and the sixteenth century in England respectively), others have been concerned with the more circumscribed analysis of individual religious personalities.[27] Some individuals who have recently been studied are the medieval contemplative, Thomis à Kempis; the American man-of-letters, Ralph Waldo Emerson; Jonathan Edwards, the eighteenth-century leader of the American 'Great Awakening'; the nineteenth-century founder of the Theosophical Society, Helena Blavatsky; Jemima Wilkinson, who formed a personality cult in America along New Light Baptist lines at the time of the Revolutionary War; and Elisabeth Kübler-Ross, who advocated the study of death and dying, and who pressed the point that we all have a lot to learn from the terminally ill.[28] This is but a short list of compelling individuals who represent different emphases of explicit/implicit religion. The list is illustrative of the range of biographical work being done in religion and the human sciences. What, then, is the basic interpretive style that is evident in such life-writing and reading?

Let us take the case of Friedrich Nietzsche, with special reference to fragments of autobiographical writings that were written during his incarceration in a mental asylum in the last decade of his life.[29] These fragments represent a vindictive exposé of the decadence of his German Lutheran heritage. His early incestuous relationship with his sister, Elisabeth, which enabled her to dominate his adult life, reveals to Nietzsche in a very painful way his inability to transcend his background in spite of his profound sensitivity to its moral bankruptcy. This brief description of what is significant in Nietzsche's relationship to his sister indicates cursorily the basic interpretive style of the 'bridge' of biography (and autobiography) as it focuses on individual personalities and their explicit and implicit religious bearings. One notices that very much in evidence in the use of biography to study the religious life is Erik Erikson's emphasis on the dynamic interaction between the *personal experiences* of the individual and the *historical milieu* to which that person may be responsive. Erikson's work on Martin Luther and Mohandas Gandhi is well known.[30] The Eriksonian emphasis can be illustrated by a study of the founder of the Theosophical Society, Helena Blavatsky.[31]

Blavatsky's restless wandering following failures as wife, mother, and novice spiritualist in Europe during the first half of her vagabond life predisposed the woman to be unusually responsive to the unstable religious climate of nineteenth-century America when she arrived there in 1873 for a stay that was to last for five years. The emotional effects stemming from the absence of clear guidance in religious matters were intensified by the historical situation: religious traditions in America, which had been sustained through years of Puritan hegemony, underwent collapse. Blavatsky stylized her founding of the Theosophical Society in 1875 according to her less than conscious identification with Russian Orthodox Christianity, which greatly guided her formative childhood years in Russia; and also according to indigenous pre-Christian Russian and Indian traditions of shamanism. The historical instability of America, touching her at that particular juncture of her life, triggered the creative act of founding the Society. In retrospect, Blavatsky looked like a Russian Orthodox 'holy woman,' a virtual female *starets*, which was a role unheard of pertaining to women in Russia and America alike. Therefore, Blavatsky's restless orthodoxy of adulthood can be understood by focusing on the interaction between important personal experience and an unstable historical milieu, and how a dynamic resolution occurred in the form of her new self-understanding and religious leadership in society.

Having noted the basic method involved in reading and writing lives as a bridge between the objective and subjective circumstances of the individual, it is now possible to indicate the value of this kind of study in the context of studying the religious life, from its explicit communal outcropping to the implicit faith of individuals. Ultimately, the proliferation of such studies will reveal the precise role played by individual religious personalities in the development of religious thought and institutions in any cultural orbit. While sociological and economic theories have become heuristic tools in historical study, psychological theories have been neglected. Thus, while our understanding of movements, organizations, and institutions, say, in the development of Christianity has reached great sophistication, our understanding of the religious individual remains crude and largely anecdotal (e.g., Luther was an 'earthy' individual; Calvin was a 'cold and distant' person, etc.). But the proliferation of these studies will have an even greater contribution to make in efforts to describe and to delineate some working hypothesis about the nature of *homo religiosus* in the West as well as in the East, and to suggest how Eastern and Western understandings may differ. By *homo religiosus* is meant the inherent spiritual responsiveness of the human character to sacred and profane dichotomies in lived experience. That is, one comes to take lessons from all the most powerful moments in living (both 'good' and 'bad') which, themselves, may lend a person meaning by which to live, intuitive direction/goal-setting, and an overall sense of spiritual empowerment.[32] The point is that humankind is to be taken as religious (not political, economic, psychological, etc.) in the first instance. More general assertions about the nature of the religious personality will be able to be made on the basis of increasing the number of individual and comparative studies. Thus, in a manner analogous to the pioneering efforts of Harold Lasswell to describe the political personality, these kinds of studies will contribute to understanding the religious personality.[33] Such studies aim at depicting implicit religion, or the 'spiritual quest.'[34]

Three ways in which progress is being made on specifying the place of the religious personality in society and culture, and on giving substance to a cross-cultural model of the religious personality, can be suggested. Each way is but a beginning, or first steps on a journey of reflection about reading and writing lives as a spiritual quest. The journey will proceed in subsequent chapters, and move to conclude that a personal appreciation of dying is the key to living more fully. Dying is an individual's most powerful, often poignant, existential focus for reckoning with a lived sense of 'otherness,' a crucial dimension that is inherent in personal experience. For now, however, we must start at the beginning of such a journey of reflection and take up the three ways that the religious personality is coming to the fore in work of scholars who are engaged in reading and writing lives.

Bridge to religious thought and institutions

The first of the three uses of life-writing and reading in religion and the human sciences relates especially to the continuities between personality and the development (at least) of Western religious thought and institutions. Preliminary investigations suggest that there are certain gross similarities in the personal experiences of such major religious personalities as Augustine, Abelard, Goethe, Schleiermacher, Newman, Kierkegaard, Nietzsche, and Schweitzer. For example, intense biographical study suggests that a significant number of these figures experienced the loss or prolonged separation from one or both parents in infancy or early childhood. In addition, the personal documents of religious figures such as Goethe, Gorky, Schweitzer, Newman, and Buber reveal the unusually decisive influence of either a grandmother or grandfather in their spiritual development. These 'findings' could have enormous implications for the study of Western religious thought and institutions. Clearly discernible links exist between these personal experiences and mature theological reflections, and the affiliative behaviour of the individuals who had these experiences. The loss of one's mother in infancy or early childhood frequently establishes in these religious individuals a lifelong pattern of yearning for maternal support. Similarly, the loss of one's father frequently appears in the adult life of the individual as a persistent longing for paternal guidance. Unusual reliance on a grandparent rather than one's natural parents (a psychological phenomenon which early Freudians called the 'reversal of generations') tends to indicate a nostalgia for an earlier, more reliable historical era than the present. Most important, these yearnings, longings, and nostalgia find their way into theological reflections of the individual. In addition, they influence not only their affiliations with existing religious institutions, but also their roles in the creation of new movements and organizations.

The Jewish theologian, Martin Buber, provides a good example of this link between the personal experiences and mature reflections of a religious individual.[35] Buber's parents were separated when he was three years old. In his earliest memory, he recalls standing on the balcony of his grandparents' home in the company of a girl several years older than himself. He had confessed to her his belief that his mother, from whom he had been separated a year earlier, would some day return to him. But the girl disagreed with him. Over the course of the next ten years, while he was being raised by his grandparents, he became increasingly convinced that not only would his mother not return but, in a more profound sense, she *could* not return. This conviction was borne out twenty years later when his mother came to visit him. He saw in this returning the tragic illustration of the word he had coined − *Vergegnung*, or 'mis-meeting' − to designate, as he put it, the failure of a real meeting between men. He said, 'I could not gaze into her still astonishingly beautiful eyes without hearing from somewhere the word "vergegnung" as a word spoken to me ... I suspect that all that I have learned about genuine meeting in the course of my life had its first origin in that hour on the balcony.'[36]

In contrast to this 'mis-meeting' between mother and son, Buber experienced the meaning of real encounter in his relationship with his grandmother. Buber's grandfather was 'a true philologist, a "lover of the word,"' but his grandmother's love for the genuine word affected the child even more strongly: because this love was so direct and so devoted.[37] This love for the 'genuine word' was especially evident in his grandmother's relationships with other people: 'To the glance of the child [Buber] it was unmistakable that when she at times addressed someone, she really addressed him.'[38] Reflecting, therefore, on her sensitivity to direct and genuine communication, Buber clearly intimates that his grandmother first wakened in him an intuitive understanding of the '*I−Thou*' relationship, the backbone of his theological thought.[39] Thus, in contrasting his relationships with his mother and grandmother in his early formative years, Buber himself noted the critical link between his personal experiences and his mature religious thought.

This example of Buber points in a rather elementary way to the continuities between the personality of the individual and the development of religious thought. On the basis of more fully developed analyses of these sorts of continuities, it would be possible to show that psychology and philosophy and theology are not simply analogous at certain points, but that the psychological dimension − the personal experience of the individual, especially insofar as it taps into what William James called 'religion,' namely, 'the feelings, acts, and experiences of individual men in their solitude, so far as they apprehend themselves to stand in relation to whatever they may consider the divine' – penetrates to the very core of such intellectual systems.[40] The contribution of such analyses would therefore be that of showing how an unusual sensitivity to personal experiences has played a decisive role in the development of religious thought.[41] A similar case could be made for the integral relation of personal experiences and the development of religious movements and institutions, where the cross-cultural study of religious leadership and particular leaders would be important.[42]

Bridge to sacred biography and hagiography

The second way of making headway in studying life-writing and reading and religious life by focusing on the individual religious personality concerns sacred biography and hagiography, more of which appears in Eastern than in Western religious traditions. There is a noticeable lack of studies about specific individuals in Hinduism, Buddhism, and other Eastern traditions. Not only do specific personalities tend to drop out of the picture, but there is also little concern for the historical development of religious thought and institutions. Possible continuities between a person's experiences and the intellectual and institutional life of Eastern cultures are not readily apparent.[43] However, the proliferation of sacred biographies in the East is remarkable. Sacred biographies, which are primarily about saviors and founders, like the Buddha and Lao-tsu, depict the embodiment of distinctly new religious ideals. Hagiographies, which mainly concern the lives of saints, kings, mystic prophets, and other charismatic figures, present subjects as individuals who have realized, perhaps in a distinctive way, an image, ideal, or attainment already recognized as worthy by some religious community. The key to understanding such a focus is to recognize that cultures carry models or paradigms within their networks of symbols and language. Members of those cultures use the images of selfhood to stabilize their lives and to reflect upon their identities. Also, these inherent patterns of culture, or 'narratives of the self,' are effective means of transmitting the life of an exemplary figure to succeeding generations. Involved is myth-making by cultures and the interpretation and appropriation of myth by individuals. The presence of sacred biographies and hagiographies within cultures potentiates the possibility of hero-worship.

For example, in the Chinese context hagiographies of various monarchs are organized to highlight the virtues (or, in some cases, the vices, as in demonologies) that are associated with the subject and with his position in the history of his dynasty. Similarly, in the Buddhist tradition biographies of the various disciples of the Buddha are organized to highlight the particular virtue, attainment, or vice which that disciple exemplified in classic form. Thus, Sariputta is presented as a paragon of wisdom; Moggallana as pre-eminent in the possession of magical power; Ananda as the prime exemplar of compassion; and Devadatta as the embodiment of evil. In the Christian tradition too there are numerous accounts of the lives of saints which are usually topically organized, with the acts of individuals recounted in terms of virtues such as 'humility,' 'obedience,' 'poverty,' and so forth.[44] An emphasis on the formulaic biographical pattern hardly precludes the use of text-critical and other objective scholarly methods for penetrating various traditions of sacred biography and hagiography in order to develop empirically accurate historical accounts of religious figures. However, this is particularly difficult to do in cases of Eastern religious figures because of their emphasis on culturally based models of individuality rather than on historical accounts of specific individuals themselves.[45] It may be the case that when searches for the historical individual 'behind' the biographical ideal fail to show clear results, we end up seeing the importance of the more devotional or, at least, existential impact that such texts necessarily have on those to whom they are sacred.

Psychological and historical issues can be effectively combined in studies of sacred biographies and hagiographies. Ernst Kris's *Psychoanalytic Explorations in Art* (1952) is a classic example.[46] Kris draws on the tradition represented by the work of Otto Rank and Joseph Campbell, namely, myths of the hero as an archetypal biographical pattern. Kris notices a connection between the biographical pattern in medieval and Renaissance biographies of artists, and the mythical ideal reflected in pre-eminent sacred biography in the religious culture. In an apocryphal gospel of Jesus, the Lord is portrayed as sculpting clay birds into which he thereupon breathed life. According to Kris, Jesus himself is the mythical ideal behind the biographical pattern of the medieval and Renaissance artist. Kris recognizes historical development within the biographical patterns, and he takes note of historical connections between such patterns, and an exemplary figure as portrayed in a sacred biography. New patterns may emerge out of older patterns, and this can lead not only to consistency but to entirely new patterns altogether. The same strategy can be easily carried over into texts within Eastern religious traditions.

Bridge to world theology and the life-writer/reader

The third and last area in which the study of life-writing and reading and religious life hold promise is the effort to describe and delineate a working hypothesis of a cross-cultural model of *homo religiosus*, one in which a world theology that binds all religions together in kind is implicit.[47] A common construct in personality theory is the typology (for example, Jung's 'introvert' and 'extrovert'). Following Lasswell's efforts to devise a typology of the political personality (he suggests three types, the agitator, administrator, and theorist), it seems reasonable to anticipate that a similar, albeit more dynamic, phenomenologically grounded typology could be devised for the religious personality. Thus, on the basis of an informal factor analysis of the personal documents of more than twenty recognized religious figures, one important example of such a study found it possible to differentiate four dominant dispositional factors of self-understanding: resigned self, chastized self, fraternal self and aesthetic self.[48] This typology, which is based on the belief that autobiographical texts express the religious personality, is but one small step toward delineating the basic and persistent conviction that at bottom individuality, or the human character as such, has profound, albeit implicit, spiritual bearing. Thus, one may speak and write about 'spirit' not only as a theologian or religious believer/ belonger, but also from the position of a humanist. In another similar study, a typology that combines the individual personality with social structures that are related to the formation of new religious movements and established traditions of religion is offered.[49] In-depth studies of many figures may reveal alternative or more fundamental characteristics of *homo religiosus*. The concern here is simply to suggest that comparative biographical studies of religious individuals in their historical contexts can be expected to contribute to the attempt to specify the distinctly religious.

But the anticipation of a proliferation of such studies, leading to more profound understandings of the role of the individual in the development of religious thought and institutions and contributing to specifying the nature of *homo religiosus*, is not the only justification for engaging in this kind of academic enterprise. Each biography is intrinsically valuable and is able to shed light on other academic approaches to the study of the individual. Consider the work of the biographers of Ralph Waldo Emerson, the nineteenth-century American man-of-letters. Curiosity about the man has been deflected by scholars into tracking only Emerson's literary reputation, in spite of any intentions they might have to understand the man himself.[50] For a start, in 1949 Ralph Rusk published a treasure-trove of a biography about all aspects of Emerson's life. However, Emerson's individuality is obscured by this chronicle of overwhelming detail about his historical epoch. Henry Pommer similarly neglected Emerson's indivi- duality in favor of focusing on his first marriage, a period of only two years, in a short biographical vignette of 1967. Psychological analysis is unwittingly invited by Edward Wagenknecht in 1974 when, without much psychological sophistication, he tells us that he wishes to deal with the character and personality of Emerson. However, Wagenknecht ends up by portraying Emerson only as a balanced soul, which would seem to leave poor Emerson as a lifeless bore! Joel Porte's biography of 1979 carries on as the others did. Emerson is portrayed in terms of his literature, and that is taken as a symbolic expression of Emerson's life which Porte reduces to nothing other than all that is typically American, whatever that means. Hence, Porte's study further obscures Emerson's individuality by turning the record of his life into moderate hagiography. Generally, Emerson biographers have all but invited comparative biographical approaches to the study of the religious individual.[51] Such approaches, added to the previous ones, could renew efforts to evaluate Emerson's contributions not only to American literature, but also to Western religious experience.

Another equally important justification for the study of the religious individual is its contribution to the intellectual and emotional integration of the investigators themselves. This issue was mentioned earlier. It invites the scholar to go beyond scholarship alone. Here the scholar is beckoned to a spiritual quest. That biographical study can contribute to the *general* intellectual integration of the researcher should be self-evident, inasmuch as the comparative study of religious figures will require a broad familiarity with the theological, political, and literary currents of an era. But it is also likely to enable intellectual integration in more concrete, perhaps unanticipated ways. For example, in ways that I myself could not have anticipated in advance (and here I must be personal regarding the suggestion being made about reading and writing lives in this section), my own biography of Ralph Waldo Emerson in 1983 carried me into some of the concerns of the history of religions and specifically the concern of cross-cultural studies of religious leadership. Emerson's trip to England immediately prior to his entry into American public life in the mid-1830s raised the whole problem of the mythical significance of travel in general and ritual pilgrimage in particular. Also, Emerson's peculiar preoccupation with his eyes and all things visual, including a traumatic period of psychogenic blindness when he was twenty-two years old, made him particularly responsive to Plato's allegory of the cave as a personal worldview. Allusions to that allegory occur throughout his writings and it is itself another myth and ritual complex that cuts across many religious traditions, especially those of Western antiquity.

In addition to the mythical and ritual dimensions of Emerson's vocational conflicts, his leadership of the Transcendental Movement in American cultural history articulates another area of scholarship within the history of religions, namely, the typological study of religious leaders. While his contemporaries like Søren Kierkegaard, Freiderich Nietzsche, and John Henry Newman may have identified with martyr images, Emerson identified with the image of the seer, a type of religious authority and leadership that was highly valued in pre-Christian and gnostic religions of the ancient Greco-Roman world. The troubling limitations that Emerson perceived within Boston Unitarianism, in which he had labored as a minister for about a decade, can be understood in the light of his identification with the role of the classic seer, with his view that 'faith is a telescope,' which permitted a wide horizon of personal and historical meaning.[52] Thus, life-writing and reading may enable the student of individuality to integrate seemingly diffuse and unrelated intellectual interests.

The study of individuals, especially with a view to making comparisons between individuals, may also contribute to the personal growth and spiritual formation of the scholar/biographer. In the field of religion and the human sciences, the value of 'examining' one's actions and responses in encounters with oneself and with others as a means of achieving greater understanding is frequently stressed. The study of significant religious figures sets the stage for a similar kind of examined experience. It provides an effective means of cultivating in the investigator a sensitivity to the deeper psychological nuances of his or her own response to the 'Other.' As Leon Edel suggests, even the choice of a subject for study raises the question of the investigator's own emotional involvement, and this goes for any field of intellectual endeavor.[53] Erik Erikson adds that the choice of a subject reveals personal biases which cannot and ought not to be expunged by a methodology which is faultless. On the other hand, inasmuch as 'any *reviewer* of a bit of history makes it his own by the mere circumstances of his selective attention, a reviewer trained in clinical observation must account — at least to himself — for his own initial writing of history.'[54] Such accounting is itself a spiritual quest.

Thus, the process of reading and writing lives requires the scholar not to remove his or her subjective involvement or empathic engagement from the study of lives. Rather, it is the mandate of the investigator to examine the whole gamut of conflicting attitudes and motives that enter into an intense and prolonged encounter with a notable religious figure, or a similar encounter with several at once. Whatever the outcome may be, the methodological clarity of the future depends on one's present capacity to challenge the limits of specific fields of scholarship, and to exercise the capacity to work beyond the boundaries of tried and true approaches to biography, individuality, and the study of religious life, or some other field. This bridge links together texts for objective scientific study about individuals and appropriates these for personal integration and growth. Such implicit religious integration and growth of the individual is called throughout this book the 'spiritual quest.' Such an endeavor, I believe, is a worthy hedge against the impoverishment of contemporary postmodern literary and religious thought. Such studies in literature and religion, which would claim to be interdisciplinary, even multicultural in nature, bear little moral impact, and thus leave the student of lives adrift in an existential vacuum. Such a condition can be arrested insofar as we learn to read and write lives as a personal spiritual quest, one that will involve learning through the lives we study that 'dying' together is a means to 'live' more fully. However, we must first begin as life-writers and readers of lives, and then learn how to take hold of and constitute an *individual as a text*, one that can be written and read as a personal means of filling our existential vacuums with meaning, direction, and a sense of spiritual empowerment. How to construct the individual as a text is what Chapters 2 and 3 offer. Later, how such *biographical construction* ('reading/writing' lives) may actually become *autobiographical reflection* ('living' life) for the reader and writer of lives will be considered. As this shift occurs, the spiritual quest as a trajectory of personal realization can be gradually brought to awareness. The suggestion will be that this has to do primarily with a person's appreciation of his or her body as a idiom of intuition and knowledge.

2 Searching for coherent character

What are the abiding and unique features of a life? How might these be ascertained? These questions arise out of the biographical interest to bring coherence to the facts of a life, and to suggest some sort of overall pattern of sameness and continuity that appears to the intelligent reader and writer of lives to be evident in that life over time. In the history of biography studies, this coherence has been traditionally called a person's 'character.' Character is one of two components in the biographical construction of an individual as a text. The other component is 'irony,' which will be taken up in Chapter 3. Two biographical thinkers in particular bring the search for coherent character into sharp focus, namely, Henry A. Murray and Gamaliel Bradford.

Not only does each thinker raise the question of coherent character. They also represent twentieth-century expressions of the touchstone in the history of reflection on the nature of biography that was articulated by James Stanfield a hundred years earlier. Stanfield, of course, sought to write a life with a view to its overall moral meaning, which itself would be worthy of emulation by readers, especially young ones who were undergoing education for life.[1] We have noted in Chapter 1 that Stanfield's work came close to foreshadowing the complicity of biography and implicit religion, and was in part a precursor of reading and writing lives as a spiritual quest in a way that James Boswell's work was not.

Henry A. Murray, the psychologist of Harvard University, was thirty years the junior of Gamaliel Bradford, a relatively obscure early twentieth-century biographer from Wellesley, Massachusetts. Murray's reputation has become well known, especially since the publication of his now famous book, *Explorations in Personality*, in 1938. As if he wished to rank amongst the giants of the early days of psychological science, Murray dedicated his book to several of them: Morton Prince, 'who had the vision, raised the endowment and was the first director of the Harvard Clinic,' to Sigmund Freud, 'whose genius contributed the most fruitful working hypotheses,' to Lawrence J. Henderson, 'whose expositions of scientific procedure established a methodological standard,' to Alfred N. Whitehead, 'whose philosophy of organism supplied the underlying generalities,' and to Carl

G. Jung, 'whose writings were a hive of great suggestiveness.'[2] Each graphic characterization was an expression of a part of Murray's sense of himself as a multifaceted psychologist and, more significantly, a student of lives in a less than professional or technical sense.

However, few people today have heard of Gamaliel Bradford, and he hardly ranked himself amongst the greats of any single academic discipline, let alone the discipline of psychology. None the less, his biographies were extremely popular amongst Americans who were nostalgic for the waning Victorian era when hero-worship, which was made popular by the biographies written by Ralph Waldo Emerson (and by Emerson's 'hero,' Thomas Carlyle in England), was rife. (Such a cultural backdrop goes far to explain the Olympian nature of Murray's dedication above.) After the First World War, however, such nostalgia could be readily identified by the new burgeoning psychological establishment as 'neurotic' and 'regressive.' Biographies like those Bradford wrote might all too easily be pushed aside, or relegated to a nineteenth-century style, and therefore considered to be only archaic psychologizing at best or useless idolatry at worst. Bradford was a humanist and a man-of-letters in an Emersonian sense. He believed that discovering the coherence of a person's character would open a window to the truth of human nature in general. Not one to regard his work as inferior to any, Bradford considered *all* humanistic disciplines his special province: he considered himself a scholar of human 'Character,' as he himself put it. As a scholar on the look-out for a person's essential character, Bradford was concerned about such things as 'temperament,' 'demeanor,' and 'mood.' A generalizable trait appeared, he believed, throughout a person's life, even within the purportedly least significant events of that life. Just as Murray could so easily characterize the meanings of his mentors in single lines of dedication, so too did Bradford labor before him to offer portraits of the essential personality styles of individuals whom he studied. A similar concern for characterological description appeared about the same time in anthropological discussions. They were concerned less with individuals and more with the character of entire cultures. Perhaps the most outstanding representatives of such a trend were Ruth Benedict and Clyde Kluckhohn. Benedict's *Patterns of Culture* (1934) and Kluckhohn's study, 'Myths and Rituals: A General Theory' (1942), served to counter the usually unwitting nineteenth-century bias toward employing historical and evolutionary presuppositions in ethnographic research. Such thinking appeared in the work of anthropologists like E.B. Tylor and J.G. Frazer, and it undergirded their descriptions of so-called 'uncivilized,' 'primitive,' or 'savage' races. Nowhere in the work of Bradford or Murray does evidence of a similar elitist intellectual style of the past century appear.

Bradford's greatness lies in the fact that his work in biography was a portent of ideas generated in the field of psychology, indeed, amongst biographers and psychobiographers, almost a decade after his death in 1932. It is this mode of inquiry, the mode of searching for a person's coherent character, which not only is a vestige of nineteenth-century hagiography and the 'hero-worship' implied by the 'Great Man' theory of historiography, but also the major avenue of investigation of the American biographer, Bradford (1863–1932), and the American psychologist, Murray (1893–1988). It is possible to suggest that Murray's psychological notions were prefigured in Bradford's biographical sketches. Moreover, Murray's psychology, when taken as a whole, can be understood to be contained within the domain of Bradford's original biographical program. Therefore, Murray's psychology can be understood more as an elaboration of Bradford's notions about biography, perhaps, than as a unique construction outside the boundaries in which turn-of-the-century biographers, at least Bradford, found themselves. The integrity of historical reflection that traces its lineage back to Stanfield's work would thereby be sustained.

Both Bradford and Murray came to their professions later than their peers, and after failing to find satisfying successes doing other things. Their lives evidence fairly clear 'turning points' which were not without similarities.

It was not until 1912 and the publication of *Lee the American* that Bradford's career as a biographer suddenly crystallized and set him to the task that would command his fullest attention for the next two decades of his life. Frail and shy, Bradford adopted literature as his life's work at the age of nineteen when ill-health obliged him to leave Harvard College. This was at the outset of his first year there. His mother had died of tuberculosis by this time and his attachment to her had been special and very important, if only by dint of their shared constitutional frailty. However, there seems to be more to it than physical frailty. By dropping out of Harvard, Bradford symbolically withdrew from a father's aspirations for a son and joined his mother in a fitting obscurity. Bradford's father was the fifth Gamaliel Bradford in succession of a line that extended back through seven generations to Governor William Bradford of Plymouth Colony. Young Gamaliel's father considered the career of a poet and man-of-letters to be 'unpatriotic.'[3] Bradford's father had made a success of himself in banking and political writing, and he was probably disappointed that he could not expect the same sort of success of his only remaining son, who was more like his wife than himself.

For about thirty years after withdrawing from Harvard, Bradford labored passionately in the face of constant discouragement, and largely in vain, writing poems, novels, and plays until after his fiftieth year, 1912. After 1912, the year he happened on to the biographical genre, his literary work in the area makes an impressive list:

On men in the Civil War:

Confederate Portraits (1914)
Union Portraits (1916)

On women:

Portraits of Women (1916)
Portraits of American Women (1919)
Daughters of Eve (1930)

On English poets:

A Naturalist of Souls (1917)

On Americans:

American Portraits (1922)
Damaged Souls (1923)

On varied figures:

Bare Souls (1924)
As God Made Them (1929)
The Quick and the Dead (1931)
Saints and Sinners (1932)

Longer studies:

The Soul of Samuel Pepys (1924)
Darwin (1926)
Dwight L. Moody: A Worker in Souls (1927)

Posthumous publications:

Biography and the Human Heart (1932)
Elizabethan Women (1963)

Perhaps it was his odd little book of 1895, *Types of American Character*, that predisposed him to try to express biographically the possible national personality types which he believed were available to Americans of his day − 'The American Pessimist,' 'The American Idealist,' 'The American Epicurean,' 'The American Philanthropist,' 'The American Man of Letters,' 'The American Out of Doors,' and, with notable international zest, 'The Scholar.' In the Preface to this particular book he writes, 'I am afraid that some of the essays breathe a spirit of gloom and melancholy. This I am sorry for; for I have come to feel that the two things most desirable and most to be cultivated in this world are love and joy, and I believe that it is possible to cultivate these things far more than we now do.'[4] Like Ralph Waldo Emerson, Bradford thought of himself as a 'naturalist of souls,' an astute observer of humanity. We shall return to this in a moment. In any event, when he happened on to biography he discovered his most fulfilling vocation, and probably cultivated love and joy to boot.

If Bradford's life suggests the designation of 'sudden blossoming' after years of waiting, the life of Henry A. Murray can be characterized as one of 'gradual unfolding,' especially after 1927. In 1915 Murray graduated from Harvard with a major in history, after which he enrolled in the Columbia College of Physicians and Surgeons, graduating at the head of his class in 1919. He received a master's degree in biology at Columbia and taught physiology at Harvard for a brief period. In a not insignificant sense, Murray's early career as a physiologist, all while on his way to teaching psychology at Harvard, parallels the career of a predecessor there several decades before, namely, the philosopher of pragmatism and psychologist, William James. It is a curious omission from Murray's list of dedication that James's name is not included there. James's personal and professional interests were tied up in reading and writing lives that had religious bearing. The treatise of his Gifford Lectures, *The Varieties of Religious Experience: A Study in Human Nature* (1902), is an outstanding example of such an intellectual focus. The book is a classic in the field of study known as the psychology of religion. Nevertheless, James's life and work will figure prominently in a subsequent chapter, as not only is Murray connected to the Jamesian style of biographical interests that are linked to religious experience, but James himself, as we will suggest, points the way for those readers and writers of lives who come to realize that their work involves cultivating an implicit religious life for oneself, or engaging in a 'spiritual quest.'

After two years of internship at Presbyterian Hospital in New York City, Henry Murray took a position on the staff of the Rockefeller Institute for Medical Research. He then went to England where he received a Ph.D. degree in biochemistry in 1927. Of his experience as an intern, Murray recalls that he spent more time than was considered proper for a surgeon 'inquisitively seeking psychogenic factors in my patients.'[5] His career required, however, that psychology be put aside, and it did not come up again, he reported, 'until I began to wonder, after several years of research in biochemistry and physiology, why some of the men with whom I was associated at Rockefeller Institute clung so tenaciously to diametrically opposing views about the simplest phenomena.'[6] It was Carl Jung's book, *Psychological Types* (1933), which, he continued recalling, provided 'a partial answer to my question' and 'started me off in earnest toward psychology.'[7]

After conversing with Jung in Switzerland about this matter, Murray returned to the Rockefeller Institute. A year later, in 1927, a man with a transformed outlook accepted an invitation from Morton Prince (who had recently founded the Harvard Psychological Clinic) to become an instructor of psychology at Harvard. In 1928 Murray became Director of the Psychological Clinic and by 1935 he had completed training in psychoanalysis, helping to found the Boston Psychoanalytic Association.

The publication of *Explorations in Personality* (1938) occurred during Murray's forty-fifth year. His career unfolded swiftly thereafter. No doubt his long-standing interest in Herman Melville's novel, *Moby Dick* (1851), had much to do not only with the mythological dimensions of American culture, but also with his own vocational queries. According to Murray's interpretation of the novel, Ahab represented the primitive and largely evil forces that operate in humankind, and these clashed with the moral forces within each and every individual and within the institutions which they have created, their society. These moral forces, of course, are represented by the white whale. Just as Ahab sought to subdue the spirit of the whale, so too did early studies attempt to thwart Murray's fullest creativity: 'At college a bud of interest in psychology was nipped by the chill of Professor Munsterberg's approach.' Murray continues to report that during the second lecture he looked constantly toward the nearest exit and, besides, he reasoned at the time, 'there was more bread (and fewer stones) in biology and chemistry and afterwards in medicine.'[8] By 1928, Murray had begun to free himself from the harpoons of his earlier vocational commitments. At that time he began to flourish, so to speak, in the deep and largely uncharted sea of psychology.

What, then, is the nature of Bradford's method in biography and Murray's method in psychology? In what sense does Murray's work serve to elaborate the work of Bradford in the general search for coherent character in the lives of biographical subjects? How would each begin the work of the biographical construction of an individual as a text?

After 1912 Bradford worked his trade in biographical sketches in his solitary office in Wellesly Hills, Massachusetts, amongst 'the sum qualities or generalized habits of action' of many well-known people from Robert E. Lee to Saint Francis of Assisi.[9] Bradford called his biographical sketches 'psychographs' or, more specifically, 'condensed, essential artistic presentations of character.'[10] He was convinced that although a person might appear to a biographer to perform in inconsistent ways from time to time throughout his or her life, underneath such apparently random activity lay an essential and enduring coherent 'character' which could be recognized and adequately stated by the sensitive biographer. The result of doing so would be to draw together or to unify the subject's life by pointing to a central line of continuity within it, that is, a general theme which would provide the form for the story that a psychographer could tell about that particular individual's life. Out of the perpetual flux of actions and circumstances that constitute a person's whole life, Bradford suggests, psychography 'seeks to extract what is essential, what is permanent and so vitally characteristic' of a life that, to simplify it a bit, the 'psychographer endeavours to grasp as many particular moments as he can and to give his reader not one but the enduring sum total of them all.'[11] Indeed, Bradford implies that this totality is greater than the sum of its parts, greater than the events of a life which may lend it occasions for expression.

An illustration of Bradford's psychographic method should suffice to crystallize and convey the nature of his particular biographical style. One sketch, published in 1922, is of Mark Twain, whom Bradford recognizes as one of America's most popular humorists. After examining the course of Twain's life and literature in the space of a twenty-five-page essay, he declares Twain's 'essential character' to be one of qualified 'desolation,' at least more so than one of basic laughter by which, incidentally, Bradford felt Twain's life was mistakenly remembered by most Americans. Attempting to set the record straight, Bradford becomes the dramatic artist when he thinks about Twain. Bradford reported that he himself 'cannot escape' the image of 'a person grasping in the dark' with his hands 'blindly stretched before him, ignorant of whence he comes and whither he is going, yet with it all suddenly bursting out into peals of laughter' which, Bradford suggests, in such a situation, have the 'oddest and most painful' affect.[12] No, the source of Twain's humor cannot be his propensity towards laughter that the public so commonly attributed to him. Bradford points to Twain's own writings in order to lend cogency to his argument. He suggests that Twain himself could turn his own attention to his basic melancholy: 'Everything human is pathetic. The secret source of humour is not joy, but sorrow. There is no humour in heaven.'[13] Therefore, the thematic line of Twain's life might read like the following psychograph, namely, 'desolation' or, more pointedly, 'laughter masking sorrow.' This, then, would be the essence of Mark Twain's coherent character, or a typical pattern of sameness and continuity over time that could be evident to the intelligent reader. Even though the life has an ironic flavor, Bradford is not concerned about dealing with any sort of sustained ambiguity or contradiction. After all, the unity or coherence of character is the paramount object of Bradford's scholarly searchings.

What of Henry Murray's work? The question is, how does Murray appear unwittingly, but perhaps explicitly, to formulate Bradford's biographical program of 'psychography' in more up-to-date psychological ways? How does Murray himself get down to the work of the biographical construction of an individual as a text?

In his Introduction to 'The Case of Earnst' by R.W. White, Murray suggests that the method White uses in discussing that case follows this simple principle, namely, that 'by observation of many parts one finally arrives at a conception of the whole and, then, having grasped the latter, one can reinterpret and understand the former.'[14] Murray refers to the psychological investigator who uses this line of investigation as a 'biographer.'[15] The biographer writes up his report on a particular case and then brings it into a group discussion where it is analyzed and elaborated. The goal sought by all the discussants is 'insight.' After this was completed in the case of Earnst, 'the biographer,' according to Murray, 'read his "psychograph" of the case.'[16] Though the word 'psychograph' is shared with Bradford, Murray evidently took no account of the fact that his psychological use of the term had been preceded by its use within the scholarly tradition of literary biography, specifically by Bradford several decades before. Murray explains that although 'the term "psychograph" has been used by G.W. Allport, A.A. Roback and others to stand for a list of rated traits (comparable to our list of scored variables),' he and his group of researchers used it 'to mean "abstract biography." '[17] Abstract biography is later understood to be the same thing as the answer to the question, What is personality? – 'since the proper conceptualization of a human life (abstract biography) *is* the personality so far as it can be scientifically formulated.'[18] Keeping this in mind, one needs to pay greater attention to Murray's psychological notions so that his concept of personality comes more clearly into view, and hence becomes available for use by readers and writers of lives.

Murray never referred to his general psychological approach as 'psychography,' as Bradford did in regard to his own particular biographical approach to reading and writing about individual lives. Bradford entitles the lead essay in his book, *A Naturalist of Souls*, 'Psychography.' Instead, Murray refers to his psychology as 'personology,' because his emphasis as a psychologist is about the 'study of human lives and the factors that influence their course, which investigates individual differences and types of personality ... the science of men taken as gross units (*sic?*).'[19] Therefore, personality is defined as 'the hypothetical structure of the mind, the consistent establishments and processes which are manifested over and over again (together with some unique or novel elements) in the internal and external proceedings which constitute a person's life.' Murray summarizes this by saying, 'personality is not a series of biographical facts but something more general and enduring that is inferred from the facts.'[20] Reading lives and life-writing involve not reducing a life to terms of coherence that are extraneous to it, a view of sameness and continuity over time that just does not add up or 'fit' the facts. Rather, character formulations grow organically out of the rich surfaces, and also usually from the deep subsoil, of how an individual 'presents' to a biographer. This also involves how he or she is 'presented' by reading and writing that life over time.

Bradford and Murray share the term and the general meaning of 'psychograph.' They also share self-understandings as 'biographers.' In addition, Murray's idea of 'personality' and Bradford's idea of 'character' are virtually identical. Therefore, at the level of basic definition, coincidences between Murray's personology and Bradford's psychography serve to make each thinker appear as a version of the other. However, though it would be proper to say that Murray was a biographer, it would be less appropriate to refer to Bradford as a psychologist. For a start, Bradford never claimed to be a psychologist. Perhaps claiming to be a psychologist never entered his mind. At the turn of the century, Havelock Ellis was calling biography a branch of 'applied psychology,' and bewailing the fact that most life-writing and reading appeared to be uninformed about the work of psychologists like 'Wundt, G. Stanley Hall, Munsterberg, and Jastrow.'[21] Explicit familiarity with psychologists and psychological terms and concepts is not evident in Bradford's work.

Furthermore, if Bradford was aware of the existence of biographies written by psychologists, then he perhaps unwittingly disclaimed any similarity between his professional creativity and their output. For example, Freud's psychoanalytic biography of Leonardo da Vinci appeared in 1916.[22] At the same time, Bradford's works were beginning to be published. However, Bradford makes no mention of Freud's important biography of Leonardo, which started an entire sub-genre, namely, psychoanalytic biography; and he continued to show no influence in his later life-writing and reading from the more precise methodological work subsequently developed for biography by the entire psychological establishment. According to John Garraty, who writes about the interrelationships between psychology and biography, although the organized discipline of psychology since the late nineteenth century has had an impact on biography, this impact occurred only during the 1920s, of which Katherine Anthony's *Margaret Fuller* (1920) and Leon Clark's *Abraham Lincoln* (1933) may be the most popular.[23] This was considerably after Bradford's well-forged die had been cast. However, Henry Murray's work developed within this new professional context of psychoanalytic biography (the harbinger of modern psychobiography), and he claimed himself to be a biographer as Bradford before him had been bound to be. Insofar as Gamaliel Bradford understood himself clearly as a biographer, one could argue that his work represents a long-standing tradition in life-writing and reading, namely, the search for coherent character. Moreover, a case could also be made following this that Henry Murray's psychological contribution aligns with this particular biographical tradition. How, one might ask, does Murray himself elaborate the coincidence suggested above without being quite aware of doing so?

Murray's contribution to the biographical tradition can be recognized in the form of his theoretical suggestions regarding inherent structural characteristics of the personality. None the less, because the history of the personality *is* personality, as he suggests, then structural considerations must never be allowed to be viewed as separable from the dynamics of individual life-histories. Murray's structural theory of personality dynamics is clear. Essentially a theory of motivation, 'needs' are forces which either act upon or avoid internal or external sources of 'press.' These Murray has listed, and his list includes such needs as 'achievement,' 'affiliation,' 'play,' 'order,' 'sex,' and the like. All of these human needs are determinants of behavior within the individual personality. Press, on the other hand, represents the significant determinants of individual behavior within the environment. For example, presses may include such ones as 'family discord,' 'inclement weather,' and 'religious training.' The way in which configurations of presses and needs are handled by the investigator so as to arrive at abstract biographies is by using the structural concepts with which Murray organizes lives. These structural concepts are 'thema' and 'unity-thema.'

A thema, says Murray, is the 'dynamical structure of an event,' involving a combination of a particular press and a particular need 'on a molar level.'[24] In other words, it is a pattern or a thematic structure that is evident in specific events of one's life, but which can also be said to typify a life over time (for example, 'She is a pushy woman'; 'He is a manipulative man'). While it would be possible to apprehend a thema for any particular fleeting moment of a person's life within the confines of Murray's definition, a thema becomes more significant for purposes at hand when it is wrenched out of the context of particular presses and particular needs. This is precisely what Bradford urged by emphasizing that his psychographic 'portraits' were not really portraits of persons as they appeared only at one moment during their lives. Instead, Bradford claimed that his psychographs were sketches of how individuals appeared throughout the entire course of life – their 'essential character' or their characteristic thematic lines, as psychological thinker, Erik Erikson, might put it.[25] With the notion of 'unity-thema,' Murray attempts to meet a similar requirement in the context of his personology.

By unity-thema Murray means a 'compound of interrelated – collaborating and conflicting – dominant needs that are linked to press and to which the individual was exposed on one or more particular occasions, gratifying or traumatic, in early childhood.' Murray continues, 'The thema may stand for a primary infantile experience or a subsequent reaction formation to that experience.' Then he arrives at the most significant point for purposes at hand by suggesting that whatever the nature and genesis of a unity-thema, 'it repeats itself in many forms in later life.'[26] This last suggestion is crucial if one is to employ Murray's concept of unity-thema in its explicit form in the biographical context established by Bradford. Though it would appear that Murray is staging his discussion upon Freudian planks, his last sentence permits one to regard the dynamic nature of a coherent character, as the axis of a personality, in non-Freudian terms as well. This maneuver enables one at the same time to apprehend the unity-thema of an individual's life in terms of needs and presses. Thematic lines of individual lives can now be explained explicitly by pointing to their location within the concrete and unfolding history of particular lives, from birth to death (as well as from within possible transpersonal and non-Occidental parameters of living) without dwelling on any single event which may differ somehow from all other life events. In other words, while themas characterize a single need and press combination (it might be referred to as a life 'event'), unity-themas trace lines of continuity and sameness between those combinations, from 'event' to 'event.' This happens in the context of an entire life, not merely during the first five or six years (as Freud believed) or during any other specific 'moment' thereafter.

Incidentally, here is one dominant pillar supporting Erik Erikson's particular psychohistorical style of biography. A pillar, by the way, that permits him, for example, to talk about sixteenth-century Protestant reformer Martin Luther's 'fit in the choir,' and thereby speculate about Luther's fainting episodes when he was required at choir duties in his monastery – as discussed by Erikson though all other Luther experts remain in great disagreement about whether Luther ever actually underwent such peculiar and unnerving personal experiences. Erikson points to the 'characteristic' nature of the event of Luther fainting in the choir of his monastery in the overall context of Luther's life. Thus, Erikson permits himself to 'read into' Luther's early years probable psychological and social realities on the basis of firmer historical and biographical knowledge about Luther's later years. Structurally speaking, this is a reasonable means of approaching the problem faced by readers and writers of lives, professional biographers, personologists, psychographers, and other thinkers alike, namely, having only scant recorded 'evidence' to go on.[27]

Erikson aside (his own important work on reading and writing lives will be taken up in a subsequent chapter), the work of Gamaliel Bradford and Henry Murray may also be located as part of one of two major traditions that, as we noted briefly in Chapter 1, constitute the broad tradition of reading lives and life-writing in general. The two traditions that are referred to are those initiated generally by James Boswell and James Stanfield. The final point to be made is that Bradford and Murray appear to pick up on and lend voice to the Stanfieldian tradition of reading and writing lives. At its base, searching for coherent character in lives is what this particular tradition is all about, and it has in the past come closest to expressing implicit religion in motion, so to speak, or on its way to becoming a 'spiritual quest.' Gamaliel Bradford found his major inspiration in the nineteenth-century 'naturalist of souls,' Charles Augustin Sainte-Beuve (1804–69). 'The man is so profoundly interesting to me,' writes Bradford in 1921, that

> his work has been, on the whole, so much more stimulating and suggestive than any other books whatsoever and has been such a main factor in the evaluation of my own psychography, that I feel as if I want to be intimately acquainted with every fibre of his nature, and rarely has there been a soul so subtle, so complicated, and so difficult to become acquainted with.[28]

If this is the man whose work so inspired Bradford, even compelling him to embrace it as his own, then attention should be given to what this first 'naturalist of souls' had to say in his own right during the early part of the nineteenth century.

Briefly put, Sainte-Beuve emphasized sketches, or short pieces ('portraits') instead of lengthy narratives, in which other life-writers include much historical documentation and pieces of conversation taken from the writings of their subjects. Another way of putting it would be to say that Sainte-Beuve hedged on reading and writing lives solely on the basis of a Boswellian historical-critical preoccupation, or with an emphasis on 'scientific' chronicle biography. As a literary critic, Sainte-Beuve believed that criticism was 'the study of character as that was revealed in literature'; and the motto seized upon later by Bradford, and which he used to characterize his own style as a man-of-letters, was this: '*J'analyze, j'herborize, je suis un naturaliste des esprits.*'[29] This motto was that of Sainte-Beuve, perhaps the only idol who would have inspired Bradford to pen a line of prose in French. Sante-Beuve sketched individuals for the purpose of depicting the essential dimension of his *own* humanity in a mode of romanticism. Rudiments of the introspective art of biography are evident here. However, although the literary genre of biography gets close to 'life simulation,' it cannot be said to achieve it.[30] It stalls on the mark of 'literary' critical biography insofar as the romantic cultural consciousness of Bradford's times held sway. As Bradford himself put it years afterwards, the basis of biography is 'solidly established in the common identity of the human heart.'[31] He and Sainte-Beuve were spiritual brothers.

By subordinating narrative to his shorter pieces, Sainte-Beuve (and, for that matter, Bradford too), though extensively researching diaries, letters, and so forth, relied mainly upon intuition rather than methodical inferences from the facts of lives as he went about forming his creations. As he developed this emphasis, Sainte-Beuve displayed an affinity toward the work of his contemporary, Thomas Carlyle. Of Carlyle's method in biography, the report of Richard Altick, a literary scholar, lends insight. Altick believes that Carlyle's biographies were 'spiritual profiles,' or the 'imagined result' of his passion to discover men 'larger than life,' who were governed by 'super-human gifts and missions.' Carlyle's conception of human personality, Altick believes, was 'too feverish' ever to be confined to the 'facts as they appeared in the historical records.' Instead, 'the Carlylean obsession with a reality that lies behind appearances transfigured his subjects into simulacra at once unhistorical and unreal, visions rather than images.'[32] Therefore, not only did Bradford look to Sainte-Beuve for inspiration, but also to Thomas Carlyle, whom Bradford believed was also infused with the same tradition of intuition in reading and writing lives, and also in professional biographical scholarship.

It can be said that the tradition of biography which is expressed both in Bradford's psychography and in Murray's personology is fundamentally an intuitive one, even though this is less clear in regard to Murray than it is in regard to Bradford. After all, Murray's personology has had vast implications for empirical psychological testing.[33] However, Murray's own personal formation, which was almost protean in scope, suggests that he, like Carlyle, insisted that 'the substance and spirit of a man's life demanded to be explored, not with the pedantic charts provided by the formulas and categories of "mental philosophy" but with the intuition of the sensitive human being responding to the records of another.'[34] Murray himself intimates the Carlylean position when he suggests that 'a psychologist who believes that he can tell the truth without being "literary" has only to try writing a case history or biography, and then compare what he has done to a character sketch by any novelist of the first order.' Murray adds the insight and its subsequent lesson that 'a little humility here would add to our stature as psychologists.'[35] When intuition issues forth in creative imagination then academics, and psychologists in particular, can discover that they too might approximate literary subtlety. The qualitative balance tips in the direction of the biographical genre: psychologists can learn much from creative literature, but 'biography,' concludes John Garraty, 'with its stress on both artistry *and* accuracy, can, in its finest form, be a still better teacher.'[36] Bradford, and Murray after him, represent two fine examples of teachers within this tradition who would seek coherent human character through their art of life-writing and reading lives.

3 Sensing fateful irony

If a reader and writer of lives was able to ascertain a coherent character in an individual subject, would that be the end of accessing a life? Individuals often act, so to say, 'out of character.' Their anomalous behavior, and other aspects of demeanor, cause investigators to wonder whether the character portrayed is really adequate to the task. Thus, any investigators who are worth their salt must stand in readiness to interrogate their subjects again and again, and also to do so in the spirit of developing an empathic bond with another human being. A question mark arises from evidence – even the possibility of evidence – of an individual's life that would fly in the face of the coherent character that was originally, or initially, postulated by the reader/life-writer. While one may search for character coherence in a life, one must also keep open the possibility of alternatives as a life is researched and written. In spite of an expected reaction, a biographical subject may often be overtaken by an opposing fate, or by the power of an irony that appears to have preordained events. Life has some unexpected twists, ones that challenge a reader and writer of lives always to sense the fateful irony that would subvert the coherent character of a subject. Searching for such subversions is linked to the interrelationships between biography and psychology in the recent history of biography studies, a history that goes back about a century.

The response of life-writers/readers to modern psychological science and discourse has been a topic of considerable interest to scholars since the Second World War. Halting efforts to use psychological ideas in reading and writing lives were made early in the century, but they proliferated in the postwar era.[1] The work of John Garraty on the interrelationships between psychology and biography is well known, as is that of Leon Edel on the use of psychoanalytic ideas, especially the idea of 'transference,' in the art of biography.[2] The language of scientific psychology, however, must be recognized to be erected unwittingly upon older, longer-standing traditions of reading and writing lives. Psychological reductionism is easy to slip into, and thus is a great danger faced by the biographer (*cum* autobiographer). But an appreciation of the nature of the literary genre of biography, especially of some of the major historical and structural trends of life-writing in the nineteenth and twentieth centuries, can serve to check inappropriate 'psychologizing.'

The point pressed here is that best use can be made of psychological insights into biographical subjects, or the individuals who are read and written about, if those insights are offered in the spirit in which they first entered into the history of such undertakings in Western culture. While the achievements of James Stanfield and James Boswell (viz., the historical critical accuracy of biography, or the genre of the 'chronicle'), along with the permutations of these by the likes of Bradford, Murray, Sainte-Beuve, Carlyle, Emerson, and others, were noted in Chapter 2, a similar suggestion is made in this chapter. Here, it is argued that such a moment in the history of biography when psychological insights proper get wedded to the study of lives by professional literary biographers is represented by the life and work of the Englishman, Lytton Strachey; and that his use of what can be called 'fateful irony' in writing about figures of Victorian England virtually opened the door to post-Second World War interest in possible connections between psychology and biography. Strachey's almost melancholic preoccupation with himself, as this was gradually displaced onto the stage of literary production, was transformed into a new distinct style of reading and writing lives, that is, strategic deployment of hostility toward professional authority as a literary device for analyzing individual lives. Strachey virtually single-handedly gave consummate expression to the ironies of his subjects' lives, and thereby further developed the art of biography.

Fateful 'irony' was to become, after coherent 'character,' the second of two major components of the biographical construction of an individual as a text. The fullness of a life text would now be a combination of portraying 'character' and suggesting the nature of any of its inherent 'irony.' What is irony, and how is it fateful in Strachey's approach? Irony is a sophisticated form of hostility, defined as a feigned ignorance that is designed to confound or provoke.[3] Such hostility can range from light humor to sarcasm or satire. It probes human weaknesses, not strengths, and seeks out the subterranean opposites that constitute the 'depth' of a life, surface appearances notwithstanding. The strategy of using irony in his biographical narratives maintained (sometimes created) a distinction between Strachey the working biographer and the subjects towards whom his hostility was directed, and upon whom his unique literary craft worked. Yet, such a distinction was not given but achieved, and the achievement was never as clear and as permanent for Strachey as he might have hoped.

Lytton Strachey unwittingly introduced fateful irony into life-writing and reading lives at the turn of the century. Irony, or the sense that something exists to render a life ironic in whole or in part, has become a powerful device by which the analysis of an individual subject becomes an interminable activity of interpretation and participation in a life (a position toward which Stanfield inclined), or just a life's records (the less ambitious Boswellian project). Strachey's contribution to the history of reflection on reading and writing lives amounts to a cultural hermeneutic, or guidelines according to which the writer and reader of lives can claim personal meaning from the text by identifying with the circumstances that contributed to its creation. And remember, by 'text' is meant not only the story that one reads, but also the person more or less 'simulated' by the writer and reader alike.[4] The individual whose life is narrated is thus said to 'live' or to 'come alive.'

As a strategy of expressed hostility, irony is perfect for portraying ambivalence in greatness. Irony is marked by a revealed play of unseen but deeply sensed opposites. It denies any univocal meaning, theme, appearance, or characterization that a life-writer/reader may possibly invoke in order to construct a description of a life. Strachey's legacy to us – what Leon Edel calls 'New Biography' – is that by means of sensing and seeking out the ironic in what is popularly believed about an individual, by implying something markedly different from first impressions, occasionally even the opposite of what is the public's general view, Strachey 'made space,' so to speak, in how individuals may now be encountered in texts about them.[5] Such space, as an 'empathic opening,' is evident in Strachey's biographical narratives, and the space becomes a threshold to a new kind of discourse about reading and writing lives. The use of psychology in biography is one current attempt to give shape and force to this emergent discourse.

Backdrop: two approaches to lives

Most of those who read and write lives fall short of Strachey's hermeneutical mark, perhaps because the time was not, or currently is not, as historically potent for them as it had been for him.[6] According to Eileen Overend, Strachey's literary reputation rests traditionally on *Queen Victoria* (1921), and his general popularity is due to *Eminent Victorians* (1918). Strachey became secure in his person and art so that, says Overend, 'the distancing irony' of his early Victorian portraits mellowed into 'sheer warmth' by 1928 when *Elizabeth and Essex* appeared.[7] Other readers and writers of lives, however, failed then as they may fail now to find such a secure place within themselves and within the practice of their art. The problem is that students of lives, including professional (usually literary) biographers, are prone to stereotyping. Henry Murray describes a parallel situation in psychology. What he calls 'trait psychology' is to psychology what stereotyping is to life-writing and reading lives. Says Murray,

According to my prejudice, trait psychology is overconcerned with recurrences, with consistency, with what is clearly manifested (the surface of personality), with what is conscious, ordered, rational. It minimizes the importance of physiological occurrences, irrational impulses and beliefs, infantile experiences, unconscious and inhibited drives as well as environmental (sociological) factors. Hence, it does not seem fitted to cope with such phenomena as: dreams and fantasies, the behavior and thought of children and savages, neurotic symptoms (morbid anxiety, phobias, compulsions, delusions), insanity and creative activity (artistic and religious). It stops short precisely at the point where a psychology is needed, the point at which it begins to be difficult to understand what is going on.[8]

To seize upon traits, or recurrent and continuous patterns that are evident in a life, or what earlier was called coherent character, precludes genuine understanding of the rich and variegated nature of individuals. While claims are usually made that the depth-dimension of a figure is presented, what remains is merely a stereotypical description of the 'surface of personality.'

It is useful to distinguish two approaches by which readers and writers of lives construe their subjects and face up to the problem of 'surfaces and depths' in lives. On the one hand, there is what can be called the *unidimensional biography*. This approach emphasizes traits and engages in stereotyping for the purpose of locating a subject's single most motivational value(s), predominant personal style in all things, or specifying a person's coherent character over time. Many recent life-writers have crafted their subjects in terms of an 'identity crisis,' an 'approach/avoidance conflict,' 'depressive episodes,' and the like. To use Edel's phrase from psychoanalysis, the 'transference relationship' between a life-writer and the subject breaks down, with the life-writer virtually 'constructing' his or her subject by using an intuitive psychological method, almost like a novelist creating a protagonist or a psychoanalyst submitting to a 'counter-transference.' Such a method lends itself to the charge of projectionism, where there is a tendency toward uncritical construction, or construing a life so that it fits into and illustrates some prior conception or didactic point that the life-writer wishes to make, often the facts of a life notwithstanding. 'Projective tests' in psychological diagnoses are based on similar assumptions about what counts in a life.

The approach of unidimensional construction is not new. Culture-bound models or paradigms of the ideal (or less than ideal) self are notable in ancient sacred biographies and hagiographies. Life-writers, including autobiographers in Greco-Roman antiquity, have long been in the habit of stylizing lives according to the current cultural and historical horizons of meaning that are represented by models of selfhood, or popular images of what constitutes a good or bad person.[9] This approach has as its major nineteenth-century proponent and spokesman not only the famous Thomas Carlyle who espoused biographical 'hero-worship,' but also the less well-known theorist of biography, James Stanfield.[10] For Stanfield, of course, people's characters are conditioned by the ideals with which they associate (for example, Abraham Lincoln, associated with honesty, is portrayed as 'Honest Abe'). The particular association that is described by the life-writer/reader is of his or her own making, constructed usually for didactic ends. As Stanfield puts it, the biographer's job is 'not only to describe, but connect; not only to narrate, but philosophize.'[11] In this way, reading/ writing lives is used to sharpen the cutting edge of the particular worldview, along with its inherent values, mainly of the investigator. Here is present the 'literary' critical biography, but by the same token the 'scientific' chronicle and the 'simulated life' types of biography are noticeably absent.[12] Moreover, when faced with modern psychology the unidimensional approach risks charges of being reductionistic insofar as psychological concepts contribute grist to the mill of construction, by which itself a life is rendered in ways perhaps not wholly in accord with the actual life lived.

On the other hand, the second way to construe a life and to manage the problem of 'surfaces and depths' in lives can be called the *multidimensional approach*, where biases more like those of Henry Murray may prevail. Here, anything like biographical hero-worship is eschewed in favor of sustaining that 'point,' as Murray puts it, 'at which it begins to be difficult to understand what is going on.'[13] Lytton Strachey laid the foundations for this approach to professional literary biography. His interest in the strategic deployment of fateful irony, when directed at his subjects as a guideline for critically scanning their lives, themselves all stylized in the public mind's eye according to proper Victorian canons of selfhood, served not only to 'debunk' those subjects, but also to establish the viability of an alternative to biographical hero-worship. Exactly what constituted such an alternative remained unclear, however. This was because, as Strachey so well demonstrated, it is not easy to manage effectively, or in any standard manner, the tricky business of the transference relationship, which is well known and taken for granted as a maxim of practice by the psychoanalytic establishment. Doing so is quite personal; there are no models, no paradigms, and no real guidelines to follow. Nevertheless, Strachey achieved what Edmund Wilson described as 'a rare attitude of humility, of astonishment and admiration, before the unpredictable of life.'[14] Reductionism of any kind, with its implicit risk of 'getting a life wrong,' so to speak, was far from his interests.

Whereas the unidimensional approach suggests the viability of biographical construction, the multidimensional approach is more iconoclastic and concerned with deconstruction. This means that portraits of lives which have resulted from prior modeling (i.e., the constructionist tactic) are now taken apart or, at least, seen for what they are; and so become available to the reader and writer of lives to live over afresh. Such a process, as noted earlier, was well put by James Boswell who described his own approach to writing the life of Samuel Johnson. One must see Johnson 'live,' and '"live o'er each scene" with him, as he actually advanced through the several stages of his life,' and thus 'to see him as he really was.'[15] Boswell said that his purpose was not to write Johnson's 'panegyric, which must be all praise' but, instead, 'his life, which, great and good as it was, must not be supposed to be entirely perfect.'[16] Amongst other possible formulae of selfhood, a panegyric here represents the kind of unidimensional construction, or stereotyping, that any good multidimensional deconstructionist would avoid, or declare to be wooden, even trite.

Discussions about construction and deconstruction are prevalent in recent literary criticism. The two terms are not intended to be technical ones when related to reading and writing lives. They indicate attitudes toward what to expect from the life studied. Construction means a limited expectation, one that seeks to discover within or read into a life some univocal meaning. The assumption is that a life can be 'boiled down,' so to speak, to a fairly circumscribed single point about how the individual lived. Deconstruction means an expanded expectation, one that simultaneously challenges all univocal meanings that are attributed to a life (and the possibility of such), and holds out for something less than (or more than) consistency about a person's lifestyle, patterns of thought, relationships, and the like. Here there is no assumption that a life can be boiled down to anything that in itself can be conveyed conceptually. Rather, deconstruction means that the biographer and the reader of biographies must be open to encounter the text of a person's life itself, perhaps by means of sustaining an empathic readiness to affirm 'Hail fellow, well met!' And this requires a critical suspension of disbelief, along with an appreciation of everyday situational ambiguities.

Put differently, construction establishes a relationship between the life-writer/reader and the person studied that renders that subject an 'it,' or a fabrication, at least in part, by the student of a life. Having to confine a life within a textual genre necessitates this, though the artistry of the student of a life may work to ameliorate it. The life-writer/reader may incline to control and construct that life, often using discourse and concepts from psychological science or any other idiom of human inquiry. A criticism of construction is that the person, as a living text, gets lost, or becomes substituted by an alternative text that is built by the reader and writer of lives.

Deconstruction, on the other hand, establishes a relationship between the investigator and the person studied which converts that person, hitherto an 'it,' now into a 'thou,' which is not a fabrication by the student of a life but, rather, an *evocation of the possibility of human encounter*. The text of the person's life, not the perhaps heavy-handed life-writer/reader, takes charge so as to preclude a search for univocal meaning or some other such stereotypical reduction. No alternative text is fabricated; the human text presses itself upon students of lives, and it makes its ready availability to them apparent. At least, we read the life and can see how it was put together by the biographer and autobiographer; and, perhaps, gain personal insight into the circumstances that went into the formation of the individual's life and times. Generally, the debate between constructionists and deconstructionists pertains to attitudes toward objects of study in the humanities, the former being somewhat more chauvinistic than the latter.[17]

We can now say that each of the major two approaches to the art of reading and writing lives should be kept in mind if Lytton Strachey's unique achievement is to be recognized as the 'high water mark' of connections between life-writing/reading and the creative use of psychological insights into lives up to the Second World War. Clearly, Strachey's sensing of fateful irony, which is so well recognized in his work by commentators and critics, stands at the crossroads of unidimensional construction and multidimensional deconstruction. How did Strachey achieve this in his own person first, and then finally express it in his art?

Strachey's achievement: from character to irony

The formation of a coherent character with personal moral impact is one thing, but irony with its subversive effect is another. Leon Edel has called Lytton Strachey a 'master of biographical irony,' a less poignant expression of ancient Greek 'tragedy.'[18] The strategic use of irony means that any theoretical reduction of the facts of a life, say, to a statement about a person's 'character' or personality 'type,' ought to be forestalled. Herein lies the incipient deconstructionist posture in Strachey's biographies. The posture guarantees that the human quality of a subject is rendered available to a reader by means of the irony of juxtaposed facts, a sophisticated form of hostility that Strachey directs toward professional authority, especially those literary giants of the generation before his own, such as Carlyle and others.

Strachey's approach to biography is no better seen than in his short essay of 1930 on the historian and biographer, James Anthony Froude (1818–94).[19] Martin Kallich astutely observes that Strachey's sketch of Froude 'reads like a study of Queen Victoria in miniature.'[20] Kallich makes this observation because of the similarity which he believes that Strachey implied between the queen's 'unconscious search for a father substitute, someone to satisfy her craving for authority,' and Strachey's peculiar interpretation of Froude's life.[21] If as Eileen Overend implies, namely, that Strachey's *Queen Victoria* stands as his first clearly multidimensional biography, perhaps with psychoanalytic overtones, then his essay on Froude represents the culmination of the multidimensional approach in which construction is abandoned and a process of sensing fateful irony, itself posing as incipient deconstruction, is activated.

If Kallich is correct, then we can ask, why did Strachey find this a necessary line of continuity to draw upon, that is, a personal encounter with his own search for coherence of character and moral authority as a person and as a writer, whether deliberately conceived as such or not? Could it be that Strachey is pressing the Queen into the service of his own personal needs or, at least, finds such a connection useful for grappling with his sense of identity? Were Froude and Queen Victoria, somehow, to serve as the forge on which, through such grappling, Strachey would craft his method of sensing fateful irony in a life? Behind the work of Strachey the professional literary biographer is the person who harbors an intelligent curiosity about the lives of others. Doing so is a means of finding out the truth about himself, or a meditation on comparing and contrasting his life with the lives of others. The magnitude of his final achievement for reading and writing lives in our era can hardly be overestimated.

Strachey's life itself is a paragon of irony that has been recognized by a number of scholars. Great emotional distance separated Strachey from his father, Sir Richard, a general who had been active in the economic development of India and was sixty-three years old when Lytton was born. His mother was twenty-four years younger than his father, and she dominated Strachey's life, in spite of his being the eleventh of thirteen children. Physically frail and with precarious health, Strachey became preoccupied with increasingly frequent and troubling homoerotic thoughts and feelings during school, and he engaged in homosexual relations throughout his life, usually falling deeply in love with robust, athletic men. According to Michael Holroyd, the irony was that 'Strachey's tendency was to fall in love with the sort of person he would like to have been.'[22] This served time and again to heighten the irony of his most intense personal relationships. The virtual impossibility of exercising effectively any capacity for growth beyond his most deeply felt and intimate personal relationships underscores the pathos of Strachey's personal irony. However, it was precisely this that he creatively converted into a unique method for reading and writing lives. Namely, Strachey emphasized the importance of sensing fateful irony as an important component in the overall process of the biographical construction of an individual as a text.

It was no coincidence, for example, that sometime around 1910 he was overcome by a period of stagnation and general literary obscurity. He had moved away from Duncan Grant, an articulate cousin and lover, with whom he spent holidays, and soon filled the emptiness in his life by associating with the bewitching writer, Henry Lamb. Lamb launched Strachey into the world of Bohemian life and thought, so much so that in 1913 Strachey dedicated his *Ermyntrude and Esmeralda* to Lamb as 'pornographic entertainment.'[23] Strachey's life was driven by a quest for some kind of suitable authority but, when the issue was put to the test, anything other than ironic failure seemed impossible. His quest for lovers, and the authority they seemed to bear for him, was really a search for heroes, or, as Holroyd has put it, for individuals he himself would like to have been, or at least to have resembled. However (and ironically), the impossibility of success in such a personal endeavor would eventually serve to release him not only from the debilitating prison of his 'hateful physique,' but also from the narrow confines of a hateful and constrained Victorian milieu.[24] Herein lay the personal origins of Strachey's skill of discerning fateful irony in a life, and then deploying it strategically as a literary device in life-writing and reading.

All this is to say that the appearance of Strachey's essay on Froude so late in his life is more than a simple coincidence. The essay is significant because it points to Strachey's own personal confusion about the degree to which Froude was Carlylean or, put differently, because it reveals Strachey's wrestling with his own quest for authoritative heroes of one sort or another. Within this confusion were posed the two approaches to construing a life and managing the problem of 'surfaces and depths' in life-writing/reading described above: whether to side with Carlyle, the nineteenth-century and unidimensional construction, or to keep the issue open and to allow for the genesis of multidimensional deconstruction, spurred along by the psychoanalytically tinged intellectual temper of twentieth-century times? For Carlyle, far above all others within English literary circles of his century, was famous as both a hero and a maker of heroes, at least insofar as Strachey himself was a biographer and was able to identify with Carlyle on this score. Strachey's person and profession were coming together, with the identity of each at stake.

Carlyle represented strength, and no recent British (albeit Scottish) writer up to Strachey's day commanded as much attention and respect for his person and his work from the general public. We can suppose that Strachey felt compelled to address himself to Carlyle's work, and to encounter the man in that corpus, if only vicariously. The intriguing suggestion here is that Strachey accomplished this encounter by attending to an essay on Froude, who was Carlyle's student and biographer. Froude, like Strachey, was himself troubled by nineteenth-century literary constraints. The point is that scholarly opinion of Froude is much more positive and laudatory in terms of all that Strachey himself later came to stand for in biography than is the opinion conveyed about Froude in Strachey's essay.

How is this to be explained? Might this odd incongruity point to an ambivalence that lies at the heart of Strachey's own greatness? In order to account for this seeming discrepancy, the suggestion here is that personal factors entered into Strachey's writing which eventuated in such peculiarities, and which served to clarify just who Strachey understood himself to be as a man and as a biographer. The essay on Froude was Strachey's way of lending coherence to his character, or a means of working out his own identity; and this would turn on the discovery and use of irony as a strategic literary device. It also points to how *biographical construction* of an individual as a text (for example, Froude) may actually become *autobiographical reflection* (in this case, by Strachey himself). However, it is clear that Strachey probably had less insight into this shift of personal focus than may have been available to him at the time had he become introspective.

Between 1882 and 1884 Froude came out with a four-volume life of Carlyle, following the instructions of his master that his life was to be portrayed not in the manner of 'mealymouthed biography' but 'truly as he was.'[25] This biography followed *Reminiscences* of Carlyle in 1881; and the *Letters and Memorials of Jane Welch Carlyle* appeared in 1883. Froude was at first denounced as a traitor to the public's memory of his master. The exact nature of the breach is described by Richard Altick:

> In his pages the man who was the veritable conscience and scourge of Britain, whose eightieth birthday in 1875 had been a national occasion, turned out to have been an extremely difficult man to get along with, selfish, grim, irritable, even violent. From first to last his domestic life had been marked by tensions and fierce outbursts. The spirited Jane Welch Carlyle, as was revealed by her letters which Froude published, had been a martyr to the bearded prophet – but far from an uncomplaining one. And Froude, had he chosen to do so, could have presented an even darker picture of unrest in Cheyne Row, for in a passage in her diary which he suppressed she recorded that her arms bore blue marks from her husband's abuse.[26]

Surely Froude's work served the history of reading and writing lives as a prefiguration of Strachey's popular writing later in the twentieth century. While it was not as subtle as the strategic use of fateful irony that later came to be buoyed up by psychoanalytic notions for Strachey, Froude's approach to biography rested on a fresh, almost cheeky style of 'debunking,' which became popular in his own day, and that stood as a precursor to Strachey's style. One wonders, therefore, why Strachey found it necessary to be less than enthusiastic about Froude's life and work than we ourselves may be, at least when confronted by Strachey's short essay about this writer.

Strachey knew about Froude's accomplishments and it is easy for one to suppose that, being the kind of twentieth-century biographer that he was, Strachey's desire to be like Carlyle's student and biographer was intense. Was Strachey unwittingly jealous of Froude? If so, would this not be ironic in that Strachey and Froude were separated by a generation, and Froude long dead and buried? Once Froude was placed in the position of resembling a hero, if only because Strachey had selected him as a subject, the narrative about Froude reveals nothing short of ambivalence toward Froude's accomplishments as an historian and biographer. In this way, Strachey the student of lives engages his own transference relationship, or encounter, with his subject. And, too, the gradual methodological shift from a unidimensional to a multidimensional approach, with an incipient emphasis on deconstruction, begins to be seen. The essay starts on a note of tribute but moves quickly to a sketch of Froude's failings; or, to put it another way, to the irony of Froude's highly acclaimed life and work. Thus, Strachey strategically distances himself from Froude, but also unwittingly reveals to the reader a deep engagement in sorting out the truth of who he himself is and who Froude is. How to deconstruct popular memories of Froude, and to tell the truth of his life, without at the same time surrendering to any univocal meaning that might be attributable to Froude's life? – that was the question.

According to Strachey, Froude was a man 'in whose presence it was impossible not to feel a hint of mystery, or strange melancholy, and an uncomfortable suggestion of enigmatic power.'[27] He asks, 'what was the explanation of it all?' Just what was the 'inner cause' of Froude's 'brio' and his 'sadness,' this 'passionate earnestness and this sardonic wit?'[28] Strachey believes that it is easier to ascertain this inner cause, incidentally, than it had been for Froude's contemporaries. As he put it, the reason was because 'we know more of the facts and we have our modern psychology to give us confidence.'[29] The multidimensional approach to biography is signalled by the phrase, 'modern psychology.' However, that he gained only 'confidence' from this psychology, and did not employ any of its theoretical constructions as he might have if he had been a member of the professional psychoanalytic fold (intimations of which were beginning to wash westward from Europe at this time), suggests Strachey's incipient deconstructionist stance. Prompted by a greater than usual fascination with Froude, Strachey's hostility first appears in the form of a fateful irony. This also betrays the nature of his ambivalence toward Carlyle, and thus Froude, both having been very successful biographers in Strachey's eyes, as well as authority figures unable to be embraced in fact or in fantasy. Such feigned intimacy with these literary giants, his heroes, was the price Strachey paid in order to achieve a creative advance beyond unidimensional, constructionist life-writing/reading.

'Perhaps the real explanation was old Mr. Froude,' writes Strachey, 'who was a hunting parson of a severely conventional type, with a marked talent for watercolours.'[30] We are told that Froude was brought up in an atmosphere of terror by his widower father and brothers, who were 'much older than himself'; sent off to college at Westminster, where he suffered 'indescribable torment'; then kept at home for two years as an 'outcast' and 'flogged' for 'imaginary delinquencies'; and, finally when he began enjoying himself at Oxford later on, his father broke off Froude's engagement to a young woman and 'denounced him' to the girl's father as 'little better than a common swindler.'[31] However, writes Strachey, Froude was kept from suicide by an unrelenting 'intense admiration' for his father, as Mr Froude had drawn a 'magic circle' around his son, from which escape was 'impossible.'[32] Froude's life had been almost ruined by his father's 'moral cruelty' and, though appearing to have 'thrown off the yoke,' Froude, concludes Strachey, remained in 'secret servitude.'[33]

After his father's death, Froude, suggests Strachey, 'submitted himself to Carlyle,' expressing in 'explicit dogma' the 'unconscious teaching' of his father by adopting Carlyle's philosophy of history, stress on heroes, and his provincial moral tone. Strachey then focused on the central question, how are we to account for Froude's 'adoration' of Carlyle? This adoration, Strachey believes, prevented Froude from allowing himself 'untrammelled' to play upon his subject with his native art and his 'native wit! . . . But alas! these are vain speculations; old Mr. Froude would never have permitted anything of the sort.'[34] One wonders if the same thing could not be said about Strachey's unspoken opinion of old Sir Richard, his own father, who permitted him so much of his mother's time and attentions. Multi-dimensional life-writing, and a maneuver of deconstruction, are incipient here. By declaring ironic his predecessor's relationship to Carlyle, Strachey managed to tarnish the lustre of Froude's most significant contribution to reading and writing lives up to that time. However, the point is that this tarnishing was in Strachey's eyes alone. By pointing to the negative aspects of Froude's life, Strachey unwittingly accentuated the positive aspects of his own budding art. By putting down a hero (Froude), Strachey himself, as an innovative biographer (who builds on Froude's courageous technique!), becomes a hero too. His personal triumph consummated a hard won creative leap ahead for life-writing/reading, and for its methodological possibilities.

The genesis of Strachey's dynamic contribution to the history of the relationship between life-writing/reading and psychology, though only implicit, is most clearly observed in process in this short essay on Froude. What begins as a personal struggle, perhaps with a transference relationship with Froude (and Carlyle), ends up as a professional resolution of that subterranean tension at the level of methodological creativity in the context of biographical construction. Thus, unidimensional construction is subverted time and time again; and this persists as a literary style in all of Strachey's mature biographical writing. Leverage supplied by locating irony in a subject's life can prise open (and keep open) the possibility of real encounter, beyond projection and beyond stereotyping. The biographies that Strachey wrote drew attention away from the blinding illusions of nineteenth-century moralistic understandings of the self, or what it meant then (the Victorian era in England) to be an upstanding individual member of society. By doing so, Strachey's work stands for the open-ended reality of individuality, or for the possibility of overcoming the distortion of the encounter between a biographer and a biographical subject. It overcomes a distortion of the life-writer/reader's capacity to participate in a life, albeit at some remove in time and space.

Strachey took a giant leap forward. He allowed himself to be bound neither by the tried and true canons of the 'scientific' chronicle nor by the conventionality of the 'literary' critical type of biography, although he was, perhaps, more in tune with the latter than with the former. He paved the way for the coming of the 'simulated life' type of biography, itself a 'spiritual operation,' according to Paul Murray Kendall.[35] Simulating a life invites introspection by the student of lives in ways that the other types of biographical construction do not. Revealed is a trajectory of personal realization along which the process of biographically constructing an individual as a text may gradually turn into the living actuality of autobiographical reflection by the reader and writer of lives, who can then be said to have embarked on a 'spiritual quest.'

The strategic deployment of insight about the fateful irony of a life is thus a powerful hermeneutical tool by which others might seek restoration of the self, if only through the vicarious means of reading and writing lives, and then rehearsing the drama of the play of invisible or felt subterranean cross-currents that move lives like tides that shift sand on the beach. Such opposite forces constitute all of us as much as they do the usually famous subjects of professional biographies. Lytton Strachey's contribution to reading and writing lives is that, though it may possibly be informed by psychological science and discourse, whatever else it may admit, the process of coming to terms with a life is hardly reducible to categorical statement alone. The legacy left by Lytton Strachey is the autonomy of the art of portraying individuals, an avante-garde art that would seek not only the goal of personal coherence, but also aim to subvert it with insight into life's ironies as these come to light in the darker recesses of the lives we study.

4   Erik Erikson as a life-writer/reader

Two major biographical constructions of an individual as a 'text' have been written by the psychoanalytic thinker, Erik Erikson. The first is about Martin Luther (1958), the second Mohandas Gandhi (1969). During the eleven years separating the appearances of *Young Man Luther* and *Gandhi's Truth*, years of outbursts of violence in America and armed conflict in Southeast Asia, the scope of Erikson's project broadened and deepened to form a paradigm for intellectual inquiry. Also, that scope shifted psychologically. As 'A Study in Psychoanalysis and History,' *Young Man Luther* shows Erikson's early inclination to launch his project of what his readers called 'psychohistory' in terms of methodological clarity.[1] Erikson hoped that 'by using psychoanalysis as a historical tool' he might be able to 'throw light on psychoanalysis as a tool of history.'[2] However, when *Gandhi's Truth* appeared, it was published as being 'On the Origins of Militant Nonviolence.' In it Erikson describes 'a Westerner's and psychoanalyst's search for the historical presence of Mahatma Gandhi and for the meaning of what he called the Truth.'[3] What does Erikson's work mean for reading and writing lives, especially inasmuch as Erikson's work reflects a shift in psychological thrust? It would appear that here with Erikson we begin to observe how autobiographical reflection may start to flow from the genre of the biographical construction of individuals as texts. The shift moves from a 'text' about a life to the 'body' of an individual who is faced by violent force and learns to reckon with it.

Proposed here is the use of a psychology of the imagination in life-writing and reading, at least more so than the use of a psychology of adjustment with its scientific concern to specify motives, instincts, inhibitions, and so forth as its base.[4] From the point of view of the life-writer/reader, the major concern is how imagination is structured by the demands of the biographical genre ('coherent character,' 'fateful irony') and then inserted into his or her own life and into the lives of readers. Generally, the major concern is how a person's imagination is carried by a particular structure of continuity and discontinuity, and how this is meaningfully expressed over time. This can be said to pertain to both the subjects of biographies and to biographers themselves. In light of such an understanding of life-writing and reading lives, we can recognize the approach of Erik Erikson as a form of biography which is based on a psychology of adjustment, at least insofar as it is grounded in the tradition of psychoanalysis in which an individual is assumed to repress and sublimate biological instincts for the sake of social cohesion. For example, crisis-resolution, or attaining a state of quiescent adjustment in the cases of Luther and Gandhi led to the 'higher states' of the Protestant Reformation and Indian Independence respectively.

However, Erikson's project also goes beyond such a strict psychoanalytic view of things. It points to a vista which is greater than that of a psychology of adjustment alone. His work reveals a deeper substratum, one that embraces the body as an idiom of knowledge and an object of autobiographical reflection, this in the form of a psychology of imagination. Erikson's introspective style is a form of reverie (not unlike Freud's notion of 'free association') which is grounded in the body as *sensorium* and makes its home in the realm of cultural symbols and which effects cultural adaptation: Luther and Gandhi *for us*, as Erikson might put it.[5] Thus proposed is the view that beneath any life-writer/reader's style of biography is incipient autobiographical reverie about his or her subject. This reverie includes the legacy of life-writing and reading itself, the genre, and also the uses made by life-writers/readers of various kinds of psychology in their work. Such reverie cuts two ways. First, it moves to construe or construct the person to be written about, just short of resorting to writing fiction. Second, it reflects and serves to construct the life-writer/reader oneself. The body-based substratum of imagination in the work of Erik Erikson has the question of breaking through to new levels of human awareness, or mythic reverie.[6] This aim is shared by readers and writers of lives who are concerned not only about what biographer Stephen B. Oates calls the 'critical study' and the 'scholarly chronicle,' but also about the 'pure biography,' in which lives are put forth as having something to say to those writing and reading them.[7] People are not only 'texts' to be read, but also human beings of flesh and blood to be encountered as bodies too, bodies subjected to a number of existential (and physical) forces that are usually beyond one's deliberate control. Biographical constructions of texts may lead onward to autobiographical reflections on one's body, or the physical being-in-the-world of the student of lives. This appears to be prefigured in Erikson's work.

If by 1969 Erikson's 'search' for Gandhi's presence and for the meaning of Satyagraha represented a broadening and a deepening of his method of 'psychohistory' which he presented in 1958, then that method underwent a qualitative transformation between 1958 and 1969. The bankruptcy of any facile and exclusively academic concern with 'method,' especially with the method of 'psychohistory,' which was enthusiastically embraced by many thinkers and life-writers/readers during the 1960s and 1970s, comes clearly to light in the growth of scope between Erikson's two studies. His completed 'study' of 1958 gave rise to his agonizing 'search' of 1969. We could say that Erikson has been touched by the failure of method in the decade of the 1960s. Fittingly, therefore, he symbolized old inquiries giving rise to new ones of a more fundamental sort when, reacting to a political assassination that occurred in Memphis, Tennessee in the spring of 1968, he dedicated his book on Gandhi: 'This was to be Joan's [his wife's] book. We are now dedicating it together to the memory of Martin Luther King.'[8] Perhaps this is startling, but the focus on an individual, namely, Martin Luther King, Jr, including an implicit description of a body once alive but now dead, is unmistakably clear, and it could hardly be more poignant. Erikson is a point of embarkation to the second of the three phases of the trajectory of personal realization in which readers and writers of lives engage.

If Erikson's method of psychohistory is relevant to the moral issues of our day, its suasion derives from what he puts forth as the fundamental bodily substratum of his work, not from applying his earlier psychological work with life cycle theory to historical figures. It can be argued that this bodily substratum, or the paradigmatic quality of Erikson's project, is *introspection* (which itself cultivates empathy): of both Luther and Gandhi, he suggests in 1969 that 'it could well be ... that we must look at the self-inspection practiced by such men in public as part of an "evolutionary" trend in man to break through to new kinds of awareness.'[9] Martin Luther King, Jr turned the ambiguity of being a black man in a predominantly white America into a public drama driven by the vision, 'We shall overcome someday.' The Civil Rights Movement was often called the 'Freedom Movement' by Civil Rights workers in the American south during the early 1960s. One can only wonder whether the death of King's body was the price of the evolution of bodies that were strengthened by his vision of a new society and his compelling dedication to building up the human species writ large.

By counterpoising 'praying man' to the Church's 'philosophy and practice of meritorious works,' Luther applied introspection to the very center of his conflicts and discovered the 'technique of prayer' to be an instrument of 'faith.' Prayer eminently served to clarify the 'delineation of what we, to the best of our knowledge, really mean,' that is, 'to be at one with an ideology in the process of rejuvenation.'[10] Gandhi counterpoised 'nonviolently resisting man' to British colonial rule in India. By so doing, his own personal conviction of Hinduism's Satyagraha, of 'Truth Force,' was brought to the eye of public scrutiny. The 'technique of resistence' became for him an instrument of 'Truth' which could meet public needs. Therefore, according to Erikson, both Luther's instrument of faith and

Gandhi's lever of truth enabled humankind to break through to new kinds of awareness of itself and the world. This was nothing short of cosmological construction, a realization of the perceptual relatedness of individuals as, yes, thinking 'texts,' but also as bodily *sensoria*.

If the introspective substratum of Erikson's project lends greater significance to each of his psychohistorical studies than first sight might suggest, then the efficacy of Luther and Gandhi follows accordingly. Each figure was part of the cutting edge of the evolution of human consciousness, or what Erikson has called 'speciation,' or how the collective human body is affirmed as it evolves through the generations. 'Gandhi,' writes Erikson, 'in his immense intuition for historical actuality and his capacity to assume leadership in "truth in action," may have created a ritualization through which men, equipped with both realism and spiritual strength, can face each other with mutual confidence.' This, he suggests, is 'analogous to the instinctive safety built into animals' pacific rituals.'[11] Harking back to Luther's praying, Erikson states, 'indeed, only faith gives back to man the dignity of nature,' which prevents humankind from annihilating the entire species.[12] Gandhi's 'ritual' of resistance and Luther's 'ritual' of prayer, therefore, are two notable examples of how humankind projects vistas of imagination in the service of adaptation in order to resolve ambiguity and to restore peace.

The general effect is to prevent social and cultural fragmentation, which would be implied either by resorting to traditional warfare or by acceding to the Darwinian maxim, only the fit survive. The human *body*, not just a biographical 'text' (*graphos*) is at stake – the body linked intergenerationally to other bodies, that together would survive even in the face of the possibility of annihilation. After Gandhi had impressed his sense of Satyagraha upon the world, 'Asia,' according to Erikson, 'could now look Europe in the eye – not more, not less, not up to, not down on.' In the following sentence of his book, Erikson implies the inclination to render the past usable for self-inspection in the present: 'Where man can and will do that (see eye to eye) there, sooner or later, will be mutual recognition.'[13] The unity of the human species, or bonding into community, is maintained when bodies come face to face, and thus occasion empathy as the outgrowth of introspection.

It is important to understand that throughout each of his two biographical books Erikson is eager to suggest the similarity between the evolutionary contributions of Luther and Gandhi and Freud's psychoanalysis. Freud's work, of course, is also a potent expression of introspection. Both Freud and Luther 'illustrate certain regularities in the growth of a certain kind of genius.' Luther's 'specific creativity represented a late medieval precursor of some aspects of Freud's determined struggle with the father complex; even as Luther's emancipation from medieval dogma was one of the indispensable precursors both of modern philosophy and psychology.' Indeed, both Freud and Luther shared a 'grim willingness' to do the 'dirty work' of their respective ages insofar as each 'kept human conscience in focus in an era of material and scientific expansion.'[14]

Moreover, in the middle of his book on Gandhi, Erikson actively enters into the text in order to see himself more clearly. He writes a letter to the 'Mahatmaji' in which he suggests that 'psychoanalytic insights happen to complement your kind of truth by a strange reversal of the traditional roles of East and West: for you are now a model of activism in our culture, while Western thought has provided a new technique of introspection.'[15] Erikson seems to be saying, if Martin Luther King, Jr, can rise in the West while espousing a philosophy of nonviolence in the Civil Rights Movement of the 1950s and 1960s, then he (Erikson), as an American psychoanalyst, can provide the introspective insights necessary for illuminating Gandhi's politics. Erikson enters into his own process of realization, reading in the lives that he is studying a play of differences and similarities in regard to his own sense of himself. His study has become a personal process of self-understanding. Erikson is no detached scholar who would dispassionately study a 'text' alone. However, to point to the similarity between Luther, Gandhi, and Freud is one thing. To take this similarity to task for reading and writing lives in general is another, one that makes implicit the 'spiritual quest.'

By confronting the spiritual truth of Luther and Gandhi as each formulated and lived it with the psychological truth he himself learned and practiced, Erikson prepared for the future. He suggests that their work will spread beyond the present in 'unforeseen ways.'[16] If, as Erikson seems to assume, violence marks the unresolved ambiguities of our age, then to link together the achievements of Luther and Gandhi with Freud's insights supplies humankind with an ounce of prevention: 'therapeutic persuasion,' not power gained by warfare or coercion, can become a 'cure of man's aberrations.'[17] After all, Freud himself listened to his patients in their free associations and, with more insight than simply hearing what *they* said, he discovered that he was hearing *himself*, that is, his own inner nature speaking, this based on a perceptual relatedness that was a body sense. The similarity between Luther, Gandhi, and Freud which is alluded to in Erikson's letter to Gandhi is completed toward the end of his book. Erikson's project of tracing the course of introspection in lives, including his own when occasioned to do so by contact with another during life-writing/reading, is marked by 'man's basic need to confess the past in order to purge it.'[18] It is quite possible to call introspective purgation a basic human ritual behavior. What might this ritual have to do with the contemporary moral thrust, or stress on 'human virtues,' of Erikson's work?

The ritual of introspection means, 'historicizing *as such* appears to be a process by which man recapitulates the past in order to render – even surrender – it to the judgment of the future: an adaptive process.'[19] When the inner needs of a self-inspector match those of his or her public, any satisfaction found becomes a possible discovery of 'truth' by those watching, by those rallying around. Such a situation is the genesis of an evolutionary pay-off promised by Erikson's psychohistory. As a general 'therapeutics of history,' ritual introspection of one's human character in the broadest sense is enhanced by psychological insights. Having an introspective edge on history makes it possible for humankind to overcome certain stereotyped ways of carrying out the historical drama, 'ways,' Erikson remarks, 'which man can no longer afford,' namely, resorting to mass violence.[20] Indeed, psychohistory implies a paradigm for scholarly inquiry which takes account of the bodily task of human survival. Erikson's work invites us to exert effort to 'think clearly' in order to enter into 'an optimum of mutual activation' with others, our contemporaries; and this, Erikson suggests, calls for a combination of 'clear insight into our central motivations' and a 'pervasive faith' in the 'brotherhood of man.'[21] What all this means is that Erikson has transformed the narrow stream of 'methodology' into the deep river of 'morality.' However, by this morality is meant the 'sense of search,' or the 'spiritual quest,' for which, I argue, only a psychology of imagination suffices. Moreover, we must note that imagination, which is tied to the body as *sensorium*, is mostly visual in nature.

The direction suggested by Erikson's project is not unlike what many readers and writers of lives have assumed, albeit unwittingly, to be a fundamental criterion of their art, namely, to examine the lives of others in order to better understand oneself. The degree to which Luther's or Gandhi's self-inspection becomes significant for human adaptation depends on the degree to which each converted private rumination into public resolution. Luther did not go to his grave worrying about how to please his father. Gandhi did not feel remorse for the rest of his life after failing to be at his dying father's side. From an inward gaze Luther and Gandhi both managed to turn outward, seeking public altars in history for resolving inner conflicts (discontinuities, or the force of 'fateful irony') and for further differentiating who they understood themselves to be (continuities, or the security of a 'coherent character'), both aspects being psychological through and through.

Not everyone who reads and writes lives, or the person written about, is as famous or as historically significant as Luther or Gandhi. Nevertheless, everyone can be said to be engaged at some level in a ritualization of experience, in which (literally) one's 'body is on the line,' so to speak, and where a person reckons together with others in order to see oneself and the world more clearly. This is the 'eye-to-eye' experience that characterizes reading and writing lives as a process of coming to grips with aspects of human similarity and sameness, or the second phase of the trajectory of personal realization that is available to readers and writers of lives. Thus, ritual itself is a matter of critical vigilance moving through one's interiority and refracted in the lives of others. A person who does not 'ritualize' in Erikson's sense is fated to repeat history by re-enacting all of its impediments, all of its old avenues of awareness, and to sound the often discordant chord of human differences and alien natures. However, a person who historicizes therapeutically, though risking destruction and the 'violence of history' and the wearing down force of time, will watch the times closely, avoiding impediments and, especially, hoping to strike upon new resolve.[22] To be vigilant is to 'watch'; and watching itself emphasizes the 'visual' dimension of ritual. And rituals are not thoughts, but actions, ones in which engaged bodies, or *sensoria*, are paramount. Implicit religion, or the 'spiritual quest,' necessarily focusses on 'bodies in motion' through time and space.

Up to now, we have been attempting to look Erikson, so to speak, 'in the eye.' Any reader and writer of lives these days can benefit from conversation with Erikson's work, and receives in so doing an invitation to make personal sense out of it. The 'locking of antlers' (another Eriksonian analogy), as it were, that ensues in a ritual manner has the double message of mutual affirmation (in sameness) and mutual critique (in difference). However, we do not intend here either to 'submit to' or to 'win over' Erikson. Rather, to encounter Erikson's project is nothing less than a major effort to come to grips with the hard work of building one's identity.[23] Those who have attempted either of the following two tactics have banished themselves from meaningful continued engagement with the impact of Erikson's project in Western culture, with Erikson and his work standing side by side with Luther, Gandhi, and Freud, all 'transhistorical colleagues.'

On the one hand, referred to in particular are those thinkers who employ Erikson's 'Eight Ages of Man' (his theory of psychosocial personality development) explicitly and directly by applying them to an historical figure. This tactic is not unlike some Freudians' search for 'Oedipal Complexes,' or biographical stereotypes, standard keys that are believed to unlock explanations of great men's and women's lives. This is a reductionistic approach. It tries to explain lives by reducing them to terms that are extraneous to them. On the other hand, some have tried to invalidate Erikson's approach. The critique of *Young Man Luther* by Roland Bainton is one example of this academic attack.[24] Jacques Barzun has joined in the attack by questioning whether the term 'psychohistory' lends any new dimension to our understanding of the past.[25] Generally speaking, and not to belabor the point, Erikson has been thought of as a poor historian by historians and a psychologist out of his field by psychologists. Without saying more to substantiate these admittedly impressionistic comments, this level of popular criticism has not adequately taken into account a 'mutual recognition' of Erikson's whole project, and its implications for the meaning of lives in general. Reductionistic reading strategies nip imagination in the bud. They do not allow the body and the forces at work on the body enough leeway to embody reflection about living, which is itself an autobiographical task.

How is the slant that is being argued here about the nature of Erikson's project for life-writing and reading lives different from Erikson's psychohistories? In order that Erikson's project continues to be 'recognized' as such, it is necessary to remove his work from the battlefield upon which the war between historians and psychologists has been waged. Clearly, Erikson's work involves a 'spiritual operation,' one that implies a 'moral tenor.'[26] This unique feature makes his effort qualitatively different from the kinds of work usually done by historians and psychologists. Given this difference, we can view the thrust of Erikson's work to be more in accord with the thrust of traditional biography. Biography is a literary genre that is distinct from purely 'historical' or purely 'psychological' kinds of life-writing/reading. It is neither a 'life and times' chronicle nor a 'clinical case study' alone. Once Erikson's psychohistorical work is understood as *biograpical construction* in the first instance, then it is possible to do two things. First, the moral impulse activating current expressions of the biographical genre can be taken into account. Second, Erikson's psychohistorical 'method' can be understood as involving more than just another particular 'tactical' approach to reading and writing lives. Autobiographical reflection about the body as *sensorium* is evoked.

Life-writing and cultivating moral virtue

On what grounds is one justified in suggesting that it is more within the genre of biography, less in historiography or psychology *per se*, that life-writing bears a deliberate and tangible 'moral impulse?' In other words, why does biography invite introspection, or that inward gaze, perhaps refracted through the life of another, that works toward the integration of the self in a cohesive community (for example, the accomplishments of Luther and Gandhi)? An answer to these questions will confirm the point that during Erikson's shift from *Young Man Luther* to *Gandhi's Truth* he became more explicit in acknowledging his fundamental spiritual quest (and the moral virtue that goes with it), this being grounded in the importance he placed on relating perceptually to his subjects, Gandhi especially. This is not to say that his very early psychological work, *Childhood and Society*, was without a moral thrust. Nor is it to suggest that when compared to

Gandhi's Truth his study of Luther is out of character. Erikson has sustained his interest in human strengths, or what he calls 'virtues,' in tandem with his methodological reflection on his theory of the eight crises of the life cycle.[27] The point is that in his study of Gandhi, Erikson is more explicit about the nature of his moral search than in his previous work. An answer to the questions above will supply a new point of view as to the nature of life-writing/reading itself. Within Erikson's project of introspection lies a 'psychological' approach to studying lives, based on perceptual relatedness to his subjects, which forms the basis upon which his own use of his earlier psychological notions occurs (for example, Luther's crisis of 'identity versus identity diffusion'; Gandhi's crisis of 'generativity versus stagnation'). This can be called 'life-writing eye-to-eye.' Visual perception is the major way in which Erikson relates perceptually to his subjects. After all, he began his search for a fitting career as a landscape painter in Europe. Erikson uses his own body as a *sensorium* as an idiom of knowledge and as an object of autobiographical reflection.

Why might biography produce 'introspection,' a word Erikson himself introduces into the discussion? Philosopher and historiographer Wilhelm Dilthey (1833–1911) wrote that self-biography, or autobiography, is the literary expression of the individual's reflection on life: 'When this reflection is transferred to the understanding of another's existence it emerges in the form of biography.'[28] Autobiographical reflection is widened not only when introspection commands reflection on one's own life, but also when that reflection becomes the window through which someone else's life is viewed. It develops, therefore, into what can be called *biographical introspection*, which is a zone of transition between the process of biographical construction ('text') and autobiographical reflection ('body'). Enlarging self-inspection to include the lives of others as a part of one's own common humanity affirms one of Dilthey's basic beliefs, namely, that the value of reading and writing lives lies in the fact that one may scan a repertory of lives, and this may differentiate and further clarify one's own identity. One compares and contrasts one's life with another's. Identification with lives by means of empathy born of introspection facilitates the development of a unique self, this on the backdrop of human sameness.

The advantage of biography remains true to introspection because, says Dilthey, 'the course of a life preserves the relation between the outer and something inner,' which, he adds, 'is the meaning of that life.'[29] When this particular artful balance is reached, this point of view or the *meaning of lives*, it becomes possible to see the 'general historical horizon of a life.'[30] What was possible for a Luther or a Gandhi in their times, their histories, may or may not be possible in the contemporary era. None the less, going hand-in-hand with the widening of an historical horizon is clarification of a subject, an individual, who 'must remain in the center of a dynamic and meaningful system' of historical forces.[31] Biographical introspection is another way of pointing to some of the less explicit dimensions of Erikson's work. But more than that, the caption is not unlike Dilthey's notion of 'historical understanding,' which itself bears a double relation: 'Understanding presupposes experience (*Erlebnis*) and experience only becomes insight into a life if understanding leads us from the narrowness and subjectivity of experience to the whole and the general.'[32] If the biographer's intention is to turn from the narrowness of one's own experience to the narrowness of the lives of others, then one does so with the potential for carrying understanding both of oneself and others to some meaningful transhistorical level of insight. Life-writing and reading lives compares meaningful identities of the past with identities of today.

To the degree that a reader and writer of lives is further actualized or completed by means of clarifying his or her own 'pattern of meaning,' the pattern organizes itself in terms of the inputs of biographical introspection, or in terms of the lives scrutinized. The pattern that organizes 'comes from within,' writes James Olney: 'As Gestalt psychology maintains,' he suggests, lives 'are *drawn* into channels, into formal relations, and in formal composite they make ... the individual.'[33] This construction is the output of biographical introspection with its incipient autobiographical impulse. Evidently Erikson is clearly engaged in the process. The interval between his two psychohistorical studies reveals a broadening and deepening of his overall project. The fundamental channels remain connected, but as life goes on his stream, so to speak, flows into a river. In fact, as a psychoanalyst, Erikson readily identifies with Freud and then suggests the essential likeness of Freud, Luther, and Gandhi. Erikson implies that his own name might very well be tacked on to the list. Erikson engaged in biographical introspection because of his own embedded, perceptually based style of life-writing/reading, and also because he believed that the insights of Luther, Freud, and Gandhi weighed significantly into contemporary culture. It is to this more implicit dimension of Erikson's psychohistorical approach to life-writing and reading lives that we can now turn. It is the grist of his implicit religion, or the substance of his own 'spiritual quest.'

What we aim to articulate is the implicit method of life-writing used by Erikson as the basis on which his explicit psychoanalytic, or ego-psychological insights into lives play out themselves. We shall want to keep attuned to signs of Erikson's imagination, his introspective reverie, in the broadest sense of that term.

Erikson's art as biographical introspection

Because his moral searchings are most clearly expressed in *Gandhi's Truth*, it is to that psychohistorical study that we turn. If in *Young Man Luther* Erikson emphasized the need to see the complex interrelationships between individual psychological crises and historical forces which shaped and were invigorated by them, then it can be said that that particular book was his more 'methodological' book on the art of his psychohistory.[34] Erikson employs the 'Epilogue,' in fact, in order to teach the reader about the psychological theory of epigenesis, which he had developed earlier in previous works.[35] By way of contrast, *Gandhi's Truth* appears to be less didactic in the traditional sense of that term. It does not specifically teach a 'method.' The tome is clearly an extended invitation to join Erikson in his search for the origins of militant nonviolence, not only to sit back and to watch the display of his methodological wares. Thus, the style of each book is different and this difference presses one into a personal 'quest' for the reason.

In *Gandhi's Truth* Erikson takes for granted what he was impelled to reiterate time and time again in *Young Man Luther*, namely, that the key to psychohistorical awareness is noting the fit between individual development and historical tides, and how history sets a stage on which a person enacts their life. In the later book, however, although he carries through a psychoanalyst's preoccupation with issues such as sexual repression, guilt, and generativity, another kind of psychology flows between these sorts of lines.[36] The title of the extensive Prologue, 'Echoes of an Event,' anticipates the fact that soon afterwards Erikson will devote the rest of his efforts to an understanding of the Ahmedabad mill strike of 1918, during which Gandhi's 'Truth' was vividly displayed in capsule form. But what of the title itself? What might it suggest about Erikson's qualitative shift of emphasis in his psychohistorical approach?

Young Man Luther begins with the sentence, 'The literature on Luther, and by Luther, is stupendous in volume. Yet it adds up to very few reliable data on his childhood and youth.'[37] Erikson goes on to reconstruct Luther's childhood and youth on the basis of the legacy of Luther's literature, scant as it is on such topics. But *Gandhi's Truth* begins on a different note, a note of sensation and adventure: 'As the plane sets down in Delhi airport before dawn, the newcomer is enveloped in a new world of sights, sounds, and smells which darkly command him to reset all his senses before asking any questions.'[38] A clear difference appears: of Luther, Erikson asks a scholar's questions from the start. However, with regard to Gandhi, and due in part to the eleven-year-long interval between the two books, he engages in a much more rigorous and risky task of personal involvement, one that implies a perceptual relatedness to Gandhi which 'darkly command[ed] him to reset all his senses.' Erikson withholds questioning in favor of opening himself intuitively. That he should use his own subjective experience of meeting the mill owner, Ambalal Sarabhai, for example, is characteristic.[39] Therefore, understanding the task posed by his intuitive capacity, based as it is on using his body as a *sensorium*, is a key to understanding Erikson's artistry.

Perhaps because he himself searched somewhat in vain for a vocational identity as an artist and painter before coming to the psychoanalyst's profession, Erikson betrays his adherence to such an early goal in the first sentence of 'Echoes of an Event' (the name of this chapter itself also suggests an implicit perceptual agenda, this time the sense of hearing). He emphasizes from the outset the necessity of readjusting perceptual capacities in order to arrive at the essential tones of Indian life, so that the seemingly insignificant Ahmedabad event can still be noticed reverberating across the land and faces of contemporary Indian life. Unlike his previous psychohistorical study of Luther, in this one Erikson is first the artist engaged in an experience of the senses and only afterwards is he a psychoanalyst, historian, and cultural thinker. His 'sensory' engagement propels him along a trajectory toward autobiographical reflection on his body as a valuable resource for self-understanding. Only after acknowledging the central importance of his *senses* does he claim to have an appropriate starting-point for seeing similarities between Freud's psychoanalysis on the one hand, and Gandhi's Stayagraha on the other hand.

The implication of such a basic tactic in the context of his entire project of psychohistory does not simply end there. By emphasizing a 'resetting of the senses,' a point of entry into the substratum of introspection is opened. Taking seriously the *perceptual dimension* of Erikson's project is to recognize an implicit psychology in his work, a priori to his well-known and subtle enough theory of personality development, namely, his list of eight 'life crises,' or epigenetic schedule of growth by which human strengths and values are bestowed on living. Moreover, when made explicit this psychology affirms and refines matters of method for biographical and autobiographical scholarship. All this is to say that we must recognize the dimension of 'biographical introspection' as it emerged in Erikson's eleven-year-long psychohistorical project: as his work clarified into a 'quest,' he came to realize its evolutionary purport, namely, a consciousness of the adaptive value of militant nonviolence in a global sense. In order to study this dimension which is 'deeper than psychology, deeper than history' awareness, then, Erikson seems to have resorted to his earlier, perhaps more fundamental artistic mode of apprehending the world. Erikson's lesson for life-writers and readers of lives requires that this tacit dimension be made explicit. James Olney signaled the tacit dimension of Erikson's work when he introduced Gestalt psychology into our discussion earlier. Gestalt psychology has been foremost in the study of the inner organization of sensation and human perception. We turn to *Gandhi's Truth* in order to substantiate the perceptual preoccupation that Erikson finds to be his special methodological forté.

Erikson's perceptual preoccupation lends a certain kind of form to his biographical introspection, itself sitting halfway between biographical construction of an individual as a 'text' and autobiographical reflection on the 'body' as a source of life. It is not unlike the form presented by Dilthey, namely, a life becomes the point of convergence of larger historical vectors. Gandhi stands out as a central 'figure' only to the degree the historical 'ground' in which his life had meaning (and, for the purpose of biographical introspection, still has meaning) is adequately represented. His approach to an understanding of the Ahmedabad event is a singularly important example of this. Erikson writes, 'I had work to do; and work is a welcome counterbalance when impressions become too varied and too crowded.'[40] He had been invited to India — Ahmedabad in particular — to give a seminar on the human life cycle in relation to the conception of the cycle of life prevailing in India's culture of Hinduism. Though 'echoes of an event' sounded for Erikson during the seminar, he reports that his senses were further stirred by spending time with children in a combined school and clinic. Not only were arrangements made for him to attend the seminar-like discussions of case histories. He reported with considerable enthusiasm that arrangements were also made for him 'to "listen" to Indian school children by seeing them repeat a play performance which,' he added, 'has taught me much about our children.'[41] By listening with his eyes, Erikson was being synaesthetic, or mixing sensory modes.

The point of Indian children in the process of play-construction is not simply that they — unlike American children who select a few toys in order to put together a scene — use all of the toys at their disposal, but, more fundamentally, the way in which Erikson himself reports his own engagement in the process, as an observer behind a one-way mirror. Once he knows from the children's reports where and what the 'exciting scene' or 'event' is, he commences to employ a certain and specific kind of process of biographical introspection. This is an activity of knowing that is the precursor of a combined process of biographical construction and autobiographical reflection. 'Once it is located,' he writes, 'a Gestalt emerges and suggests some relation to the child's history and background — as do the scenes at home.' He continues revealingly, 'and since, with all my wordiness, I am a "seeing" type, what the children did before my eyes merged with configurations that had impressed me in case-histories and, indeed, in Indian fiction.'[42] And, indeed, we may recall here that he watched the children while being 'enveloped in a new world of sights, sounds, and smells' which 'darkly commanded' him to reset all his senses 'before asking any questions.'

One might speculate by saying that Erikson's penchant to search for 'an over-all configurational impression' of India is one way in which he himself sought to strive for integrity in his work, his psychohistorical project. By doing so, he learns to trust the firmament under which he himself bears responsibility for human phylogenesis.[43] In this way he is able to reaffirm a strictly 'methodological' concern in his work, pointing to *Young Man Luther's* explicit reference to the combination of 'psychoanalysis' and 'history.' However, Erikson's search for viable cultural adaptation is reaffirmed also by the way in which he alters his relationship to the world around him. This is reflected in the qualitative difference between his study of Luther and his study of Gandhi. If the former book tends in the direction of Eriksonian 'orthodoxy,' then the latter book is an emblem of Eriksonian 'radicality.' Furthermore, the continuum between both can be understood as involving different levels of perception that are implied in each study, with the least in the Luther book and, of course, the most in the Gandhi book. A brief digression into a psychology of perception can help move discussion along, especially as it points to life-writing 'eye-to-eye,' or to the method of biographical introspection that Erikson articulates. For us this can serve as an example of how when the body is recognized to be a *sensorium*, biographical construction of life 'texts' leads to autobiographical reflection on the living 'body.'

Ernest G. Schachtel, who has worked extensively with interpretations of the Rorschach ('inkblot') Test, has proposed two basic modes of human perception. Each specifies a different type of relatedness between a subject and his or her phenomenal ('sensory') world, that is, different ways of 'communication' or, to employ Erikson's term, different degrees of 'mutuality' between them.[44] Schachtel likens the two respective modes to Freud's 'Pleasure' and 'Reality' principles, but not without differentiating them from Freud's notions. While Freud's principles remain more or less static and metaphysical, Schachtel's modes are intended to account for the ontogenetic development of human perception. Ontogenesis, like Erikson's epigenesis, is connected to psychic growth and maturation.[45] Schachtel's modes of perception, orchestrated as he depicts them, clarify the 'two phases' or different degrees of emphasis of Erikson's project. This is done in terms of perceptual differentiation. It pertains, on the one hand, to the 'givens' in *Young Man Luther* and, on the other hand, to the 'higher' aim of *Gandhi's Truth*.

Schachtel's first mode of human perceptual relatedness is subject-centered and called 'autocentricity.' Such relatedness implies 'little or no objectification.' This emphasis is on how and what the person 'feels'; there is a close relation, 'amounting to a fusion,' between sensory quality and pleasure or unpleasure feelings, and the perceiver 'reacts primarily to something impinging upon him (although sometimes one may have brought about the impingement, for example, by taking food into the mouth).'[46] 'Allocentricity' is the second mode of perceptual relatedness and it implies objectification: 'the emphasis is on what the object is like; there is either no relation or a less pronounced or less direct relation between perceived sensory qualities and pleasure–unpleasure feelings.' That is, such feelings are usually 'absent or less pronounced or of a different quality.' Schachtel continues with a most significant point: 'the perceiver usually approaches or turns to the object actively and in doing so either opens himself toward it receptively or, figuratively or literally, takes hold of it, tries to "grasp" it.'[47]

If it can be said that biographical introspection is linked to a style of sensory perception, then it is possible to show how Schachtel's modes provide a framework for understanding Erikson's personal perceptual engagement in the construction of *Gandhi's Truth*. His modes of perceptual relatedness can be correlated with Erikson's process of observing, that is, of gaining overall 'configurational impressions' of Indian life. The process of biographical introspection can be recognized to be carried on in terms of that specific perceptual engagement.[48] Each of Schachtel's modes, briefly, relates to the other ontogenetically and each differentiates between and cuts across the different senses. According to Schachtel, this happens in the following manner: 'developmentally the autocentric mode holds almost exclusive sway at the beginning of life in all the senses of the newborn, and later the allocentric (higher) senses can and do function also in the autocentric mode, while the autocentric (lower) senses are capable of a very limited degree of allocentricity.'[49] Sight and hearing are associated as higher senses; taste, smell, touch, and the like are grouped by dint of their shared lower order.[50]

If the opening sentence of *Gandhi's Truth* is recalled, especially as it stands in the section, 'Echoes of an Event,' then the following suggestion can be made. Erikson shifts to an autocentric mode of perceptual organization in his opening line ('The newcomer is enveloped in a new world of sights, sounds, and smells.'), but toward the end of the section, just prior to putting his finger on the 'elusive event' of Ahmedabad, when he talks about Indian children doing play constructions, he shifts into allocentricity by preparing to 'grasp' the event of 1918 ('seeing' an 'over-all configurational impression,' as he put it). When Erikson 'listens' to the children with his 'eyes,' so to speak, in order to 'hear' what he called 'echoes' of the event of 1918, his own allocentric relatedness assesses the potential worth of his autocentrically bound sense in the service of taking hold of Gandhi.

If Erikson relied on autocentric perception alone he would, as Dilthey implied, be drawn only into the vagaries of Gandhi's 'life and times.' He would only be able to offer a clinical case history (a critical biography) or a factual summary (scholarly chronicle) about the the man.[51] More regrettable, Erikson would be drawn into his own 'subjectivity.' This 'life and times' tactic might supply a method of self-inspection by dint of ready identification with Gandhi. However, it would in no way suggest 'mutuality' of identification, or an empathic connection born of artful introspection. And mutuality of regard is one major characteristic of biographical introspection. None the less, and still on the level of perceptual analysis, it is clear that Erikson is free from that sort of submission. He is able to scrutinize Gandhi and the event of 1918 without 'losing himself.' The allocentric cast of his overall 'impression' implies the kind of introspection which 'comes out of itself,' which is intended to be public, that is, to facilitate evolutionary adaptation at a cultural level, a level of symbolic meaning with an ethological impetus. Erikson's psychohistorical method can, at one level, be understood simplistically as conventional psychoanalysis, if that is how one wishes to take hold of it. However, at second sight, Erikson reveals his more abiding preoccupation with the structure of 'higher' perceptual forms, itself an artist's preoccupation: Erikson is, as he says, definitely a 'seeing type.'

If perception, and allocentric perceptual relatedness in particular, specifies the nature of Erikson's 'focal attention' on Gandhi and, to a much less explicit degree by implication, on Luther, how might a psychology which deals with perception enhance Erikson's approach to life-writing? When the efficacy of biographical instrospection is granted, the entire discussion about psychohistory can be lifted out of the 'history or psychology' debate and considered broadly as reading and writing lives proper. Thus, psychohistory can then be viewed as a form of recent life-writing with a biographical emphasis, one that is a dynamic shift of focus from 'text' (*graphos*) to 'body' (*bios*). It is within the genre of biography, as distinct from though overlapping somewhat with historiography and, more recently, with psychology, that seeing 'configurations' of meaningful interrelationships in individual lives has been going on methodically for a considerable time. This was suggested earlier in discussions of the work of Gamaliel Bradford, Henry Murray, Lytton Strachey, and their predecessors in reading and writing lives, namely, James Boswell and James Stanfield amongst others.

A search for 'configurations of meaning' is not only a way of giving expression to Dilthey's notion of biography and not only a reasonable characterization of Erikson's psychohistorical approach. If a search for 'configurations of meaning' is to be the methodological axis of biographical introspection, then it behoves us to examine the 'psychology of configurations' or, at least, to see what contributions can be made to the discussion about biography by classical Gestalt theory. Classical Gestalt theory has developed a psychology of configuration based on experimental analyses of perception, visual perception in particular. Such work has led to considerations of a psychology of imagination, at least insofar as the psychology of art has had an edge on finding Gestalt theory useful for its own work.[52] That this has not yet been made explicit by psychobiographers in particular is, at least, a surprising neglect.

5   Biography, empathy, and introspection

Erik Erikson's study of Gandhi has supplied insights that are critical for depicting the intuitive, mainly perceptual basis of his methodology as a life-writer and reader of lives. The point to be pressed here is that such an intuitive, mainly perceptual grounding is already prefigured in the genre of professional literary biography and in the history of biographical writing itself, especially as early twentieth-century life-writers are witnessed reflecting on the nature of their craft. This is so quite apart from Erikson's psychohistorical project of the 1950s and 1960s, and also from life-writing and reading lives that have since been deliberately located within the tradition initiated by Erikson's pioneering work. That Erikson and others in his tradition of reading and writing lives have not paid much attention to the literary genre of biography is, indeed, surprising. Erikson ended his project admitting that he employed a 'configurational' method but he failed as a student of biography. He did not use configurational analysis, familiar to many life-writers and readers of lives, within his own particular training in psychoanalysis. In a word, did Erikson finally 'reinvent the wheel,' so to speak?

While Erikson's emphasis on perceptual relatedness to his subjects may occasion biographical introspection, his emotional relatedness to them curiously appears to be absent from his study of Gandhi. However, emotional relatedness, or one's capacity for empathy, has been a central concern of conventional professional biographers. Building on Erikson's biographical introspection, which he grounds in human perception and in a personal analytic style of 'seeing configurations' in lives, one can suggest that professional literary biography offers a good understanding of ways to manage empathy in reading and writing lives, empathy that can be tied directly to Erikson's perceptual approach. Thus, what can be called *empathic introspection*, I suggest, accounts for the emotional relatedness between a subject and the life-writer/reader. Such a designation characterizes ideally the art of what readers and writers actually do. While introspection cultivates human difference, empathy links an individual to the possibility of a shared humanity, and it invites this as an abiding affirmation of value in living. Empathy completes the 'moral search' of Erikson's project of introspection, or his perceptual relatedness to Gandhi. This lends introspection a force of feeling that is able to elicit a feeling response from readers.

None the less, some more reflective readers and writers of lives have been concerned with empathy but approach it somewhat systematically by invoking a continuum. Life-writers and readers of lives of this inclination offer typologies by which they seek to bring a range of clarity and methodological precision to their work of stitching together a text of an individual's 'coherent character' and 'fateful irony.' This is done usually because their typologies integrate disciplines like history, literature, and psychology. The integration revolves around the documentary accuracy of the facts and the prose style of the presentation. Sometimes such typologies weigh the use of empathy in the balance, with the literary disciplines being considered (as Henry Murray himself did) to be more empathic than either the practitioners of psychology or history. However, other trends in life-writing/reading have taken a different road altogether. We ourselves shall take a road less traveled later, after several typologies of biography are described. This other path captures the spirit of biographical introspection that is the surface in Erikson's *Gandhi's Truth,* and deeper (and suppressed) in *Young Man Luther,* and it amplifies this by adding emotion and an empathic capacity to it. Typologies are limited, however, in that they offer little help in extending insight into the less technical but more fundamental process of empathic introspection.

Within the world of professional (usually literary) biography, methodological technique has not been carried to the limits that it has been taken in Erikson's corpus. However, professional life-writers and readers of lives have sought to represent lives adequately, and this has amounted to cultivating a common 'garden variety' kind of empathy with their subjects. If a cue is taken from the example of *Gandhi's Truth,* in which the question of method hovers over each of Erikson's chapters, the professional biographer should not be overly concerned with systematic thinking as such or with discussion in which method is the only consideration. Lives are lives; they are not just thoughts about living or about depicting those alive. As Samuel Johnson knew it, biography is 'of the various kinds of narrative writing, that which is most eagerly read, and most easily applied to the purposes of life.'[1] Such an appeal derives its vitality, perhaps, from a biographical concern that is more sophisticated than theorizing as such. Within the entire biographical tradition, what Wilhelm Dilthey called 'lived experience' (*Erlebnis*) is preserved as the basis of the life-writing/reading, as well as modulated beyond some current approaches to writing about lives.[2] Conveying 'lived experience' in life-writing/reading establishes a horizon of realization for those engaged in the biographical construction of an individual as a text. Such a horizon itself may occasion personal transformation insofar as an empathic and introspective study of lives helps a person to reckon with the forces inherent in existence, these being consummated, of course, in the force of dying but also in being thrown into life (natality) and in sexuality, which connects mortality to birth and to a sense of rebirth in living. Empathic introspection, or the name that is being applied here to that method of uniting perception and emotion in reading and writing lives, is itself what converts the study of lives into a 'spiritual quest' for the investigator.

Biography as configuration

Methodological discussion can be carried on about the nature of biography as long as it cultivates and refines 'lived experience,' which itself is grounded in both the perception and the emotion of empathic biographical introspection. Such a criterion of authenticity in reading and writing lives sets a high standard. It invites a clear perception of and an empathic response to existential dimensions of living. Methodological comment by biographers about their art has usually been shunned, the books they produce being their primary concerns. Two of the most notable exceptions to this general rule, however, are the famed James Boswell, whose most popular work, *The Life of Johnson*, was published in 1791 and the rather obscure James Stanfield, whose only major work on the subject, *An Essay on the Study and Composition of Biography*, appeared in 1813. The work of these writers of lives was briefly presented in Chapter 1. Here it will be expanded, because their work is allied to the empathic biographical approach to studying lives. The point is that readers and writers of lives engage in the construction of configurations, ones that make the process of the interaction between an investigator and an individual subject, so to speak, 'greater than the sum of its parts.' The configurations are based on linking together 'coherent character' and 'fateful irony,' or life's actualities, and also requisites of the genre of life-writing for presenting a life as a 'text.' Both Boswell and Stanfield sought to make clear their art, and wondered how it could best cultivate and refine 'lived experience.'

Boswell's methodology was clear: 'I cannot conceive a more perfect mode of writing any man's life,' he wrote, 'than not only relating all the most important events of it in their order, but interweaving what he [Johnson] privately wrote, and said, and thought.' By careful attention to the historical accuracy of one's portrayal, Boswell believed that he was enabling mankind, 'as it were to see him live, and to "live o'er each scene" with him, as he actually advanced through the several stages of his life.' The result of such an engagement would allow a reader to see Johnson himself 'as he really was.' Hence, Boswell professed to write not Johnson's 'panegyric,' which must be all praise, 'but his Life; which, great and good as it was, must not be supposed to be entirely perfect.'[3] In this, Boswell contributed to the currency of the life-writer's craft a concern for 'historical-critical accuracy,' which itself emerged in our century in the self-conscious form of the scholarly chronicle. Boswell believed that writers before him did not take seriously enough an accurate portrayal of all the facts of a life, however much each biographer claimed to present a life authentically. The impulse to write hagiography was to be eschewed. Boswell professed to write a life as the history of a person, not merely that person's 'panegyric.'

James Boswell was an English man-of-letters. The biographical tradition he represented was not altogether like that represented by his contemporary, James Stanfield. Educated for the priesthood in France late in the eighteenth century, Irish Stanfield went to sea aboard a slave ship and returned to England — one out of three survivors — as a dedicated abolitionist. Later he became an actor and the manager of a traveling theatrical company in Yorkshire. Stanfield's son was named after Thomas Clarkson, an anti-slavery crusader, and became a successful Victorian painter and an intimate of Charles Dickens. What did the adventurous Stanfield contribute to biographical method?

'The two great ends of biography,' Stanfield asserted, are 'to obtain a deeper insight into the principles of the human mind, and to offer examples to practical observation and improvement.' He suggests that 'for the one, accurate fidelity is necessary; and for the other, moral illustration.' He believed that for the insights into a life to be delineated with 'force and truth,' the writer 'must enter intimately into the character he would exhibit — he must, for the time, endeavour to see things from the same point of view, and conceive sentiments of the same nature and feeling.' Hearkening back to Boswell's cautions, however, Stanfield felt that it was not his 'office' to defend what he represents, not to change 'the historian into the apologist,' much less to blacken the party or characters that are found 'in opposition to the opinions and practices of his hero.'[4]

What makes Stanfield distinctive are the kinds of issues he skillfully delineated and discussed. These include scholarly impartiality, historical accuracy, and creative skepticism; issues related to his emphasis on environmental conditioning, childhood physiological and psychological factors, and inherited physical traits; and his conviction of the importance of personal details, anecdotal material (incidentally, his conviction parallels Freud's own conviction about the 'psychopathology' of everyday life), and connections between a subject and his creative work. (Stanfield's thought about biography is one of the earliest examples of biographical theorizing which makes explicit use of patently 'psychological' notions.) And Stanfield did so approximately 150 years before Erikson did.[5] What exactly did Stanfield have to say about writing and reading lives?

Stanfield published his views on the nature of biography only a few years after Boswell described his own ideas. Stanfield's thought serves as a bridge built upon but going beyond Boswell's concern for historical-critical accuracy in biography. Stanfield is concerned as well for 'practical observation and improvement,' that is, for the didactic nature of studying lives, for their 'use-value.' In Erikson's sense, 'use-value' connotes the capacity for sensing the necessity of evolutionary adaptation which is possible at a level of cultural symbolics fuelled by an ethological impetus. Such a concern has its origins in a particular kind of psychological theory for Stanfield. This is the first time in the history of biography where the theorizer is explicitly relying on insights that are recognized by others as well to be patently 'psychological' insights. Stanfield's effort in what must be called 'applied biography' is one of the first in the history of reading and writing lives to imply that there exists an expanding horizon of new awareness involved in studying lives, or what we have called a 'trajectory of personal realization.' Stanfield suggested that an investigator's life could be changed as lives were studied, or examined in certain ways.

The point of view in Stanfield's *Essay* is that of associational psychology, or that mode of inquiry which takes for granted the epistemological notions of John Locke. Stanfield believed that Boswell's accomplishment in advocating historically accurate biography made possible 'a more attentive examination of the principles of the human character' – principles which could be 'actively applied to the improvable points of education and conduct.'[6] It could work the other way too. Constellations of social and cultural associations could illuminate obscurities of the lives that were depicted strictly in the Boswellian manner:

> [T]here is no object, physical or moral, that can be presented to the conception at this susceptible period of life (i.e., childhood) but will produce correspondent emotions; and according to the nature, force, and duration of the excitement, and the aptitude, sensibility, and steadiness of the disposition, permanent habits, manners, and opinions, will be formed, affecting every aspect of the future conduct and character ....
> ... the constitutional and moral circumstances of early youth have the chief influence in the formation of character; and ... in the continuance of this process of action and reaction, a cast of permanency is given to the character.[7]

As suggested in Chapter 2, Stanfield pointed out the way taken up by Bradford and Murray and others who searched lives for 'coherent character.'

Stanfield also argues that 'meaning' should be extricated from biographical historiography. The annalistic method in biography, he says, 'presents nothing but a chequered display of occasional interest and habitual occurrence; resembling life in the mere glance at appearances, but utterly unlike it in a close view of that seemingly-interrupted, yet persevering pursuit of objects, which constitutes the very essence of rational being.' The following antidote is offered: Where an interesting process occurs,

> it should be pursued through the links of purpose, progress, and attainment, shutting out, for a time, the synchronous incidents, which would divert the attention to confused objects, and break the clue of rational investigation; ... it is [the biographer's] province not only to describe, but to connect; not only to narrate, but philosophize.'[8]

Verisimilitude serves not as the sum, but as the basis upon which the more significant themes of a life become meaningful as personal realization events for the reader and writer of lives alike; that is, both what a person 'meant' in his or her own times and what that person 'means' in the present to those investigators who engage in empathic introspection.

It would be no surprise to learn that Stanfield's model for the use of associational psychology in biography often supplied the literary biographer of the late eighteenth and early nineteenth centuries with a tool for understanding the artist who was his subject. However, if one is able to point to an example, then probably that instance, ironically, was uninformed by Stanfield's work. His 339-page *Essay* was, according to all reports, difficult to read besides being obscurely published at the Durham coastal town of Sunderland in 1813. For these reasons, Stanfield's work was 'completely neglected.'[9] Only later, after a century had passed, would these sorts of biographical concerns be reconsidered by clearly 'psychologically' oriented life-writers/readers, themselves caught up in the new psychology of psychoanalysis.

By underscoring the centrality of Boswell and Stanfield to any study of reading and writing lives, other more recent contributions to biographical method flow from their work. These contributions number two. Each revolves around the aim of preserving 'lived experience,' or immediacy in living, that which the tradition of professional biography holds as a central criterion of the authenticity of life presentations. We could say in passing that as a mark of empathic introspection, lived experience is one outgrowth of Stanfield's emphasis on 'practical observation' on the one hand, and 'practical improvement' on the other. Stanfield especially would appear to be Erikson's forerunner. 'Observation' is not very different from Erikson's perceptual method, and 'improvement' is not unlike Erikson's concern that new levels of human awareness, once recognized, facilitate cultural adaptation. At any rate, the two recent contributions to professional biographical method that flow out of Boswell's and Stanfield's work have to do with typologies of biographies, the historical nature of biographical writing, and the degree to which a student of lives engages a life 'text' empathically, if at all.

Typological approaches to biography

The first grouping of later contributions to the preservation of 'lived experience,' or the immediacy in living quality of life-writing and reading lives, is that which has offered typologies of various sorts of biographies [10] Some life-writers/readers have sought a virtual firmament of meaningful order for biography by classifying various works according to certain standards of legitimacy. By and large, typologies have been a recent, twentieth-century phenomenon. In this sense, perhaps, they parallel the concern for types of political personalities in the comparative study of governments and leaders, and 'personality types' in the study of personality theory in psychological studies.

Two general kinds of typologies have been used. On the one hand, typologies have set standards of various kinds of 'literary style' that a biographer might use to present an individual. Leon Edel's work concentrates on the possible literary styles which are contained within the whole genre of biography, especially biography about literary figures. On the other hand, the use of typologies in methodological discussions has also been of the sort that the 'historical-critical legitimacy' of the genre forms the crucial standard. Here the work of James Clifford comes to mind. Even though the 'literary' and the 'historical-critical' emphases can be pressed into the service of purposes at hand, the work of Edel and Clifford appear to be in accord, inasmuch as both strive to order the immediacy of lived experience and thus follow the mandate established by Boswell and Stanfield. However, the basic assumptions of each typology are different. 'I think at least three main Architectural Ideas can be found in the structure of biographies,' writes Leon Edel.[11] The first is the 'chronicle,' or the 'traditional documentary biography.' This particular kind of stylistic emphasis stresses 'an integrated work in which the biographer arranges the materials – Boswell did this – so as to allow the voice of the subject to be heard constantly (even when that voice is heard in converse with his own biographer, as in the case of Boswell).'[12] The chronicle style of biography implies that the life written about is 'large' and 'roomy,' in which documentation is continually in the foreground and the author is 'never so happy as when he can be quoting liberally' from it.[13] The chronicle is a work of history built around a central figure.

The second type of biographical style in Edel's scheme is the 'portrait,' or a circumscribed picture, carefully 'sketched in,' with a frame 'placed around it.'[14] Portraiture seeks to catch all the 'essential traits,' that is, all that will characterize and express the personality and 'suggest the life 'behind' the surface exhibited to the world.'[15] So-called 'critical biography' is often of the portrait type, and it can sometimes go astray and portray an individual in an all too favorable or unfavorable light, depending on the author's critical standpoint.

Edel's third and final type of biography is the 'novel,' or the 'narrative-pictorial' style.[16] Larger than the portrait and smaller that the chronicle, this type of biography aims at delimiting documentation so that 'a figure may emerge, a figure in immediate action and against changing backgrounds.'[17] One may free oneself from the bondage of documents without abandoning the pursuit of the truth. An author would communicate in the manner of a novelist, who usually seeks to say something about 'humanity.' It is evident, for example, that Erik Erikson's *Gandhi's Truth* pressed more in this direction than did *Young Man Luther*. Edel concludes his description of this last type of biography by pointing to the early twentieth-century biographer, G. Lytton Strachey, as an example of the 'novelist' biographer — the 'father of this kind of biography in our time.'[18] Strachey was a master of biographical 'irony,' says Edel, who also indicated that such irony is a less poignant expression of the ancient Greek 'tragedy.'[19] Such a tragedy, when associated with individual lives, can invoke an empathic response to the 'fate' of another. However, when taken up by his followers, Strachey's irony eventuated in the style of biography known in the latter part of the first half of the twentieth century somewhat disparagingly as 'debunking.' An empathic response to the individual subject as 'Other' disappears here in the face of critical ideological posturing by such writers and readers of lives. One example of such debunking is Herbert Gorman's 1926 biography of Henry Wadsworth Longfellow. Gorman depicts Longfellow as 'a sort of American Queen Victoria ... the emblem of Victorian America, kindly, benign, urbane, moral, and safe,' endowed with 'mental feebleness' and possessing no poetic talent whatsoever.[20] The debunkers formed a central core in the ranks of 'flapper-age' biographers trying to imitate Strachey. Unlike their master, however, their successes were based mainly on writing biographies which only 'criticized the subjects for leading the lives they did.'[21]

The other typological emphasis — namely, focusing on the 'historical-critical legitimacy' of the biography rather than on its 'literary style' — is expressed by the work of James L. Clifford. His range of types is a function of the degree to which a biographer may choose to stress the use of primary historical documentation. The degree of usage determines either the 'subjective' or the 'objective' cast which will form the basis of one's literary style. This is to say in one sense that Edel's typology rests, in part, on the sort of typology Clifford presents. Both are biographers and both are concerned with the question of the relation between 'style' and 'facts.'

Clifford distinguishes five types of biographical emphasis regarding 'historical-critical legitimacy.'[22]

First, 'objective biography' assumes that one will assemble everything relating to some person and present it without editorial comment and without imposing external interpretations. Writing biography with these strictures in mind may be next to impossible to do in its pure form, as Clifford himself avows. Edel's 'chronicle' comes to mind as a type of biography which is roughly similar to objective biography.

Second, 'scholarly historical biography' posits the selection of evidence without any unacknowledged guesswork, fictional devices, or attempts to interpret the subject's life psychologically. Selected facts and details (not *all*) are strung together in chronological order with some historical background that serves to illuminate a life.

Third, 'artistic-scholarly biography' depends on exhaustive historical-critical research. However, once all the facts are in, a process of selection occurs according to the creative imagination of the investigator. Empathy is allowed in. As an imaginative creative artist, the biographer tries to present the facts of a life in the liveliest and most interesting manner, usually as 'events' of significance to the individual. There is no conscious distortion of the evidence and no making up of conversations the subject 'might have had' or of events of his or her life for which evidence is scant. The biographer is able to suggest that what is done is something more than merely to write a 'history,' which itself embraces the emphasis of the first two types of Clifford's typology. Here Edel's portrait type seems similar.

Fourth, 'narrative biography' uses all the collected evidence and materials in such a way that the atmosphere of real life is created in imaginative and vivid ways. One might use portions of the subject's letters so that the subject 'comes to life' during the course of the narrative. Here it is often the case that concern for historical-critical legitimacy drops from the picture almost entirely and an empathic response is readily invited. However, it must be said that this may result either from the attitude of the biographer or from a paucity of biographical information. Erikson's reconstructions of 'Luther's fit in the choir' and Gandhi's engagement with the mill owner during the Ahmedabad strike are of this order.

Fifth and last, 'fictional biography' is usually constructed upon pure fabrications about crucial details and events of the life of the subject. Most concern for historical-critical legitimacy is suspended. Biographies about figures for whom little historical information is available are often written fictionally for limited didactic purposes. (Erikson, of course, was often accused of this by 'psychologists' and 'historians' alike.) Here materials can be rewritten with an eye not only to novel-like style, but also to pointing out and embellishing exemplary lives. *Aesop's Fables* have this quality as do sacred biographies of Jesus and the Buddha, for example.

More recently, Stephen B. Oates offers a typology of biography which lays special emphasis on empathy, introspection, and simulating in the present the 'lived experience' of an individual as a 'text.' Thus, Oates's list includes the 'Chronicle Biography,' or an extensive accumulation of facts about a subject with a minimum amount of the biographer's presence being evident in the narrative; the 'Pure Biography,' which retains the chronicle's detailed accuracy, but also aims to simulate a life in the heat of the biographer's empathy; and the 'Critical Biography,' in which the story of a subject's life, far from being 'brought to life,' becomes only the occasion for airing the biographer's opinions.[23] Oates himself has written a considerable number of biographies about American Civil War leaders and other more contemporary figures associated with the contentious issue of race in American life. He has done so as a self-conscious advocate of the 'Pure Biography,' which he believes to be the most compelling type.

If professional biographers are to be applauded for the efforts they have made to preserve the integrity of 'lived experience,' or immediacy-in-living, by means of their work, then it behooves the modern, late twentieth-century interpreter of the biographical tradition to do no less. This would apply particularly to professional biographers and to intelligent readers and writers of lives who avail themselves of psychology and its often wooden, abstract, and reductionistic ideas about the human personality and interpersonal relationships. How, then, might methodological discussions be extended without losing the immediacy of lived experience? Does any kind of theoretical structure exist, aside from the work of Boswell and Stanfield and the typological approaches represented by Edel, Clifford, and Oates which might lend appropriate expression to such issues? An examination of the historical tradition of recent biographical efforts provides the kind of framework that is needed. By this means the work of Erik Erikson will be able to guide us further into genuine autobiographical interests.

Biography as history

In spite of typological considerations, Edel writes that the biographer 'may be as imaginative as he pleases — the more imaginative the better — in the way in which he brings together his materials, but he must not imagine the materials. He must read himself into the past; but he must also read that past into the present.'[24] Biography not only serves to report the nature of the past, but it also serves to clarify who individuals living in the present are. We could suggest that because he 'reads' into and out of the past, Edel operates perceptually and emotionally as a working biographer, somewhat in the manner of Erikson. However, what is most important here is that Edel is calling for careful hermeneutics. He asks, what does the life studied disclose to the writer and reader of lives, or what affirms a shared humanity, and hence is morally efficacious? Both Stanfield and Edel stress the importance of a 'biographical imagination,' while being well aware of the responsibility to report history accurately, or at least to interpret the past as fairly as possible. Edel (and Stanfield by implication) has characterized in a sentence the morally efficacious nature of empathic introspection. It is a mark of Erikson's introspective biographical approach, now charged with empathy, and not merely the result of juggling 'psychology' and 'history' together and coming up with something that could be viewed to fall short of the standards of those two disciplines.

Another way of saying this is to suggest that Clifford's typology is one expression among many other possibilities of the Boswellian tradition of reading and writing lives. Emphasis is placed on 'historical-critical legitimacy,' or doing away with 'panegyric.' Edel's typology, then, presents itself as an expression of the tradition of Stanfield and its concern for the 'use-value' of biography, or the 'educational' (i.e., 'psychological') value of biography in our own times. Stanfield's tradition, which is the more explicitly 'educational' tradition, remains truer to the intention of Samuel Johnson than does that of Boswell, with its more explicitly 'historical' direction. These are emphases only. They are not exhaustive and exclusive ways of life-writing and reading lives as windows into history. Nevertheless, they seek to depict the backdrop of contemporary efforts by which readers and writers of lives may engage in establishing for themselves a 'trajectory of personal realization' that would transform such efforts into a 'spiritual quest.'

The following thesis can be presented at this juncture. The so-called psychohistorical work of Erikson, which is ostensibly biographical in form, can be viewed as an extension of the biographical tradition of James Stanfield (which, of course, takes for granted the historical-critical emphasis of Boswell). What does this entail? When the work of Erikson and Stanfield are combined, better recognition of the insights of Gestalt theory as being implicit in the development of the biographical tradition is possible. An empathic response to life texts is the key. We ask, how is Erikson an engaged reader and writer of lives, neither a psychoanalyst *per se*, nor an historian *per se*? An answer has to do with the way attention is paid to the non-typological tradition of life-writing/reading, in which the moral efficacy of lives, accessed by means of empathic introspection, is a major hallmark. As we move beyond Boswellian verisimilitude as a benchmark of the biographical construction of an individual as a 'text,' attention can be focussed on the legacy of 'lived experience' as a criterion for the biographical construction of texts of lives. In Chapter 6 this will be called *soteriological biography*. By this is meant that process of reading and writing lives which invites a change of attitudes and awareness that aims at increased personal realization in the life of the investigator.

Leon Edel anticipates what is to follow as he speaks particularly about the use of Freud's psychoanalysis in biography: 'It is fairly obvious,' he writes, 'that we can handle it only after we have studied and mastered that part of psychology useful to us, as we must master any learning. Our success will depend,' he believes, 'on the extent to which we know what we are about and the way in which we use these shiny new tools. We must not run amuck; above all we must beware of the terminology and jargon of psychoanalysts. What we must try to do,' Edel proposes, 'is to translate the terms in a meaningful way and into the language proper to ourselves.'[25] Only in this way will modern reading and writing of lives which make use of non-literary, recent psychological formulations – be they psychoanalytic ones or not – be 'that which is most eagerly read, and most easily applied to the purposes of life,' as Samuel Johnson required of the art.

We have said that the work of James Stanfield remains a high watermark in nineteenth-century thought about the nature of life-writing/reading. As we have seen, other biographical thinkers coming after Stanfield relied unwittingly on much of the groundwork he laid for discussions, especially in literary circles in England at first and later in America. Though subsequent thinkers and biographers probably did not all read Stanfield's *Essay*, they were none the less quite aware of the general tenor of opinion about the biographical art that Stanfield expressed. Erikson, for one, does in fact provide such a step ahead along the way towards a more sufficient conception of reading and writing lives. His view differs substantively from and qualitatively transcends 'typologies' (the alleged highpoint of theorizing by literary scholars). By way of foreshadowing more from Erikson's approach, we have already noted in previous chapters the almost uncanny similarities of method and style between the enterprise of professional literary biography and psychology during the first half of the twentieth century. This was clearly evident in the apposition of the work of Gamaliel Bradford and Henry Murray, and Lytton Strachey and Sigmund Freud. Similar questions to those put to these four readers and writers of lives – two biographers and two psychologists – continue to fuel reflection in contemporary times. Do we see relationships of similarity between what was happening in the field of biography in the late nineteenth century and what was beginning to happen in the nascent field of psychology? Or, at least, can the different structures of inquiry of each domain into the 'individual life' be meaningfully correlated in retrospect? Are literary biographers and psychologists working in different ways on a common project and not quite realizing that they were doing so? Not only are they working on a common project, but are they even going so far as to be employing similar methods without knowing it? By seeking answers to these questions, connections between the two domains of inquiry form threads. These threads have been woven together into an overall theoretical structure which, as suggested previously, is perhaps largely consummated, represented and expressed in Erik Erikson's work of biographical introspection. However, as already noted as well, that particular structure in Erikson's work remains implicit or embedded far from the surface in his two psychohistorical studies of Luther and Gandhi.

A model of empathic introspection

Let us recall the point made by Richard Holmes about the elusiveness of a biographical subject, in his case, Robert Louis Stevenson. Instead of pursuing another person's footsteps, biography brings alive a life by other sorts of skills and crafts and sensible magic. One can never catch the footsteps of another; no, never quite catch them: 'But maybe, if you were lucky, you might write about the pursuit of that fleeting figure in such a way as to bring it alive in the present.'[26] Our job now is to try to specify such luck, the luck cherished by Holmes's methodological insight. The sort of magic required is Erikson's art. A return to the Eriksonian style of reading and writing lives may now be undertaken.[27]

The purpose of such a return is to underscore the perceptual basis of Erikson's style, and to use this basis to suggest that reading and writing lives is a sensuous activity; it is a matter of embodiment and body-based intuition. Not everyone is adept at using their own bodies as idioms of knowledge, but for those so skilled at embodied knowing, this appears as a capacity to be empathic. Empathic introspection, based on a capacity to feel an intuitive connection to other people, can be defined as the retrieval by a life-writer/reader of the lived experience of a biographical subject. The moral mandate of reading and writing lives, namely, to cultivate the immediacy of lived experience in a life that can elicit an empathic response, is the criterion by which searching for 'coherent character' and sensing 'fateful irony' are best focused. The perceptual basis of this art makes possible retrieving the experiential quality of the life 'text' that results from biographical construction. The student of lives is readied to enter into autobiographical reflection, this process being 'mirrored' in the constructed 'text' of a biographical subject.

How do the chief genre characteristics of writing and reading about individuals, namely, coherent character and fateful irony, come together to form the perceptual context of Erikson's work? How might we make explicit what in his works remains implicit, or go about revealing the perceptual basis of them by seeking out the threads of character and irony that appear in the recent traditions of professional literary biography? How, in other words, is Erikson a representative and exemplary life-writer and reader of lives? A hint is to be found in his essay, 'The Nature of Clinical Evidence,' where he writes that '(from the direct observation of children and perception experiments to "metapsychological" discussion), it stands to reason that clinical evidence is characterized by an immediacy which transcends formulations ultimately derived from mechanistic patterns of thought,' by which he means psychiatric and clinical psychological points of view.[28] One might be able to bring forth the implicit perceptual immediacy of Erikson's style and, perhaps, incline to rename his article 'The Nature of Biographical Evidence,' which would then be more accurate. How does Erikson as a life-writer/reader join together in his work the search for coherent character and a sense of fateful irony in order to bring about an authentic sense of lived experience, 'immediacy in living,' or the hallmark of genuine empathy and introspection for oneself?

Erikson accomplishes the task of bringing together character and irony by using a particular model of psychotherapeutic experience. His model is an analog of the threads that make up the broad tradition of life-writing/ reading. Seeking an individual's 'text,' and noting how different it may be from one's own life story, must also include a search for dimensions of a shared humanity, or a sense of existential reckoning with life – what it means to be born (natality), to age and die (mortality) and to rehearse during living these two outer limits of life by means of sexual activity (sexuality). An accentuation of sexuality, and sexual behavior in particular, intensifies the experiences of being alive (for example, full orgasmic functioning) and facing dying (for example, post-coital quiescence). What the biographer should deal with, says Erikson, is 'grounded in what is "unique" to the "individual" case,' including the personal involvement of the investigator.[29] Two considerations derive from this. First, Erikson's model of psychotherapeutic change suggests a way for life-writing and reading to approximate more closely to the criterion of the immediacy of lived experience than the approaches of Bradford and Murray, or Strachey and Freud. Second, an analysis of character and irony, itself implicit in Erikson's model, clarifies or makes explicit the 'psychological' nature of that structure when it is understood in terms of the model. The wider and deeper river of inquiry into an individual's life, within which the narrower and shallower streams of character portrayal and scenes of dramatic irony flow, is provided by Erikson's model of psychotherapy.

Within the context of the clinical situation or, as Erikson puts it, in the 'special case of the "psychotherapeutic", encounter,' three items crowd out all others. These are *'complaint,' 'anamnesis,'* and *'interpretation.'* Erikson indicates that what goes on in the therapist's mind between the 'verbal complaint addressed to him' and the 'verbal interpretation given in return' is, as he takes it, 'the question' of psychotherapy, the subject of his essay.[30] The reader/writer of lives is like a psychotherapist when he or she responds

to the presentation of a particular life. One comes across what can be taken
to be 'events' in the subject's life, whether they are recorded as such or only
discerned, perhaps imaginatively, by the investigator.

These 'events' then provoke the investigator's curiosity (i.e., the subject's
'complaints'). Spread out for review are letters, journals, memoirs,
autobiographies, histories, and other sorts of documentation that make
up the constellation of materials out of which a life is to be reconstructed
(i.e., the investigator's 'anamnesis,' or the beginning of biographical
introspection). The 'interpretation' of events is critical because this is the
point at which the life studied opens up the horizon of the investigator's
self-knowledge. Not just simple biography, or a 'life and times' study of a
distant figure, is produced, rather, an experience of introspection is invited.
To interpret a life is to address its 'meaning' in the present, not only what it
'meant' for the subject to have lived as he or she did. Just what does *this* life
mean to the life-writer and reader of lives? That is the nub of empathic
biographical introspection. Erikson specifies three guidelines for the
interpretation of lives. They are loosely in sequential order: (1) searching
for 'recurring themes'; (2) recognizing 'evidential continuity'; and (3)
creating a 'unitary theme.' These guidelines, or active processes of
engaging with source materials, bring together the threads of character and
irony in Erikson's pioneering biographical (and autobiographical) work.

Assuming that a subject has been selected (for whatever reasons), the
reader and writer of lives has access to all the materials needed to
reconstruct the contours of the life and the major events in it, and is about
to commence sorting through the materials and his or her own sense of
engagement in the subject's life. Such is the beginning of interpretation, at
which point Erikson has something to say: 'I must ask you to join me,' he
beckons,

> in what Freud has called 'free-floating attention', which — as I must now add —
> turns inward to the observer's ruminations even as it attends the patient's 'free
> associations' and which, far from focusing on any one item too intentionally,
> rather waits to be impressed by recurring themes.[31]

Such themes are faint at first, but come with increasing force and signal the
patient's 'message and meaning': The 'gradual establishment' of 'strategic
intersections' on a 'number of tangents' eventually makes it possible to
locate in the observed phenomena that 'central core which comprises the
"evidence."'[32] Those 'strategic intersections' often appear to be contra-
dictory, like the patient who says one thing but really means the opposite,
for example, '*Of course*, I love you!' While we might be led to think that
Erikson operates mostly with a view to establishing a person's character,
we must realize that his understanding of the start of empathic biographical

interpretation takes in contradiction, or also embraces the need to establish irony.

When interpretation begins to yield such 'evidence,' then a second concern overrides the first. A life possesses what Erikson calls 'a basic synthesizing trend,' which provides a line of continuity between one event and another.[33] This concern for continuity amidst recurring themes or 'evidence' is similar to Henry Murray's concern to develop 'themas' into 'unity-themas.' However, Erikson believes that recognizing 'evidential continuity' is the necessary second step of interpretation; it is not a quick shift directly into developing 'unity-themas.'

His unwillingness to sacrifice the immediacy which is characteristic of the psychotherapeutic encounter to hasty theoretical considerations is demonstrated by Erikson. No doubt Gamaliel Bradford would have applauded the effort. The second level of the process of interpretation places 'apprehending' before 'comprehending.' By doing so, Erikson approximates the phenomenology of reading and writing lives more so, perhaps, than Murray does. As evidence of often conflicting connections begins to mount out of all that is presented by his 'sources' (his patients), Erikson moves from 'apprehension' to fuller understanding (*Verstehen*) or 'comprehending.'

The third and last stage of interpretation is the transformation of apprehensions of evidential continuity into a unitary pattern which gives the fullest possible meaning to the eventfulness of the life of one's subject. A 'unitary theme,' Erikson believes, involves a pattern common at the same time to a 'significant portion of his (the patient's) symptomology, to an important conflict of his childhood,' and to 'corresponding facets of his work and love life.'[34] The whole quality of the parts of evidence under consideration is greater than the mere sum of them in the eye of the life-writer/reader artist. The stature of this as insight would override the classic psychoanalytic move to reduce a life to early childhood trauma alone. Moreover, this is precisely what the reader and writer of lives can also strive to achieve. Be that as it may, how does Erikson actually preserve the quality of lived experience, immediacy-in-living, in the context of life 'texts'?

What 'metapsychological discussion' lacks that 'clinical evidence' (i.e., 'interpretations,' mentioned above) does not, writes Erikson, is 'an immediacy which transcends formulations ultimately derived from mechanistic patterns of thought.'[35] This immediacy inheres in life-writing/reading. What does such a focus suggest? One may talk about the use of psychoanalysis, or 'psychography' (Bradford), or 'personology' (Murray), or 'debunking' (Strachey) in relation to life-writing/reading as Erikson has in the subtitle of his *Young Man Luther*, 'Psychoanalysis and History.' However, the heart of the matter is the process of investigating the individual as a 'text' itself. The specific and peculiar psychological infrastructure of the process forms the tacit dimension of the life-writer/reader's task (especially for the psychobiographer). A style of dealing with lives which exists prior to the application of any one particular point of view, or a 'psychology' to a life is our aim. This tacit aim will concern us in the next part of this chapter. For now we need to ask, if Eriksonian 'immediacy' is the criterion of authenticity in life-writing and reading lives, then how does it emerge, for instance, in the context of Erikson's studies of Luther and Gandhi?

Just as psychotherapy goes on in a series, one session after the other, and so forth, so too moves the course of life-writing/reading. The task requires more than a single brush with the materials and more than a single sitting if a life is to be adequately represented. Sustaining clinical-like 'immediacy' is not only difficult because a living subject is usually not present, but is also even more strenuous because the imagination of the life-writer/reader must be continually vitalized and open to corrective evidence and fresh insights. Nevertheless, 'immediacy' occurs when attention is paid, as Erikson says, to 'series of such encounters' with one's materials, with one's evidence.[36] It would be easier to allow one mode of inquiry to dominate the other, stressing either the 'structural pattern(s)' of character or the 'critical event(s)' of irony of a life, and calling one's task finished at that. However, empathic biographical introspection is like the psychotherapeutic encounter: one keeps one's *own* thematic inclinations in check as well as one's *own* sense of the 'eventfulness' of writing series in one's *own* life. The matter is hardly easy. A life-writer/reader comes to ask continually, how does the process of writing itself determine the life being represented? Only when this question is answered will the investigator be in a position to say that the past has been successfully 'encountered' and has been readied for use in the present. This use is defined as the moral mandate to ensure that lived experience in its immediacy (*Erlebnis*) is continually inserted into human discourse and affairs in the form of 'truth,' at least as a shared search for forthright, open human encounter.

Let us turn to Erikson's studies of Martin Luther and Mohandas Gandhi in order to see how he weaves together a configuration of interpretation on the basis of a search for 'coherent character' and a sense of 'fateful irony' in his reading of lives and life-writing. We shall also want to note how he achieves the living fabric of a life according to the criterion of retrieving the immediacy of lived experience, which henceforth can simply be called the 'truth,' or the 'truth of lives.' How, then, does Erikson interpret Luther and Gandhi? One can take for granted that he progressed through the first stage of receiving a 'complaint.' Since he was interested in adolescents' 'identity crises' at the time, Erikson became interested in Luther when it occurred to him that the young man was not immune to one of the eight major psychosocial life crises which he had not long before articulated in his theory of personality development, namely, 'identity versus identity diffusion.'

Adolescence was the focus of Erikson's early clinical studies at the Austen Riggs Center in Stockbridge, Massachusetts and at the Western Psychiatric Institute in the School of Medicine at the University of Pittsburg during most of the 1950s, when the so-called 'identity crisis' formed the 'complaints' of the adolescents in his care. The specific 'complaint' which Erikson recognized in his later work with adolescents pertained to violence and the containment of violence during the era immediately after the Second World War, when rising expectations led to widespread social change. Adolescents were historically engaged in conflict and violence as the 'Beat Generation' of the 1950s, and in the civil rights and peace movements of the 1960s, that is, mainly during the decade between the appearances of the studies of Luther (1958) and Gandhi (1969). The problem of identity was central in the life of the Mahatma too. Erikson felt 'complaints,' therefore, first in the clinic and later in history. The second stage of his encounter with these foci, or 'anamnesis,' occurred as he researched each life and the times in which each individual had lived. Erikson's reconstructions soon bore the mark of 'interpretations,' two examples of which follow.

The overriding point of Luther is that he suffered from a 'protracted identity crisis.'[37] Only half seriously, Erikson suggests, 'it would be much too easy (although some stalwart opponents of all interpretation would consider even this easiest and most obvious explanation far-fetched) that Hans' son was seeking in religion what he could not find in Hans.' If one is to understand the 'deepest nostalgia of lonely youth,' Erikson continues (and surely Hans Luther's son was one of them), psychosocial development requires the 'search for mutual recognition, the meeting *face to face*,' which is an aspect in Luther's worldview and in all religion.[38] If Luther was pushed into precocity by his stern father, and if such a parental stance thwarted Luther's infantile reliance upon the 'generous breast and the eyes that care' of his mother and other possible sources of maternal support, then his 'once-bornness' was incomplete. His protracted identity crisis during adolescence, therefore, had to do with wanting 'to have another chance at being born.'[39] According to Erikson's interpretation, Luther 'wanted God's recognition,' God's trust.[40] Thus, concluded Erikson, 'A long way stretched ahead of him before he was able to experience, through Christ rather than through Mary, the relevance of the theme of mother and child in addition to that of father and son.'[41] However, once Luther realized intellectually the 'bipolarity of recognition,' the ambiguity of such life themes was mitigated by a new-found identity. Luther's identity grew out of the thematic unity represented specifically by the theological principle of justification by faith alone: 'then he could say that Christ was defined by two images: one of the infant lying in a manger, "hanging on a virgin's tits" (*hanget an einer Jungfrau Zitzen*); and one of a man sitting at his Father's right hand.'[42] Erikson captured the 'truth' of Luther's life in terms of the power inherent in early family life, with which most of his readers would be familiar.

Mohandas Gandhi, one knows, suffered from a 'crisis of generativity' according to Erikson.[43] Gandhi managed to create new choices about what and whom the Indian people could care for, what they could do well as Indians, and what the future held in store for the expression of the nation's independence. Less a matter of ideological construction than it was for Luther, Gandhi's program of *Satyagraha*, or truthful action, was governed by the readiness to get hurt and yet not to hurt others. The overall aim was to further realize individuals together, at bottom, as one species ('speciation'). A sense of speciation was prefigured in Gandhi's widely inclusive relationship with his father. 'Nursing' a stricken father early in life became the basis of the 'calling forth' of the integrity of Ambalal Sarabhai, the operator of the textile mill against which Gandhi led a protracted non-violent strike action, in Ahmedabad in 1918. The sense of inner tension, of a life lived under a 'curse,' says Erikson, to which Gandhi's life attests, was mitigated only 'when that pattern would be set for a style of leadership which can defeat a superior adversary only non-violently and with the express intent of saving him as well as those whom he oppressed.'[44]

Erikson admits that some of this interpretation, in fact, corresponds to what the Mahatma would have unhesitatingly 'acknowledged as his conscious intention.'[45] It is interesting that generativity, defined as 'nursing India out of the sickness of colonial status,' became Erikson's way of portraying Gandhi's character. By his own avowal, Erikson's interpretation of Gandhi's coherent character as pertaining to the theme of 'generativity,' as nursing, also sounds a note of fateful irony. Even though Gandhi himself would say that 'some' of Erikson's interpretation was at his own ready awareness, Erikson, acting as a reader and writer of lives, argues that Gandhi did not see the whole of it. The many seemingly unconnected parts of his life, as well as the characterological theme of 'nursing,' escaped most of the Mahatma's conscious awareness, at least in part.

It is theoretically safe to seek the configurational structure of a life wherever sources exist but, more helpful, it is also possible to employ the structure speculatively where sources do not fully suffice. This would lend weight to typologies of biography by adding the dynamics of empathy and introspection to the task of biographical construction. Increased use of Leon Edel's 'narrative-pictorial' type, James Clifford's 'narrative' and 'fictional' types, and Stephen B. Oates's 'pure biography' type of life-writing/reading would be possible. Each of these types of reading and writing lives poses a life theme that has been gleaned from periods when evidence is available and solid, and then can be 'read back' into the sparsely depicted years and inconclusive events. Principles of configurational analysis (Gestalt) come into play to guide biographical construction here. For example, principles such as 'nearness,' 'likeness,' 'common destiny,' 'good form,' and 'closure' suggest the nature of the dynamics of introspection and empathy as a configuration of inquiry into a life. In terms of Gestalt psychological theory, perhaps the principle of 'nearness' does not suffice to connect an episode about which one knows clear details, with an important earlier episode that is clouded by the lack of source materials. The biographer's configuration of the life tends to break down; and a search for more information and/or a 'reading into' the life is undertaken. Moreover, on the basis of the principle of 'likeness,' the life-writer can shift the whole period of time considered to a new level that, as 'configurational' thinkers would say, has 'common destiny' with facts that can be clearly substantiated. This allows the biographer to avoid the charge that he or she is 'projecting' his or her own narrative line into a life. In the end, 'good form' and 'closure' for the whole of a life would result. Norman Mailer's biographical speculations (many purely imagined, without configurational or Gestalt guidelines) about the circumstances surrounding the death of Marilyn Monroe move roughly in this sort of direction.[46]

Brief demonstration

Our aim now is to show just what can be done to understand lives when emphasis is placed on seeking configurations of meaning, and deriving dominant structures of character from them, while at the same time weighing up any countervailing winds of irony. Coherent character and fateful irony create the tension by which the configuration of a life is sustained as lived experience (*Erlebnis*). Character predominates, but irony not only lends it support. A discovery of irony may threaten or even shatter a subject's self-understanding when placed in the hands of the life-writer/reader. So be it. I wish here to consider an event in the life of the nineteenth-century American writer Ralph Waldo Emerson, himself a visual type. The event (or, better put, the coincidental acquaintance) is Emerson's relationship with his fellow-classmate at Harvard College, Martin Gay, which lasted from 1820 to 1822. The approach of empathic introspection, based on seeking configurational structures that link together the reader/ writer of lives with his or her subject as a life 'text' will be compared with that of one of Emerson's chief biographers, Ralph L. Rusk.

Rusk's narrative, *The Life of Ralph Waldo Emerson* (1949), is 504 pages in length. Out of these pages, Rusk reserved one paragraph of less than half a page for dealing with the person whom, Emerson reported, students at the college called 'Cool Gay.'[47] The reasons Rusk includes mention of Gay at all is for the purpose of suggesting that Emerson was disappointed by his own social achievement which, we are told, was meagre. Emerson did not easily make close friends. Thus, 'his infatuation, in his junior and senior years, for Martin Gay, a student of his own age but two classes behind him,' says Rusk, 'had no social results.' However, quoting from Emerson's journals, Rusk portrayed young Emerson as being a 'dozen times a day, and as often by night' wrapped in 'conjectures' about Gay's 'character and inclinations,' for Emerson and Gay had only 'two or three long profound stares at each other.' Concluding this paragraph, and thus his treatment of the Emerson–Gay relationship (an odd, even ironic one indeed, based on the scant information he offers), Rusk speculates about what the two-year-long experience may have meant: 'The whole experience struck him [Emerson] chiefly as an interesting psychological problem. The problem, however, was doubtless mainly his own. He was delving slightly into his unconscious self.' In 1949, Rusk, a professional historian and literary biographer, could wax provocatively in terms of interrelationships between biography and psychology but leave them undeveloped.

However, Rusk fails to mention one critical fact about the objective or 'artifact-like' nature of Emerson's report about the relationship with Martin Gay. Though he wrote about the relationship in his journals, it is clear from an examination of the manuscripts themselves that Emerson went back to those entries and more often than not, with methodical vigor, either scratched out or disguised portions of the reports, especially Martin Gay's name. In addition, for the first time in the journals, pencil sketches of male faces are drawn in the margins next to his references to Gay. This occurs nowhere else. Clearly, the relationship is unique. Could it concentrate and crystallize the overall configurational structure of Emerson's character and its ironic aspects? Does an opportunity to use empathic introspection present itself to the reader and writer of Emerson's life? Might such an approach invite a life-writer/reader to grow aware of and cultivate a personal horizon of realization? Reconfiguring the Emerson–Gay relationship suggests that an affirmative answer can be given to such questions.

One can take Ralph Rusk to task on two points, each about his neglect of some facts of Emerson's report. First, the fact that Emerson never exchanged a word at all with Gay and only engaged with him in a visual manner, marked by 'long stares,' is dismissed by Rusk. Second, that Emerson betrayed his extreme ambivalence about his 'infatuation' over Gay, along with the tell-tale alteration of his journals by disguising and eliminating Gay from the record (so to say), is not pursued by Rusk. Perhaps the biographer is not as much of a psychobiographer as he may attempt to be about the Emerson–Gay relationship. What adds to the significance of this relationship in Emerson's life is that he himself refrained from talking to Gay and vice versa (and there is no record whatsoever that after 1822 Emerson even knew that Gay became a prominent Boston physician). When the student body at Harvard at that time numbered only around 250 students, it seems likely that some effort had to be exerted in order to keep at a distance from classmates, especially from those to whom one felt an almost uncontrollable emotional attachment.[48] Had Rusk deliberately asked himself, 'How is Emerson's life like my own?' these two human experiences might have given rise to useful speculation about Emerson's motives. Thoughts about Emerson's motives would be based on the biographer's own introspective awareness and on an empathic response to the life 'text' of one's subject. However, Rusk chose to construct a narrative life 'text' that assumed a relationship of difference, perhaps based on the century or so that separated them in time between Emerson and himself.

Though Emerson believed he was removing a most baffling relationship from his journals, he actually left an indelible record of his intense ambivalence toward Gay. Moreover, that he remained at 'arm's length' distance from Gay discloses the fact that for two years Emerson was engaged in a most meaningful communication with the young man. This was definitely not unlike the manner of being attracted by what the phenomenologist of religion, Rudolf Otto, has called the 'mysterium,' which was simultaneously 'tremendum' and 'fascinans.'[49] A reader and writer of lives is able to *perceive* (for example, marginal doodlings, etc.) and *feel* (for example, anxiety over Gay, etc.) Emerson's 'approach/avoidance' conflict, especially as it lasted for so long. Though Rusk appears to be on the brink of declaring that Emerson's 'infatuation' was of a homosexual (at least, homoerotic) nature, the young man's own record and behavior — 'objective' material — must be given topmost consideration. One should pay particular attention to Emerson's ambivalence (as the form of the original manuscripts suggests) and to his use of a visual mode of expression (as the substance of his entries tells). These foci, unlike Rusk's emphases (and lack of emphases) about Emerson, fulfill the requirement that irony (i.e., instances of ambivalence) finds its tension by being linked to a theme about character (i.e., habitual use of a visual mode of expression), which together bestow unity on a life, and thus 'hold it together,' so to speak. Constructing a configuration of Emerson requires that the 'whole' of his life be greater than the sum of its 'parts.'

In other words, the tension in the relationship with Gay points to irony in Emerson's life. It was ironic that even though he was infatuated with Gay, Emerson could hardly bring himself to talk to him. Rusk misses the ironic element because he does not ask the right questions about the records Emerson left behind, or he hardly asks enough questions that call into question Emerson's record and behavior in such an event. The way Emerson dealt with his ambivalence rests on the overall thematic structure of his character in action then. A coherence was supplied to his character by his reliance on *visual* communication with Gay's presence, and on fantasy-like 'conjectures' when separated from his classmate. Emerson persisted in emphasizing vision and visual metaphors as an idiom of communication throughout his life. In passing, we could add that the combination of irony and character here implies nothing short of a religious engagement with Gay, mediated visually, indeed specularly in fact and in fantasy. Gay becomes the 'mysterium.' Emerson is gradually able to open his eyes to see the young man as such in the light of day.

Thus, Emerson's character took precedence over his ironic interpersonal engagement (or deliberate 'non-engagement') with Gay. The emotional ambivalence of their relationship, such as it was, diffused insofar as it could be managed visually at a distance. Later in his life the same configuration would appear time and again. His reliance on vision is his character: every time he was faced with situational ambiguities (for example, *free* to talk to Gay or *not*) or with inner emotional ambivalence (for example, to *talk* to Gay or *not*) he is noticed constructing himself in terms of utmost provocation and fascination in such instances according to a visual modality (often literally), 'seeing' his way clear of conflict. Emerson visually structures the configuration of his coherent character and countervailing fateful irony over the course of his life. The event with Gay of 1820–22 prefigures Emerson's later life, when he would continually search visually for an inner sense of numinosity, one intimately tied to nature, almost in a magical manner. Only as his worldview developed in terms of an apotheotic vision did his understanding of nature undergo *theosis*, or become an idiom of divinity. And on such a basis a distinctive American culture emerged during the nineteenth century.

6 Soteriological biography

Reading by the public in recent times indicates that interest in reading and writing lives in particular, is rife. A Library of Congress survey indicates that in the 1980s biography was the 'most popular category of non-fiction in the United States,' and it rivalled 'action/adventure fiction and historical novels.'[1] In the past decade more people read a biography than any other kind of book.[2] The number of titles of biographies published each year has almost doubled since the 1960s. During the twelve-month period from August 1983 through July 1984, they accounted for 15 percent of the total nonfiction books bought, a close second to reference/instruction books, the leading type of nonfiction book (16 percent).[3] This 1983–4 increase in popularity – from 14 percent to 17 percent for that period – is characteristic of the growth in the popularity of life-writing over the past two decades, about 3 percent per year.[4] One might well ask, why this upsurge of appeal for biography, or studies of lives? An answer to such a question turns in large measure on a shift from biographical construction of an individual as a 'text' to what can be learned from a life. In other words, the shift is to autobiographical reflection about how best to live.

Of particular interest in the context of this chapter, one notes with surprise that gift purchases of biographies (and autobiographies) for this typical period are especially high among adults aged thirty-five and over (17 percent), while it drops to only 9 percent among those aged between eighteen and thirty-four.[5] However, this should come as little surprise to a reader and writer of lives who engages in empathic introspection. For as aging takes its toll on one's body and as death grows palpable, autobiographical reflection and a desire for increased spiritual awareness quickens. For some, this is propellant enough to speed a reader and writer of lives along a trajectory of personal realization, one that makes such a pursuit into a 'spiritual quest.' What does the overall upsurge in the public's interest in the study of lives mean for reading and writing lives in general? This upsurge of appeal represents psychological data that readers and writers of lives neglect at their peril.

The spirit of the appeal is not unlike what psychologist Henry Murray affirmed in his work. We can recall from Chapter 2 that Murray was always responsive to wide horizons of inquiry in the humanities. In his Introduction to 'The Case of Earnst' by R.W. White, Murray suggests that the method used in discussing the case follows the simple principle, that 'by observation of many parts one finally arrives at a conception of the whole and, then, having grasped the latter, one can reinterpret and understand the former.'[6] Generating a 'configuration' of a life as a 'text' is what the initial stage of reading and writing lives is all about. Murray refers to the psychological investigator who uses such a line of inquiry as a 'biographer,' and to what is learned as something lying 'between biology (science) and literature (art).'[7] The biographer writes a report and brings it into group discussion, where it is analyzed and elaborated for 'insight,' or an awareness of the principles or themes of coherence and irony by which the life is said to 'hold together,' so to speak.

This chapter is an effort in the spirit of Henry Murray, an avowed biographer, or reader and writer of lives.[8] It seeks the configurational 'whole,' or a law, by which reading and writing lives may be understood. Are there invariants or constants which may ultimately constitute human nature for this field of investigation? Noting that literature has recently become a 'science,' we shall want to keep in mind Murray-like questions which follow, namely, might biology become an 'art'? And how might 'biological art' find expression in the 'whole' of reading and writing lives? The answers which result will suggest that autobiographical reflection by the life-writer/reader is conducted best when efforts are made to achieve 'embodied' thought about oneself.

Biography's complicity in postmodern thought

The work of Murray and his colleagues is largely neglected these days. However, any comprehensive endeavor of reading and writing lives is in a good position to revive Murray's interests in studying lives, and thus should take into account literary and aesthetic criticism in contemporary culture, but in an unusual way. The postmodern condition of knowledge itself prompts the public to flee to testaments about the fullness of life.[9] The ideology of postmodernism declares impossible the pursuit of 'invariants' by which 'human nature' might be specified. This somewhat elitist position, which only underscores cultural differences (never sameness) and absence (never presence) of a shared existence across human history, is intellectually repugnant to the public at large. It removes what is known from the life of the knower.

Postmodern thought, which was identified first in literary criticism during the 1970s and 1980s, denies the existence of a full-bodied autonomous individual and enthrones the disembodied Cartesian *cogito* as the apex of knowing. The emphasis is on cognitive *meaning*, or systems of symbols and discourse (for example, biographical 'texts'). Postmodern thinkers hold that cognitive meaning is sufficient as a focus for research. From a strictly scientific vantage point of experimental detachment – and even of correlational studies – the phenomenon of the public avidly reading and writing lives would appear to be simply a default position. None the less, the phenomenon suggests that the masses are in subtle revolt – disenchanted with postmodern knowledge, including scientific historical studies, but having renewed interest in life, which must include the 'body' (*bios*), as well as the 'mind' (*cogito*) as a source of knowledge.

The argument put in this chapter goes against the grain of most postmodern thought in the humanities. It supports the experience of those who simply enjoy studying lives. Embodied knowing usually gets pushed aside by academic reflection on the differences of culturally constructed 'selves' as loci of 'meaning.' What is thought to be important to most postmodern thinkers is not any firm basis for embodied knowing, but a *text* of individuality (even if one of an infinite number). This 'text' is a fiction, or semiotic category – a cipher by which the public's faith in human sameness, based on a lived sense of the sameness of human bodies, is recognized and 'spoken about,' only to be emptied or 'deconstructed' into a recognition of cultural differences by critics. The living body vanishes. A version of this is psychological reductionism in biography. However, one might well ask in alarm, does individuality not bear a force within culture that bespeaks of embodiment? The answer is yes: individuality, or 'personhood,' resists all the tangles of postmodern semiotic encoding. It implies a recognition of the sheer materiality of humankind itself. Thus, this is where such a new, postmodern 'science' of literature gives way to the emerging 'art' of biology, or embodied knowing in reading and writing lives. This view represents in part an update of the overall intellectual project initiated by Henry Murray.

However, workers in biographical studies have not pursued embodied knowing because it has itself been tied up in postmodernism and a 'disembodied' style of thought. The body has been neglected both as an object of study *and also* as an investigator's best tool. Attention to embodiment could foster a comprehensive theoretical reconstruction of the goals of life-writing/reading, one that works beyond ethnocentric limitations. However, the questions most readers and writers of lives ask impede answers which support a commanding interest in 'embodiment.' I argue that better questions would probe how to live, specifically, how to live with a *mortal body*, and how to know and respond daily to this fact of life. Implied are the questions: How would a life be studied with a view to its embodiment? How might the mortal body of the investigator itself serve studying lives? While cognitive *meaning*, or systems of symbols and discourse ('texts'), are necessary in academic study, they are not sufficient.

Human *needs* and *acts* – aspects of embodied knowing – must also be considered as essential components of meaning. Only when the right kinds of questions are asked will the mortal body be restored to how one goes about the task of reading and writing lives, or engaging in the science of being human. Correct questioning would first ask not what life 'means' in the face of death but, instead, how a person 'acts' with regard to the 'need' to give way to the next generation. How does a subject of biographical construction accede to or resist (or combine these behaviors) the inexorability and inevitability of death, and dying as a palpable dimension of lived experience from day to day? Only when such an interrogation results in useful answers will the force of Henry Murray's legacy of the need to become a 'biographer' working between biology and literature command fitting attention.

How does a person capitalize on their natality, and especially on ways bodies convey mortality? Body management prompts religious questions: Is the mortal body a condition to be transcended, a source of devout courage, or just what is it? What constraints are imposed on a person by their mortal body and by one's deliberate consciousness of such? Mainly ignored by most academics, such questions are, none the less, taken seriously by a number of studies in religion scholars, theologians, and especially those interested in sacred biography and hagiography. In her presidential address to the Society for the Scientific Study of Religion in 1989, sociologist Meredith McGuire called for transforming the social sciences by taking seriously the fact that human beings are embodied.[10] The editors of *History of Religions* devoted an entire issue of 1990 to 'The Body.'[11] Moral philosopher Edith Wyschogrod urges a restoration of the body to thought. In times of possible global catastrophe it is critical, she argues, to embrace 'body-vulnerability' – a fragility that manifests itself as an ethical appeal to refrain from acts of violence which, in itself, unites 'moral subjects' in a new community.[12] Thus, work elsewhere (most notably by women) makes the mortal body a pressing topic for research, but not so far, it seems, for biography and autobiography.

Laws of the mortal body

I argue that awareness of the body as being mortal is a key to directing investigations of how best to read and write lives. Studying lives – configuring a biographical (and autobiographical) process – is an important way to place the mortal body on the agenda of thought in terms of *needs* and *acts*. Indeed, it becomes foundational. Two points for the agenda can be inferred from one's awareness of the mortal body. Each is a methodological fundamental, or a law to be abided, when lives are considered to be religious and studied as such. These invariant laws express the spirit of

Henry Murray's important but neglected work: they suggest a 'whole quality' for research, or a 'configuration' of the meaning of a life in terms of the broad aspects of coherent character and fateful irony. Together the laws suggest a *need/acts complex*, or how the first law posits a basic human need and how the second law suggests responsive and fulfilling acts. A need/ acts complex embodies a life. When this complex is expressed narratively a *textual valence*, or realization event, occurs: a text elicits the fuller life of the reader and writer of lives. Thus, a phenomenology of literature is invoked (*Verstehen*). A textual valence is an explicit or implicit orchestration of the laws of the mortal body in sources used to study a life (for example, diaries, letters). The overall methodological aim is a non-reductive functionalism that seizes upon such realizations and restores *eros* to the process of reading and writing lives.

The first law of the mortal body is that of the *turnover of generations*. It is grounded not in any cultural system but in the 'need' (*thanatos*, 'pass up life/accede to dying law') to make way for the next generation. One passes up a sense of unlimited ego-mastery, or personal immortality, by sensing mortality in all things. The mortal body is an idiom of the past and the future, through which the young are linked to ancestors and the elderly are linked to progeny. At the very least, the body is a link in a genetic chain. Set in motion is a biological dynamic that links mortality to natality through sexuality, and which eventuates in the construction of cultural 'texts.' The mortal body is also the locus of human values.

For example, Erik Erikson attends to the 'cycle of generations' and, in particular, to what he calls the human strength of 'wisdom,' or 'detached concern with life itself, in the face of death itself.'[13] Not only is biological reproduction prompted by an awareness of the mortal body, but also activated is a reproduction of those enduring cultural values in which new generations are nurtured.[14] Only insofar as the law of the succession of generations is taken into account will the study of lives become embodied. Locating a life within cultural meanings of the necessary ethological trajectory, or 'need,' of generational succession/turnover is a first step towards reckoning with the mortal body in the study of lives. One would ask: How do subjects construe their pasts and futures, and their changing location in temporality?

The second law of the mortal body is that of *active biological/gender complementarity*. This is not a 'legal equality of the sexes' in society, but the complementary differences women and men offer each other insofar as they 'act' (*eros*, 'pass on life/create living law') in obedience to the law of the succession or turnover of generations, along with care for the future, including stewardship for the ecological integrity of the planet. Sexuality is located within mortality. It is the agent of natality, or the prospect of unlimited ego-mastery, passed on to the future. Practical sexuality between women and men, which reflects biological mutuality along with 'maternal thinking,' turns the past into the present and ensures the human future.[15] While obedience to the first law is absolutely necessary, the second law is less binding. Sexual intercourse, and the reproductive capacity it implies, is actually a rehearsal of conjoined idioms of natality and mortality. For example, becoming a parent entails a repositioning of the generations: one now becomes a part of the 'older' generation and the next in line to die.

Although everybody *must* die, having and caring for children, or pledging oneself to the future in some other creative manner (as, for example, in the care of HIV/AIDS sufferers by their homosexual lovers), are not similar givens. However, adults come into a fullness of their own through reproduction and change according to the second law, and this happens in terms of the first (and absolute) law of the mortal body. If the law of active biological/gender complementarity is taken into account, then the study of lives will be embodied further. Under the mandate of generational succession, practical gender differences prompt a creative response through 'acts,' sexual or otherwise. Coming to grips with the cultural meanings of such responsive and fulfilling acts in lives is the second and final step to take to reckon with the mortal body in reading and writing lives.[16] One would ask: How do subjects link themselves to their pasts and futures in terms of overall strategies and practical tactics for living in the present?

Therefore, how might these two laws of the mortal body best direct work on reading and writing lives? When we read or write about a life, how do we recognize and respond phenomenologically to its embodied 'textual valence'? Verisimilitude embodied by the laws of the mortal body, not in fragments and fictions, is the *sine qua non* of studying lives. A soteriological intention to address the 'need' to make way for the next generation with responsive and fulfilling 'acts' arises. The 'need/acts complex' is activated as an intellectual focus within the biographical construction of an individual as a 'text.' This is a call to serious introspection under the laws of the mortal body, especially the constraint of the first law, *thanatos*, which resists all action to the contrary. Yet, one acts in obedience to the first law only by means of invoking the second law. From the biographical construction of an individual as a 'text' to autobiographical reflection on how oneself might best live, a vision of the future may flow from one's past.

Questions arise: how is the 'need/acts complex' activated by means of studying lives? How might 'passing on' natality occur by means of 'passing up' a personal sense of immortality? What responsive and fulfilling acts of reading and writing lives will comply with the first law of the mortal body? Answers to these questions have not been forthcoming. *Eros*, the 'sexy' hallmark of the second law of the mortal body, has somehow gone missing from the life-writing/reading process. Recognizing the valence of a life as a personal horizon of realization, one which orchestrates the laws of the mortal body and is based on embodiment (for example, Murray's reflections on the 'Case of Earnst'), seems halted. Movement along the entire trajectory of possible personal realization needs to be activated by new strategies for reading and writing lives.

Another way of putting it is to interpret Freud's idea of the 'death instinct' as the return of *eros* to its narcissistic origins. It is an introspective return to an undifferentiated self, to an infantile existence in which the child/researcher is master of a universe which he or she now 'embodies.' However, an interruption of such introspection has somehow occurred as reading and writing lives occurs. A 'failure of nerve' in the face of such embodiment has paralyzed the study of the individual life as a religious phenomenon.[17] Nevertheless, might new courage to act (*eros*) be found? Might the present moment become a sexualized rehearsal of the impact of birth and death in a life, as biographical construction converts itself into the life-writer/reader's own autobiographical reflection on living?

Daimon or dysdaimon?

Modern humanistic psychology has been popular among some psychologically inclined readers and writers of lives, and especially among investigators who have been eager to protect Henry Murray's goal of 'personology' from theoretical reductionism by means of exalting the self as an exclusive object of study. However, in spite of its exalted self, the intellectual roots of humanistic psychology have remained too shallow. A basis for individuality in reading and writing lives — sounder than merely exalting the self — must be found.[18] David L. Norton, a philosophical thinker, argues that the conviction of an individual's intrinsic, irreplaceable worth is a positive cultural residue from Greco-Roman antiquity.[19] There was a close proximity between 'genius' and ordinary personhood in the past. In classical Roman belief, *genii* were tutelary gods or attendant spirits allotted to all persons at birth, determining their character and governing the fortune of each individual. The Greek equivalent of genius is *daimon*, and 'eudaimonism' is the term for the ethical doctrine (first systematically formulated in the words of Socrates and the writings of Plato and Aristotle) that each person is obliged to know and live in truth to his or her *daimon*. Thereby one progressively actualizes 'an excellence that is innately and potentially' linked to a sense of an Other.[20]

This is not an exaltation of 'self-actualization' or 'fulfilling one's potential' espoused by the human potential movement of a decade or more ago. 'Ego-mastery' as we know it today as an overriding personal value was avoided in Greco-Roman antiquity. Rather, one's 'excellence' was recognized only insofar as it contributed to the pool of excellences comprising some shared vision of the 'common good.' We can well ask, what is the 'common good' today? Basic to any such common good is our mostly unconscious sense of connection to the natural environment through our bodies.[21] Bodies are biological capsules which contain individuals, and out of which issue life stories, themselves, when subjected to writing, becoming 'texts.' The mortal body makes personal the epic of evolution, itself a saga of the normative ethology of *homo sapiens*. Living becomes a serious matter of moral striving (*eros*), an aspiration toward personal excellence (*arete*) and the common good. Such a shared recognition is expressed in studying lives. Human solidarity in accordance with the laws of the mortal body is thereby evident.

An individual's small intuition of their own irreplaceable worth in the human family is not the result of today's tendency toward bureaucratic rationalization, itself a condition of 'dysdaimonia,' or failure to follow moral necessity, the 'I must' of one's *daimon*.[22] Rather, that conviction is qualitative, and, following Freud, pertains to the mind, or more accurately, the soul (*psyche*), or that which is 'most valuable' in a person while he or she 'is alive.'[23] It identifies each person's *arete*, or personal excellence, as unique. By eudaimonism is meant self-authenticating norms of social life, which is itself an expression of responsive and fulfilled individuals. Such people embody the love that binds together morally empowered communities. In the Socratic meaning, love (*eros*) as desire is the aspiration to higher value. It is associated with breaking down social conventions and restoring textures of lived experience to the daily round, perhaps in erotic and even ecstatic ways. *Eros* connects every individual to his or her *daimon*, or innate excellence. This constitutes a person's 'self-enlistment,' says David Norton, 'in the service of that value for which he or she is uniquely responsible' and which 'subsists in complementarity with all other human excellences.'[24] The two laws of the mortal body go far to lend expression to the complementarity of all human excellences. The family of humankind is a community of this sort of mind or, better put, soul (*psyche*) bound by the laws of the mortal body. Might eudaimonism be available today?

The need for empathic engagement

J. Brooks Bouson, literary critic and neo-psychoanalytic thinker, believes that most transactions between a reader/researcher and a 'text' of a life, like a biography, are conditioned in contemporary times by what she calls our deep-rooted biological needs for 'empathetic responsiveness' and 'a sense of connection with others.'[25] A recognition of these human needs in studying lives makes room for the eudaimonistic impulse: Bouson, like Norton, seeks a similar 'complementarity' of the individual's *arete* with 'all other human excellences.' She uses the 'self-psychology' of Heinz Kohut to suggest that the problem of reading and writing lives today is not the classic psychoanalytic one of working out feelings of guilt but finding some urge by which to live, some basic excellence or wholeness that links 'acts' to 'need' in an embodied, or 'empathic,' mode of awareness. 'Meaning' would be lent to individuals in narcissistic self-absorption, meaning that would move toward increasing sociality, connection with others, ongoing relationships, and pooled human 'excellences.' For instance, the *act* of studying lives is itself a response to the *need* for wholeness amidst fragmentation, in which the continuity of generations is implicit. This is not the problem of Oedipus, the 'Guilty Man,' but that of Narcissus, the 'Tragic Man,' who, argues Bouson, characterizes most people today.[26] Narcissus lacked the urge, or moral power required to relate his excellence to others'. Unlike Oedipus, Narcissus failed to obey the laws of the mortal body. He rejected the calls of the nymph, Echo, who was his would-be biological and gender complement. Narcissus languished, forever gazing at himself in the mirror-like waters of a pond in a forest.

What makes studying lives serious business is that one becomes a participant observer and is thereby subject to personal change. The narcissism of our times inhibits a detached observer—scientist role. According to Bouson's interpretation of Kohut's work, what is central to the reader/text transaction (i.e., the researcher *cum* reader/text transaction) is the 'sustained empathic—introspective immersion' in the life of a biographical subject.[27] For Kohut, psychoanalysis itself banishes Freudian detachment and thereby becomes, as he himself writes, 'par excellance the science of empathy.'[28] Important here is the activity of empathy in reading and writing lives. Kohut defines empathy as 'vicarious introspection,' or the capacity to think and feel oneself into the inner life of another person while 'simultaneously retaining the stance of an objective observer.'[29] Empathy is both a passive mode of immersion and an active mode of perception and understanding, an 'instrument of cognition.'[30] It is an act of consciousness in which one orients to objects and their value in another's experience.[31] Too often, though, the life of another is approached hard-heartedly and at an unfair — or inhuman — critical distance.

Studying lives, usually in the form of narrative life 'texts,' constitutes an *empathic event* for the researcher. This is why we are so often moved by the compelling stories of the lives of others. Reviewing recent work by 'reader-response' critics, literary scholar Jonathan Culler observes that the question of control is central: Is the reader dominant over the text of a life or is the text dominant over the reader? In the view of such critics as David Bleich and Stanley Fish, the reader is the dominant force; in contrast, Wolfgang Iser and Michael Riffaterre, while admitting the active role of the reader, hold that the text is the controlling force.[32] In all this debate, what Culler finds curious is 'how easily text and reader can switch places: a story of the reader structuring the text easily becomes a story of the text provoking certain responses and actively controlling the reader.'[33]

Studying lives, like reading, is above all a subversive activity in that it creates human solidarity amongst all the underlying and reciprocal relationships one has to the subjects who populate texts. The contemporary popularity of biography and autobiography is an expression of how human solidarity — Erik Erikson's idea of 'speciation' — is affirmed as a source of value for living. Both immersion and cognition are involved:

> For the reader the work is not partially created but, on the one hand, already complete and inexhaustible — one can read and reread without ever grasping completely what has already been made — and, on the other hand, still to be created in the process of reading, without which it is only black marks on paper.[34]

Reading novels is analogous to studying lives: 'If one insists on seeing all novels as congeries of semiotic systems intricately functioning in a pure state of self-referentiality,' writes critic Robert Alter, then 'one loses the fine edge of responsiveness to the urgent human predicaments that novels seek to articulate.'[35] Alter's prose may sound complicated, but it means simply that any sort of fiction may militate against the social fabric on which conducting daily affairs depends. As Bouson herself puts it, 'Both subjective and objective, empathic reading is a dynamic process involving the critic/ reader's participation in but also active observation and interpretation of the text's intended manipulation of its audience.'[36] This is, after all, what makes texts of lives 'speak' to us, often in powerful ways.

No less is this true when lives are studied by way of discovering, says psychoanalyst Kohut, the 'nuclear essence of humanness.'[37] Along lines of psychoanalytic approaches to biography, Kohut means substituting Freud's Oedipus myth with that of Homer's Odysseus and his son: it is the *intergenerational bond* of families, or love (*eros*) as desire for a future, not intergenerational conflict, that for Kohut constitutes the 'nuclear essence of humanness' and grants the 'I must' of moral empowerment. The bond of the extended family of humankind becomes normative under the laws of the mortal body, themselves binding in the process of reading and writing lives. One could do worse than to have and care for a family in the name of seeking a personal fix or occasion for transformation in the present.

The act of introspection

Thus, studying lives is a guide for living together. It fortifies the sense of the unique irreplaceable worth of the individual. One must trust this sense, and at the same time undertake action to render it trustworthy.[38] Reading and writing lives has the capacity to personalize events and unite people in solidarity in the immediacy of empathy, albeit by means of the textual valence, or configuration of the laws of the mortal body, evident in the record of a life. Studying lives so as to live fully implies the hope that in them will be found something that outlasts life. Here 'salvation,' or soteriology, arises. Typologies of biography have not included what I propose to call *Soteriological Biography*. Usual lists include the 'Chronicle Biography,' or an extensive accumulation of facts about a subject with a minimum amount of the biographer's presence evident in the narrative; the 'Pure Biography,' which retains the chronicle's detailed accuracy, but also aims to simulate a life in the heat of the biographer's empathy; and the 'Critical Biography,' in which the story of a subject's life, far from being 'brought to life,' becomes only the occasion for airing the life-writer's opinions.[39] Reading and writing lives for the purpose of expressing eudaimonistic impulses is soteriological biography. Empathic studies of narrative life 'texts,' like autobiographies and biographies, can increase responsiveness to the 'human,' especially to the biological conditions of existence that bind the readers and writers of lives to their subjects in shared solidarity. This moves us further along the line from the scholar's task of biographical construction of an individual as a 'text' to the more personal process of autobiographical reflection on how best to conduct life.

Thus, what I call *empathic introspection* is the distinctive dynamic of soteriological biography. It is that inner empathic process by which more than basic information is gained from engaging with texts of lives. Studying lives also becomes an act of embodying the investigator's thought in a higher formative process: it is a means of playing out the 'death instinct' as a return of *eros* to its narcissistic origins for the sake of creating human solidarity.[40] This is a kind of 'spiritual martyrdom' that is internally acted out by the reader and writer of lives. What finally obtains can be called the 'truth of lives,' or an attitude of the moral subject in which the 'Other' takes precedence over the self, albeit fleetingly. Such a claim is based on what is actually experienced in the presence of another, in 'body-vulnerability,' or a fragility that manifests itself as an ethical appeal to refrain from acts of violence, including methodological reductionism. This fragility constitutes the textual valence by which the laws of the mortal body control culture, or the very discourse by which individuality is 'spoken about,' when a life is studied. Edith Wyschogrod writes, 'When I encounter the Other's susceptibility to pain, suffering and death I may resist this appeal but I cannot evade the claim itself: it is given as immediately self-warranting.'[41] The 'truth of lives' is marked by responsibility, passivity, and unworking (*désoeuvrement*), characteristics that flow from the fact of the Other's primacy. Not only is the life that is studied truly 'Other' at first sight; the Other also calls up the elusiveness of the investigator's self, a 'signifier' of the Other.[42] The elusive self is held bound in empathy with a subject out of absolute obedience to the first law of the mortal body. It seeks courage to obey the second law, *eros*, and a means by which to bring about human solidarity, this at a more insightful second sight. Soteriological biography places a trajectory of personal realization before the reader and writer of lives, one in which guidance for changing one's outlook is evident, but only insofar as one acknowledges and obeys the laws of the mortal body. How is 'salvation' of a sort available in the process of reading/writing lives? How might the reader/ writer of lives take an active part in self-transformation – 'spiritual quest' – by means of biographical and autobiographical reflection? Soteriological guidance comes in three necessary, related ways.

First, guidance for a spiritual quest would come through well-researched historical comparisons with a view to a person's moral empowerment: lives from different epochs would be sifted through and their differences from one's own life would be carefully noted. This is roughly like a 'case presentation' in psychiatry. One would grow familiar with a person's life-course, the chronology of dates of important events, travels, relationships to others, and so on. Archival research, even going to where the subject lived and worked so as to 'retrace steps,' could often facilitate the task of the reader and writer of lives here.[43] Hitherto largely neglected, but now invoked would be what I call the *body-biography*. What happened to a subject's body itself during living? How a subject responded to illnesses, growth spurts, blemishes, accidents, and chronic conditions and the like, would need to be assessed. Such an assessment would ask how the subject of a study responded to one degree or another to their body in accordance with the overall configuration of the two laws of the mortal body. (Was the body used self-consciously as a soteriological idiom in relating to the world?) People share bodies, mainly by dint of their striking and dynamic similarities and interconnected ecology. New attention to bodies in life 'texts' would signify the ties that bind all people in a common evolutionary destiny, according to the biological and ethological requisites of speciation.[44] An appreciation of the embodied basis of human motivation and behavior would exemplify a method of empathic introspection at work – self-understanding under the mandate of the laws of the mortal body. Thus, individuals would be gathered together and prepared to be identified in solidarity in this phase of the work of converting biographical construction of individuals as 'texts' to autobiographical reflection by the life-writer/reader about how best to live and, thus, how to alter one's lifestyle accordingly.[45]

Second, guidance would also come by means of inner empathic rehearsals: 'What is it like to be this person?' Here, in spite of recognizable differences between a subject and the reader and writer of lives, experiments in imagining similarities would take place. Simultaneously rehearsed would be both a person's character, or the sameness and continuity evident over time, and the irony which persists to subvert assertions of character.[46] Irony is an emblem of human mortality. It often expresses what the body in particular circumstances does in spite of a person's intentions to the contrary, as is illustrated in the Freudian idea of the 'return of the repressed' or, simply, aging (in spite of our efforts to remain fit and youthful). Such intuitive rehearsals would depend on disciplined subjectivity. Lives would not be studied outside the laws of the mortal body; nor in the belief that subjects make no active or passive choices about complying with those laws. Moreover, texts about others' lives could occasion explorations of new introspective abilities by the investigator, along with awareness of the degree of his or her own compliance with the laws of the mortal body.

Such a renewal would be a medium through which one may, so to speak, 'communicate with the dead' as if they were still alive. This reaffirms the laws of generational turnover/succession and active biological/gender complementarity as dynamics which bring about broad intergenerational bonding, or love (*eros*) as the desire for speciation. Ongoing communication between the living and the dead is an outcropping of simulating experience in life studies. An inner compensation would be activated: a subject could be envisaged, so to speak, as 'immortal,' and pointing the way to striking possibilities for new lifestyles and altered awareness. The cycle of generations itself would remind the living that they too will one day be ancestors, and looked to by mortals as inspiring sources of exemplary moral empowerment.

Third, empathic introspection could happen through unexpected powerful, sometimes life-changing, engagements with a subject which would not be easily controlled: one would feel an individual's struggles, failures, triumphs, and glories as though they were one's very own. The reader and writer of lives would be overtaken by an empathic appreciation of how a subject acknowledges humanity or consciously faces the laws of the mortal body, time and again. Here the role of 'principalities and powers,' so to speak, would enter the balance of life, and would hold untold ramifications for those who would remain faithful to the laws of the mortal body. One's spiritual quest would be at its most precarious, and it could become psychologically damaging. What is the impact of power imposed from the outside (for example, deprivations, illness, paralysis, torture) on living? The physical senses could be emphasized, along with the influence of the body on thought. Proprioception, the delicate, subliminal feedback mechanism, or 'sixth sense,' tells the brain about the position, tension, and general feeling of the body and its parts, and notes when this changes or is absent.[47] The mind (*cogito*) is one thing, but without proprioception the mind would be ruled 'out of order' if it alone claimed the necessary prerequisites for reading and writing lives.[48] Letting go, or risking a life based on intuition alone (at least experimentally), is what it takes.

Simulating lives is good as far as it goes, but soteriological biography also holds out the possibility of self-transformation as a 'spiritual operation.'[49] Not to seek one's 'excellence,' or a sense of lasting value on behalf of others now while we are still alive (i.e., *eros* in pursuit of *psyche*, by means of an individual's *arete*), is a wrongful suppression of the eudaimonistic impulse. It is a failure to acknowledge the laws of the mortal body as foundations of the long-term collective good. Moreover, such an act of acquiescing ruptures the empathic process as it works its way along the trajectory from simulations of lives past to transformations of lives present. Filling the void is a new awareness, namely, *communitas*, or a touchstone of the 'sacred,' which itself is akin to Henry Murray's experience of 'insight' in the study of lives. What is the 'salvific' bearing of this?

The religious nature of biography

In the end, empathic introspection makes the study of lives itself a religious act. The Greek roots of the word, 'biography,' are *bios* and *graphos*, or 'life' (biological life) and 'writing' respectively. That the life written about and read is truly an embodied one, grounded in human biological processes and mortality, is inescapable and must be taken seriously.[50] Not with an abstract grasp, but a kinesthetic embrace, born of engaging lives as empathic events in the life of the reader and writer of lives, is needed if lives are to be truly simulated in study and readied to transform the lives of others who engage in a 'spiritual quest' in which the full meaning of lives is at stake. Such events link together *need* and *acts* ('need/acts complex'), as these respectively combine the two laws of the mortal body as a 'textual valence' or a point(s) of power which compel attention in life-writing and reading lives ('There go I!').

In the short term, studying lives is a religious act because lives can be approached devotionally, not merely as objects of dispassionate interest. Here soteriology, or the science of human change as a spiritual process involving issues of health and healing, fits in. One studies how an individual deals with mortality as a need in living — 'body-vulnerability,' and with generating natality, or a sense of 'rebirth,' through acts of responsive and fulfilling sexuality. Our own proprioception, expressed in the laws of the mortal body, is the medium in which this knowledge is communicated best. Simulations of lives proceed as transforming magical processes for those engaged in life studies. They focus on the destruction and creation of cultural and historical meanings of embodiment.[51] This will become poignantly evident when the life of Brian Keenan in captivity is considered in Chapter 9. At any rate, attention to the laws of the mortal body, along with all hurt and healing, locates the religious centre of studying lives in a radical material, biological base.[52] A non-theological sense of incarnation – 'flesh' and 'spirit' combined – would appear to be at hand. This is especially noticeable in children for whom 'an enspirited body' is a source and focus of mental life.[53]

Notably, such simulations of lives formed the basis of the medieval hagiographer's craft. At the heart of that craft was the use of stories of past lives for the purpose of transforming lives in the present – converting 'pagans' and 'deepening the faith' of others by example. The hagiographer's 'lives of the saints' depicted exemplars of faith, or developed individuals who achieved moral insight and soteriological change because they became 'spiritual quest' success stories. Such narratological 'spiritual knowledge' could be communicated across generations and taken into the hearts of the faithful. This was an embodied kind of knowing, one that held the believer in the inexorable grip of death but with clearer purpose in living.[54] Whether the faithful argued fine theological points, or were even capable of doing so, was beside the point. What counted was fulfilling the *need* to take one's place in the turnover of generations, and to do this by means of engendering natality through *acts* of responsive and fulfilling sexuality. The 'need/acts complex' constitutes the textual valence by which the 'paper trail' or 'clinical protocol' of a life can be studied as a cultural product constituted by a specific discourse, albeit far from a disembodied one.[55]

In the long term, studying lives may begin as a magical act ('My life "mirrored" in the life of somebody else'), but it soon becomes an implicit religious endeavor because our knowledge of others is frequently related to experiences that have profound, shared religious bearing. Any person undergoes crises that affect the symbolic world in which they live: the primordial world of 'powers,' or the 'Other,' beyond the individual – deities, supernatural heroes, mythical monsters, and protohuman ancestors. These may certainly be manifested in the guise of historical and cultural forces, and some may wish to leave them at that. However, no matter how a scholar might construe the 'powers,' they still continue to have major bearing on people's lives – the 'Other' as radically material and physical, especially in the guise of mortality, itself perhaps envisaged as a cowled, skeletal, and scythe-holding 'Grim Reaper.' Whatever their historical expressions, these 'powers' derive from the destruction of primordial worlds, which gives rise to the constructed, periodic cosmos. Thus, the well-constructed life – the individual tempered by an ever-mortal *bios*, or embodied awareness – when acting properly, is an effective sign of that cosmos, itself sustained through the periodic rhythms of production, reproduction, consumption, and exchange. Bio*logy*, or the logic of biological process (and laws of the mortal body), gives rise to bio*graphy*, or the cultural 'text' which such embodiment suggests. 'Passing up' chances for ego-mastery (and empathic reading) makes way for 'passing on' natality (or individuality) to one's children and also on to all subsequent generations. This dynamic structures the narrative themes of the story of a life in soteriological biography. One joins the sacred circle of those called together by Christian theologians the *communio sanctorum*, or the body of everlasting saints of the Church.

Such is the moral force (*eros*) of the eudaimonistic impulse, 'I must.' And such is the dynamic by which a truly empathic investigator finds the story of another's life compelling as insight into one's own life, and even transforming as one's lifestyle comes under scrutiny. This process of empathic introspection at its best pursues not only the chronology of a life, but also insight into how lives of depth were lived – lives clearly engaged with the 'powers' (however they may appear) throughout the course of living. Thus, one studies lives in order to live more fully oneself – as if to outlast life – with greater purpose and with increasing wisdom in the face of the future. At least, soteriological biography, or the appropriation by a life-writer/reader of a biographical construction for comparing and contrasting it with one's own life narrative, is a mighty hedge against personal isolation and boredom.

7   Impulse to hagiography

To begin, let us suppose that we have serious interest in the possibility of becoming effective at designing conditions of life and arranging human circumstances that will contribute to people's gaining outstanding spiritual and moral achievements. Questions and direct inquiries will have to be put, ones that draw on a deeper and more detailed conceptual understanding than is presently available concerning the life events underlying actual people's individual achievements, and also concerning the course of progress toward maturity. Biographical evidence and the practice of reading lives and life-writing make it possible to chart such progress. Together they are a source of information on which further understanding will depend.[1]

An arising question is: How might biographical evidence and reading lives and life-writing implicate implicit religion ('spirituality') in portrayals of lives? Or: How are lives 'saintly' or, at least, compelling as embodiments of human value, perhaps as Erik Erikson suggests?[2] In this chapter I argue that a key to answering these questions, and also to fulfilling the general interest out of which it arises, is the *body*.[3] Biographies tell stories about bodies. These stories are not only about bodies in the 'artificial' time and space constructed by the skillful life-writer who weaves a tapestry of 'memory.'[4] They often also narrate the history of a body of flesh and blood, which is healthy or ill, old or young, and the like. A reader of lives can hardly fail to identify in his or her 'real' time and space with such a 'biology of living.'[5]

Thus, our bodies (the stories about them) are like reliquaries, or 'artificial' places in which the alleged 'real' mortal remains of saints are stored. Traditionally in the world's religions, especially in Christianity and in Australian aboriginal religions, reliquaries have been used as sacramental aids in aspiring to a 'higher life' by subsequent generations, including aspirations to a sense of 'everlasting life' among a saintly community, or at least a life of recognized 'spiritual attainment.' Like actual reliquaries in geographical time and space, biographies or life 'texts' too have for many been popular sites of 'pilgrimage' in the landscape of psychological and emotional time and space.[6] Biographies are stories about the biology of belief, as well as about the life and times of an individual. Such a fact has been missing from discussions about religious biography and hagiography. The endeavor of this chapter is to address this lack, and to explain how it can be met by what may be called an *impulse to hagiography*, or the desire to write lives in such a way that the process of writing itself confers sacred value upon them and also upon the reader and writer of those lives. An impulse to hagiography, that is, to writing and reading lives as being 'sacred' in spite of all else, confers the identity of *homo religiosus* on the student of lives. It results from autobiographical reflection upon how one may be 'mirrored' in a biographical construction of an individual as a 'text.'

Recent studies in religion and the human sciences as well as in Christian theology have given insufficient attention to the phenomenological study of the body as 'human condition,' pressing instead textual and empirical studies of religious cultures.[7] One way to address this insufficiency is to focus on the centrality of the body in research and scholarship on religion, and to examine the place of the body in biographies of outstanding individuals.[8] The aim is not only to study the religious lives of specific individuals, but also to engage the researcher in a personal encounter with his or her own body compared and contrasted over time to that of the bodies of biographical subjects. Religious and moral changes of outlook can be initiated by such systematic reflection.[9] Spiritual insights arise from connection to the body and to its wider natural context. In this way, thinking about a life lived in freedom and with a general desire for mastery and control, in which limitation by nature, death, and finitude is accepted, becomes possible. Such a mode of thought (perhaps feminine) affirms body, nature, emotion, and intuition, while at the same time it asserts autonomy, freedom, control, and the rational (perhaps masculine emphases).[10] Biographical 'fullness' and outstanding religious achievement as fruits of spiritual questing are the goals.

Biography has the Greek roots of *bios*, or the biological life of the body, and *graphos*, or life-writing which lends cultural form to embodied self-understanding. Thus, biography has two 'layers,' one being the 'mortal remains' of a body and the other being the 'reliquary' (a cultural artifact) in which they are contained. While the culture of reading and writing lives has flourished (for example, literary biographies, campaign biographies, psychobiographies, hagiographies, and sacred biographies), little attention has been paid to the biological life that cultures, presumably, express. Contemporary cultural studies, the province of literary critics (for example, Derrida) and some social scientific thinkers (for example, Deleuze), emphasize discourse analysis. That the body itself is neglected in such studies implies a moral failure to seek out and affirm enduring, life-enhancing values for living.[11] This is the goal of phenomenological understandings of human experience. These understandings identify normative patterns by which religious constants might be recognized. The value of relativity in contemporary cultural studies, so dominant in the academy, must be eschewed in favor of a struggle to give voice and cultural expression to the *body as an idiom of knowing truth*.[12]

To focus on the *bios* is to locate the self-understanding of an individual along a bodily trajectory of biological growth (natality), deliberate procreative and creative activity (sexuality), and aging/degeneration/death (mortality).[13] Of course, there are other additional forces at work on our bodies − gravity, ultraviolet radiation, magnetism, etc. However, it is the inexorable trajectory of the body, as a central locus of existence, that constitutes an experience of 'Otherness' reckoned with by the individual throughout life. Moreover, this trajectory can be immediately evident to consciousness through introspection and empathy, themselves gateways to the 'soul,' personal realization, and harbingers of enduring, life-enhancing values for living.[14] An awareness of this bodily trajectory frames the story (*graphos*) of that reckoning, that narration of a life. It is a constant struggle to keep a particular narrative, or the story of the self's engagement with this 'Otherness,' going.

So far, the *bios* has been described; and its relation to the *graphos* has been linked with such a description. *Graphos* is a focus of cultural studies (for example, literary biography), but it has not attended sufficiently to the trajectory of human biology and its parallel of personal realization. The human body *is* a human constant − everybody has one, sexual difference notwithstanding. The question now becomes: How to link together this biological trajectory and personal realization? How might life-writing and reading lives become 'embodied,' and thereby be a 'universal' human endeavor among others to engage in a 'spiritual quest'? An answer to these questions comes in telling what can be called the 'truth of lives,' or what is most valuable about them as exemplary moral and spiritual phenomena. By moral phenomena are meant those instances of lives (or in lives) where the performance of necessary species-specific functions occurs. Death-awareness, which is perhaps unique to human beings, is the starting point. A synonym for this is 'wisdom.'[15] Within the *bios*, normative standards are implied, ones that serve as benchmarks of reading and writing lives as an activity that is inherently religious. Such standards are also evident within specific biographies or life 'texts,' and they render them into religious documents that can be useful as devotional treatises.

The first standard is the turnover/succession of generations, as Chapter 6 suggested. Personal experience becomes religious insofar as present self-understanding is framed by awareness of one's ancestral present and how it gives rise to progeny and the future. Generational turnover is marked best by taking seriously the possible role played by mortality (and all other forms of human finitude) in one's life. It is difficult in living to 'learn to die,' or to give way to the next generation, but obedience to this first standard requires the courage of such a moral stance. Is the individual I read and write about 'death-aware'? Does the life-writer compose a life looking for signs of death-awareness? When I read a biography with mortality management in mind, do I find useful instruction in *ars moriendi*, or the 'art of dying,' as a lifestyle amidst my ordinary suffering?[16]

The second standard is biological/gender complementarity, which was also discussed in Chapter 6. Biological production of the future requires women and men to behave sexually. (A genetics of reproduction based on experimental genderless technologies is far from common practice.) Here sexuality leads to natality. But reproduction must also occur culturally. Any creative effort on behalf of the future must take into account not gender exclusivity, but inclusivity — that men and women reproduce the best of themselves together.[17] Learning to be biologically (as well as culturally) inclusive, perhaps by gaining an initial awareness of this through sensuality, implies courage to abide by this law.[18] Does the individual in a biography that one reads or writes embrace inclusive sensuality/sexuality as an idiom of self-understanding? Does a life-writer pen a life not only with the sex life of his or her subject in mind, but also with a view to the biologically procreative and culturally creative implications of sexuality as an embodied activity? When I read biographies with inclusive (hetero) sensuality/sexuality appreciation in mind, do I find useful instruction in how to seek extension and completion of myself while affirming the 'Other,' this on the backdrop of biologically evident incompleteness, or the recognition that women and men desire (*eros*) each other, and act to fulfill this need?

Let us speculate about constructing a theology based on the given of the body as a biological and existential fact. In other words, let us say that God has three faces — mortality, sexuality, and natality. These biological forces constitute 'Otherness' incarnate in each of us. The chief questions are: How to encounter God? How to relate effectively together over time? The formal answer to these questions is: Obey the normative guidelines for engendering religious self-understanding, namely, the laws of generational turnover/succession and biological/gender complementarity in all you think, feel, and do. Thus, selfhood is a reflexively organized endeavor. The self is not a social atom. Rather, selfhood consists in the sustaining of coherent yet continuously revised biographical and autobiographical narratives, or life 'texts,' ones that are anchored in the shared biology that bespeaks of human solidarity.[19] Awareness of such solidarity is an exercise in spiritual and moral empowerment.[20] Selfhood is a continuously revised narrative of reckonings with 'Otherness,' particularly with each and every one of God's three faces.

The process of selfhood in accordance with the standards of generational turnover/succession and active biological/gender complementarity is a task that necessitates what some scholars have called 'narratology.' By narratology is meant an ongoing study of specific individuals' stories (*graphos*) of relating to god (*bios*).[21] Narratology may also become soteriology for the investigator.[22] By means of reading and writing lives, the investigator him/herself is presented with scenarios for living a religiously responsive life: How have the individuals I have studied over the years actually faced the three faces of God time and again? Have they succeeded or failed to live according to generational turnover/succession and active biological/gender complementarity? How so? And, might any scenario studied be useful for my own relationship to God? Biographical narratology is the grist in terms of which human solidarity is generated as a touchstone of the moral and spiritual life. Engaging in reading and writing lives is subversive cultural activity in the best sense – it affirms the importance of affirming human solidarity and of looking after ongoing human 'speciation.'[23]

Thus, narratology leads to hagiography, or writing lives of saints.[24] However, these lives are not your traditional kinds of saintly ones. Rather, they are lives of saints who are more responsive to the currents of *bios* than, perhaps, they are (and have popularly been) responsive to *graphos*, or specific and isolated religious cultures and the discourses and ideals constituting them (for example, Christian, Buddhist, or Hindu 'lives of the saints').[25] Sainthood is biological.[26] Saintly moral values, on which stories of saints turn, are directly produced out of the biology of God. They are imitated by the faithful because they serve as personal strategies for managing the biological faces of God as representations of 'Otherness.'[27]

Stories of the lives of saints, perhaps like those lives themselves, press the edge of human speciation. They are instances of the power of giving life over to death as a way to produce fuller, more meaningful living. Biographies, as life 'texts' that evoke empathic introspection in the reader and writer of lives, hold 'mortal remains.' They remind us that we too remain mortal. Thus, biography is a reliquary, one due fitting reverence for those faithful to life.

Brief illustrations

A muscle spasm in 1972 propelled Robert Murphy, a professor of anthropology at Columbia University, into the throes of human mortality in which his body itself became an inert reliquary that contained a rage for natality and life.[28] Murphy's social history of his own paralytic illness poignantly describes how he was taken slowly and inexorably from that spasm, his first symptom, to quadriplegia in 1986, the year in which he wrote his book. His paralysis resulted from a tumor inside his spinal column that eventually reduced his body to total quiescence. As he put it, nevertheless, 'But it has been an education of sorts, for in my passage into paralysis I have discovered the ebullience and power of the rage to live.'[29]

Like the anthropologist that he was, Murphy recounts in painstaking detail 'The Road to Entropy,' the title of the second chapter of his book, and along with it his reckoning with an increased sense of mortality amidst a desperate search for signs of natality. On the one hand, there were the invasive diagnostic procedures that tortured his body and subjected him to the anomie of institutionalized medicine. The electromyography measured neural damage by shooting electric currents through certain nerves. Small, Teflon-coated electrode needles were inserted into the body and conductivity responses were read. The arteriogram, in which a dye is injected into an artery and an X-ray is taken immediately of a portion of the vascular system — in his case, the spinal cord — was the most memorable. The full injection of the dye felt to Murphy as if his body temperature was being raised hundreds of degrees: 'It was like being roasted alive in a microwave oven,' which he associated with an imitation of Christ's lament from the Catholic mass, where the priest says 'They have pierced my hands and my feet, and they have numbered all my bones.'[30]

On the other hand, entropy, or the daily reality of increasing bodily inertness, literally held him bound and made him impotent. Murphy's tumor had been established for so long that it had wrapped itself around the spinal cord, making it difficult to excise without causing serious damage to the cord itself. Moreover, blood vessels ran through the tumor. If they were tied off during surgery, then the diminished supply of blood would kill the cord. Wrote Murphy, 'It was a no-win situation; every surgical risk would pose a risk greater than that of the tumor.'[31] Cobalt treatment brought on mild radiation sickness and eventually failed. A major focus is on 'The Damaged Self,' Murphy's fourth chapter that stresses the assault made by mortality on his self-esteem and masculinity. Sexuality looms as a major problem for the paraplegic male, who must 'lie still' on his back during sexual intercourse; and this, says Murphy, compromises a man's status 'far more' than the woman's status.[32] Murphy suggests that a sacrifice of the relationship between a woman and a man takes place, while at the same time something akin to a mother and infant bond, itself natal but regressed, fills the void.

Diagnostic procedures that induce helpless passivity along with a sense of becoming mindlessly spastic and vegetally inert can be humiliating and frightening. Murphy reflects on these passions while he searched within himself for renewed forces of natality and life. In his final chapter, 'There's No Cure for Life,' his hospital reverie on illness and decline left him with a 'haunting sense of having rehearsed for the present' in all his past years, of 'reliving' his history 'in hyperbole, of undergoing a savage parody of life itself.'[33] He was caught in a process from which there was no escape, one that was so inevitable that resistance was useless. He could 'only watch, spellbound.'[34] None the less, paralysis is a metaphor of death and a commentary on life, the struggle between life and love and death and alienation. This metaphor that implies the necessary turnover of generations also portends the biology of sexuality and the biological complementarity of genders. As Murphy declares, 'Disability concerns our irreducible humanity, and in the shifting sands of relativism, I believe that there are such things as Man and Woman.'[35] The biology of sexual difference, and how the socially constructed genders are linked to the future by means of complementarity and reproduction, in the end, drives the species. Robert Murphy's quadriplegia was a striking and comprehensive embodiment of the dynamics of the laws of the mortal body at work, and a focus for his compelling insights. Murphy's story is a consequence of an impulse to hagiography, he himself becoming a 'saint' amidst his autobiographical reflections on how best to live in the face of adversity.

The memoirs of the American novelist, John Updike, are a particularly good example of biographical writing that gets converted into autobiographical reflection, and which comes close to being a reliquary. This is so even though Updike's memoirs would not be immediately recognized by most readers as a religious text, or a 'container of sacred remains.'[36] Like Murphy's social history, Updike's memoirs are deliberately structured by *bios*. This makes the work into an implicit religious ('spiritual') document about an individual's changing awareness, or 'self-consciousness.' The book bears tacit soteriological impact. The change that occurs turns on Updike's awareness of his own mortality in the first instance, and how mortality is signified by a sense of his own bodily maladies – poor dental health, psoriasis, and the toll exacted on his body by cigarettes, alcohol, parenting, divorce and remarriage, and aging. He writes that two sensations about his body stood out in his childhood, 'before I discovered . . . masturbation.'[37] The first, 'the awareness of things going by, all beyond my control, sliding away toward their own destination and destiny'; and the second, an intimation of deep, cosmic joy in 'the sensation of shelter, of being out of the rain, but just *out*.'[38] Although Updike indicates that the force of his sexuality would command attention later in life, he implies that he has reckoned with mortality ('things . . . beyond my control, sliding away') and natality ('shelter . . . just out') from his earliest years, having done so in terms of powerful bodily sensations and a preoccupation with sex.

But the process involved is not only about Updike's subtle, somewhat self-absorbed internal awareness of these instances of natality, sexuality, and mortality. His memory of the living they also implied invites the reader to enter vicariously into the now embodied text. Rehearsals of empathy and introspection come into play. Particularities of time, space, and cultural context notwithstanding, a reader of Updike's self-biography is called to plumb the text for would-be or approximate universal scenarios by which the biological forces of mortality, sexuality, and natality – the three faces of 'Otherness,' or God – might be similarly engaged in one's own life. Here we enter into Updike's world and consider taking the hints he gives about how best to live.

Self-Consciousness: A Memoir (1989) can be amplified by making reference to Updike's creative writing. Not only is he considered to be an '"autobiographical" novelist' by most critics,[39] but he has also pressed the characters of his novels into serving the theme of profound spiritual searching that grows from intense despair about the body and the toll exacted from it by the ravages of nature and time. As Updike himself has said, 'Without the supernatural, the natural is a pit of horror.'[40] The 'natural' and the 'supernatural' are present explicitly or implied in all of Updike's work. As one commentator puts it, 'In his writing there is always the physical, natural world, apprehended by the body through the senses and appetites. But there is another, supernatural world ... apprehended by the soul, through faith.'[41] Things natural, when embodied by the individual, are linked to all things mortal, and the supernatural is for Updike a primary focus of natality.

However, faith pales into insignificance in the face of the bodily reality of lived experience. Although he might wish otherwise, Updike portrays scenes of generational turnover – childhood, adolescence, young adulthood, maturity, old age – that are specific, scenes set in one particular place at one particular time. We are turned from generalizations about a 'New Age' to the concrete bodily realities of daily life. The question that remains constant behind the shifting surfaces of the experiences life brings us is, 'Does the universe, blindly ruled by chance, run downward into death; or does it follow the commands of a Living God whose Will for it is life?'[42] The clear answer is that mortality always aborts any actuality of a lasting sense of natality. Resignation to a god of destruction and death, perhaps conceived as a 'cosmic euthanasia process,' is more realistic than getting carried away with faith in a god of affirmation and life. One can only wonder about the viability of any theological doctrine of bodily 'resurrection,' or a philosophical concept of cutting through 'karmic habits' by means of successive 'reincarnations.' A less sanguine story is pressed by the characters who inhabit Updike's novels.

Updike's 'lopsided' dualism, with its weight on the mortal body, is nowhere more evident than in his first novel, *The Poorhouse Fair*.[43] The characterization of Conner and Hook simplifies what is, according to Updike, humankind's basic duality, by the division of the body and the spirit into two separate individuals, devoted, accordingly, to the natural and the supernatural worlds. There is Conner, the atheist and ambitious manager of an old people's home, who concerns himself exclusively with the physical comfort and health care of his wards, and is unable to understand that the aged inmates are spiritually unfulfilled. Then there is Hook, an aged and dying inhabitant of the rest home, who has the spiritual vision and the religious insight that Conner lacks.

The novel revolves around these two opposing viewpoints, but it clearly shows society as moving toward Conner's worldview, becoming obsessed with the body, its health, its sexuality, and its comfort, believing that human beings are nothing more than physical animals. The previous manager of the home let its physical condition deteriorate to what were, for Conner, shocking standards of neglect. Conner has, consistent with his philosophy, improved the residents' food, their health records, and the appearance and comfort of the poorhouse. He has put in windows and fire escapes. But his changes have conveyed to the inmates a denial of any life after death to which they are, in spite of all Conner's improvements, so close.

Although the turnover of generations brings death to all, sexuality, based on biological/gender complementarity, is a force used to generate a sense of natality for the living as well as to produce children. Updike's characters suggest his personal view that sex is the closest to a religious experience that the physical world provides. Protagonists search for spiritual satisfaction in sexual encounters. However, writes one commentator, 'Updike is always aware that sex is, finally, a natural rather than a supernatural experience,' one that becomes 'futile and promiscuous.'[44] Almost every 'hero' in Updike's fiction – Rabbit, Joey Robinson, Peter Caldwell, Bech, Piet Hanema, Jerry Conant, the Revd Marshfield, Ellellou – associate sexuality with death.[45] On the one hand, sexual intercourse betokens a conquest of death in that it confers a quasi-immortality realizable through offspring. Or, at least, moments of heightened sensuality and intense (orgasmic) experience are often thought to be of 'mystical' bearing. On the other hand, that 'quasi' restriction is the downside, and the short-lived intensity of such acts evokes fear of death.

Thus, in *Bech: A Book* Bech's recorded reflection captures this insight succinctly from a male's point of view: 'His phallus, a counterfeit bone, a phantasmal creature, like Man, on the borderline of substance and illusion, of death and life.'[46] In *Couples*, Piet's promiscuity both strengthens and allays his fear of death. Writes Updike, 'He loved any woman he lay with, that was his strength, his appeal; but with each woman his heart was more intimidated by the counterthrust of time. Now, with Bea, he had made a ledge of guilt and hurled himself into the tranquil pool of her body and bed ... Death no longer seemed dreadful.'[47] Searching for life in his sexual encounters, Piet only manages to bring on death. When he makes Foxy pregnant, he calls upon his fierce God to kill the fetus that marks his mortal fate:

> In Foxy's silken salty loins he had planted seed that bore his face and now he wished to be small and crawl through her slippery corridors and, a murderer, strike. God forgive. No: God do. God who kills so often, with so lordly a lightness, from diatoms to whales, kill once more, obliterate from above, a whip's flick, a finger down her throat, erase this monstrous growth. For Thine is the kingdom.[48]

But the abortion is only a convenience, or as one critic writes, 'an attempt to hide the truth.'[49] Piet does not accept death but only gets near it. His modest truth is recognized in the drug-dilated eyes of John Ong, who is dying of cancer: 'how plausible it was to die, how death, far from invading earth like a meteor, occurs on the same plane as birth and marriage and the arrival of the daily mail.'[50] For Updike's characters, as perhaps also for the autobiographical novelist himself, *bios* is the dramatic baseline of narrative discourse. Thus, it would not be implausible to believe that Updike's artistry, itself an idiom of sensuality, and his creative writing have origins in part in his two early childhood sensations, those mortal and natal forces that preceded his discovery of sexuality and the sensation of masturbation. This is made clearer by returning to the consideration of *Self-Consciousness: A Memoir*, Updike's avowedly autobiographical work.

Not only is the content of this particular work evidence of a reliquary self-conscious of itself (self-biography, or autobiography), but also the memoirs' structure itself represents abiding religious concerns. Commenting upon his memoirs, Updike says that his art, like his religion, has a shabby side:

> These memoirs feel shabby. Truth should not be forced; it should simply manifest itself, like a woman who has in her privacy reflected and coolly decided to bestow herself upon a certain man. She will *dawn* upon that man. My writing here about my religion feels forced − done at the behest of others, of hypothetical 'autobiography' readers.[51]

And thus, the form of the text *dawns* on us ourselves, itself like a bodily presence.

This presence pertains specifically to human mortality and to the law of generational turnover. The title of the final and most philosophical chapter of the book is 'On Being a Self Forever.' Reflections on the mortal body make up its content. For example, Updike is continually taken by surprise by his sense of smell, especially after having given up smoking:

When I get out of bed in the morning, my own smell surprises me: stale flesh, warmed over. My body's ugly obstinacy in keeping on living strikes me as admirable, like an ungenial but impressive moral position; it makes me, still half-asleep, stop and think.[52]

Elsewhere he says that 'insomnia,' a form of bodily self-surveillance, is a paradigm for existence, where 'the mind cannot fall asleep as long as it watches itself.'[53] He suggests that traditional (explicit) religion helps the faint-hearted to shut their eyes and go to sleep in spite of existential (implicit) demands. As he stands thinking 'still half-asleep' himself, near the end of his own life, Updike teeters bodily between a life anesthetized by conventionality and one that faces death with open eyes. These embodied reflections together represent Updike coming to grips with death, sex, and 'Otherness' in the construction of his narrative of lived experience.[54] He readies himself to pass up prolonged living for the sake of distilling from memory a sense of abiding value, based on an affirmation of human solidarity as *bios*. He implies that it is this sense of human sameness, recognized by the older generation in the face of the younger one, that makes mortality not just a fact to be lived with, but a value according to which life is best steered.

Also significant as a structural aspect of the book with clear implicit religious bearing is the title (and content) of the penultimate chapter, 'A Letter to My Grandsons.' This chapter narrates a story about natality which itself suggests a ready compliance with the law of biological/gender complementarity. It also stands for Updike's explicit focus on the turnover/succession of generations and for his sense of obligation. He tells us that he needs to pass on to the future something of the very best of himself, not the least of which is his liberalism. Again, the focus is bodily, this time about his own children, their interracial marriages and his racially mixed grandchildren.[55] Here themes of sexuality and natality are linked into the future. Thus, Updike's entire text approximates a reliquary. This instance of his most self-conscious personal work is compelling religious life-writing and reading. It indeed demonstrates that biography is indeed like a 'reliquary.' It compels the attention of readers who would engage in autobiographical reflection 'mirrored' in another person's life 'text.' Such readers would thereby become faithful to the fullness of life.

8 The horror of becoming saints

William James (1842-1910) sought 'to test saintliness by common sense.'[1] He wished to use 'human standards' to decide how far the 'religious life' commends itself as 'an ideal kind of human activity.'[2] If the religious life commends itself, then any theological beliefs that may support it stand accredited. If not, then such beliefs stand discredited. Only on such a basis of 'human working principles' has religion in the long run supported life as it is, and not misled people about what life ought to be.[3] Reading and writing lives is not only about biographical narration, but it also aims at giving genuine expression to an hagiographical impulse, one that makes individuals into compelling religious role-models.

Hagiographical efforts grow out of the impulse to soteriology. Soteriology, or the study of ideas and practices associated with implicit ('spiritual') religious change or 'salvation,' emphasizes the *bios* of biography. Its focus is on the effective management of the 'mortal body' (which includes natality and sexuality) as a life is lived. Hagiography differs from soteriology. Hagiography stresses narrating 'holy lives' as venerable aspects of explicit ('institutional') religion, or leader-like or heroic role-models that are evident in the world's religious traditions as such (for example, Muhammad, Buddha, Christ). Hagiography emphasizes the *graphos* of biography, and is a step removed from the *bios*, itself the bodily basis of a person's 'spiritual quest.'

James's story is an example of how the trajectory of personal realization is traversed. He illustrates how biographical construction gives rise to autobiographical reflection on the body, which is a springboard into his 'spiritual quest.' Ever present in his philosophical, psychological, and religious writings is a preoccupation with the *body* as an idiom of knowledge about existence. This chapter specifies what two such 'human working principles,' or 'human standards,' are in the context of James's life and work, as these are particularly expressed in his important work, *The Varieties of Religious Experience: A Study in Human Nature* (1902; 1961). These two guidelines frame the impulse to hagiography, and are the means by which the 'religious life' commends itself as an exemplary lifestyle, one that is available to anyone sensitive enough to the vicissitudes of lived experience as the inner terrain of the 'spiritual quest.'

The argument advanced in this chapter is that these two principles are associated with James's experience of his body.[4] James always worried about bodily fitness, perhaps as an emblem of his fragile philosophical hope that goodness would triumph over evil, that life would outweigh death. His philosophical hope notwithstanding, he was even more powerfully haunted by what his chief biographer, Ralph Barton Perry, called 'a ghost or premonition of disability': James was declared physically unfit for military service during the Civil War, lost the use of his eyes for two long periods, once as a youth and again in old age, suffered from chronic insomnia, weakness of the back, digestive disorders, grippe, nervous fatigue, and, in 1898, not long before giving the Gifford Lectures that led to the publication of *The Varieties of Religious Experience*, severe heart strain.[5]

But it was the death from tuberculosis in 1870 of his beloved cousin, Minny Temple, that devastated James most and had a lasting effect on his life. He was twenty-eight years old at the time, and had just taken out his MD degree from Harvard the year before. She was twenty-five years old, and had been an orphan who was raised by the Tweedys, neighbors of the James family in Newport, Rhode Island. Young Minny Temple had captivated James as no other woman ever did in his life except, perhaps, in later years, his mother-in-law, Eliza Putnam Gibbens, with whom he shared 'complete mutual trust.'[6] James himself had suffered a 'nervous collapse' late in 1869 just prior to Minny's death.[7] This was in part related to his experimentation with the hypnotic drug, chloral. His physical and emotional disablement set him up to be overwhelmed by the force of circumstances which served only to exacerbate his grief.

Shortly after Minny's death, James revealed a considerable personal engagement with death. In his diary for 22 March 1870 there appeared an entry about the positive value that he associated with death, while also obviously engaged empathically in Minny's life:

> By that big part of me that's in the tomb with you, may I realize and believe in the immediacy of death! May I feel that every torment suffered here passes and is as a breath of wind, – every pleasure too. Acts and examples stay. Time is long. One human life is an instant. Is our patience so short-winded, our curiosity so dead or our grit so loose, that one instant snatched out of the endless age should not be cheerfully sat out. Minny, your death makes me feel the nothingness of all our egoistic fury. The inevitable release is sure; wherefore take our turn kindly whatever it contain. Ascend to some sort of partnership with fate, and since tragedy is at the heart of us, go to meet it, work it in to our ends, instead of dodging it all our days, and being run down by it at last. *Use* your death (or your life, it's all one meaning), 'tut twam asi.'[8] ('Thou art that.')

Evidently, death was a preoccupation that James sought to convert into a constructive moral force for living, or compensation for his 'ghost' or 'premonition' of disability. The linkage between James's nervous collapse of 1869 and his bereavement of 1870, itself linked to a young woman and her death, created a potent symbolic nexus, or 'power point,' that would affect his personal and professional life into the new century. Converging in that nexus were the forces of life and death, men and women – the power of beginnings and endings, and sexuality. James's bereavement became a source of spiritual power, or the compelling moral force evident in all of his activities.

He spent the rest of his life (1869/70-1910) trying to negotiate an inner settlement with this traumatic confluence of Minny's death and his own disability, or the frailty of his body as a haunting 'ghost' or 'premonition.' His feelings as a man, his sense of Minny as a woman and their strong empathic connection from childhood served James as a microcosm of a personal drama of life and death combined with a virtual archetypal sense of relations between women and men in general. Men and women at their best share projects based on complementary self-reliance and moral freedom, while always on death's door, or sensing the fragility of life. James's grief and feeling of personal devastation were, perhaps, intergenerational counterpoints to his father's inspiring 'vastation' near Windsor Castle when William was a baby, sometime around 1844.[9] Knowledge of the mystical episode of Henry James, Sr in England set a youthful William on a course of curiosity about religious experience, a preoccupation with lived experience and its inherent patterns, rather than with theological beliefs *per se*. Soon after his father's death, James wrote to his wife, 'you must not leave me till I understand a little more of the value and meaning of religion in Father's sense, in the mental life and destiny of men.'[10] Thus, filial piety also pressed James to undertake the Gifford Lectures on religion.

The turnover or succession of the generations placed a father's spiritual legacy on the agenda of a son's life of self-reliance and moral freedom.[11] This self-conscious legacy floated on the surface of the less than self-conscious powerful current composed of James's persistent and poignant sense of disability and grief that carried over from the 1869–70 episode. All of this was inserted into his marriage and given form as a shared intellectual project in which reckoning with women figured prominently. But Alice Howe Gibbens, James's wife, fell in second behind her mother, to whom *The Varieties of Religious Experience* is dedicated. His mother-in-law took him to seances, inspired his studies of psychic phenomena, and was his constant and reassuring correspondent during his time overseas (1899–1902). He was then recovering from serious heart strain and other illnesses and also preparing to give the Gifford Lectures (1901–02). James himself often conflated the identities of his wife and her mother, and continually sought their shared maternal support.[12] Writing to his mother-in-law from London as he was preparing the Gifford Lectures, James said that his wife 'had almost come to feeding me. ... After you, Dear Mother, she is the blessedest phenomenon I have struck upon this earth.'[13] Although influences mediated to him by parents formed a significant immediate backdrop behind the Gifford Lectures, they were not the most powerful ones. Lingering and unresolved grief over the death of Minny Temple in 1870, though removed in time, conflated with his relationship with his wife and especially with her mother and commanded James most as the Gifford Lectures neared, this in spite of a current of scholarly thought that lays emphasis on the influence of James's relationship with his father.[14]

James's nervous collapse of 1869 and his devastation and sustained grief over Minny Temple's death in 1870, together converging as a 'bodily grounding of meaning,' are the torments to which his famous 'panic fear' vision of the so-called 'French sufferer' in *The Varieties of Religious Experience* is attributed.[15] This anguished portrayal is central to the lecture entitled 'The Sick Soul,' and I dare say to all of the Gifford Lectures, and it has attracted wide-ranging scholarly interest.[16] It has also been called a 'hallucinatory' experience, and has been directly linked to James's '"Crisis" texts' from his diary of 1870.[17] The 'panic fear' vision is recognized by scholars to be thoroughly and characteristically autobiographical, and the personal inner source of the energy conveyed by James's entire lecture series.[18] Thus, disability and death, or the body in decline and dying, formed the undercurrent of James's study of religious experience, and this was associated intimately with women and intergenerational forces. A standard test of saintliness by 'common sense,' James believed, would eliminate the humanly unfit and promote the survival of the humanly fittest, applied to religious beliefs. But fitness depended on facing disability and death, and wresting value from it. This was a struggle with implicit 'spiritual' religion that continually sought explicit 'institutional' expression.

Although this chapter focuses specifically on James's lectures, 'Saintliness' and 'The Value of Saintliness,' it is also evoked by my own readings and rereadings of *The Varieties of Religious Experience* as a devotional text in my pursuit of the truth of life. In this sense, my empathy toward James and his project is also introspective in nature. Reading and writing the life and work of James is tantamount to an experiment in autobiographical reflection and personal realization. Thus, my project is about how *I myself have been reflected in James's text and instructed by it*, about how reflection on saintliness and the cultivation of a 'saintly character' together have become professional and personal endeavors for me, this in spite of postmodern critics who claim that such pursuits are impossible in principle.[19] James calls the fundamental mystery of religious experience 'the satisfaction found in absolute surrender to the larger power.'[20] Such a power, I now foreshadow, gripped me suddenly about twenty-five years ago, and it has held me in awe and fascination ever since. It was nothing short of a religious 'vision,' and it will be described in Jamesian fashion soon so as to exemplify further the trajectory of personal realization that carries us into a 'spiritual quest,' if we allow it to do so.

As a result, like James, I too find the specter of disability and death, or the body in decline and dying, to be an affirmation of what he called the 'Sick Soul,' or that kind of person who accepts all that would put us asunder (what he refers to as 'evil'). Such a person accepts evil 'not only as incurable but as *essential*,' says James, and has 'made his peace with the world on terms which evil dictates.'[21] Evil is not just a social condition that, like an injustice, could be eliminated. Rather, it is an ontological faultline, or a condition of human existence that would limit life, and even destroy it.[22] The opposite temperament, 'healthy-mindedness,' to my thinking, flies in the face of my personal experience (as it also did for James), and hence pales in contrast.[23] If the lectures on 'The Divided Self,' 'Conversion,' and 'Conversion Concluded' are viewed as elaborations of the lecture, 'The Sick Soul,' then it is clear that on quantitative grounds alone James himself was much less interested in 'The Religion of Healthy-mindedness' than he was in the faultlines and deep rumblings of psychological morbidity as an opportunity to engender saintliness. He was bringing his impulse to hagiography 'down to earth,' so to speak.

Suffering, the emblem of the 'Sick Soul,' is for James a part of the deeper meaning of life, sublimated into what his chief biographer rightly called the 'exaltation of self-sacrifice.'[24] Death and dying loomed large as a crucible in which the saintly character is formed: 'No matter what a man's frailties otherwise may be,' writes James about saintly value, 'if he be willing to risk death, and still more if he suffer it heroically, in the service he has chosen, the fact consecrates him forever.'[25] It is a mystery recognized by common sense, he avows, that 'he who feeds on death that feeds on men possesses life supereminently and excellently, and meets best the secret demands of the universe.'[26] Such is saintliness. But this takes place, says James, only insofar as a person is 'congenitally fated to suffer from its presence,' that is, to suffer from 'consciousness of evil,' or our complicity in all human suffering, dying, and death.[27]

How such a process works psychologically is to recognize, as Ralph Barton Perry puts it, an 'exaltation of self-sacrifice' as a practical Jamesian strategy for living. This is accomplished by means of acceding to the natural trajectory of our bodies toward disability and death, or bodily decline and dying (and aligning our wills with these inexorable forces). As this occurs, certain indicators appear by which saintliness can be compellingly understood, cultivated, and tested. The abiding questions for me have become: How might one, indeed, be said to have a saintly character? And furthermore: How might 'human standards' or 'human working principles' – what James called 'common sense' – be used to test it for living? A preliminary answer to these questions involves my conviction that saintliness should not be based upon a 'forensic metaphor,' in which individual and social merit (sin/guilt) is the issue, but, instead, its grounding in human *'mortality'* needs to be recognized – a recognition which calls into question systems of merit themselves.[28]

The keys are our perceptual field and human embodiment, which together compose an intuitive backdrop that emphasizes saintly corporeality.[29] 'The body is the storm centre,' writes James, 'the origin of coordinates, the constant place of stress. ... Everything circles round it and is felt from its point of view.'[30] In other words, the body 'as a *whole*' functions as a 'sensorium.'[31] The extremes of ecstasy and distress express the 'organic range of saintly corporeality,' quite literally the 'systole and the diastole of saintly consciousness,' in which 'the body as a whole expresses itself.'[32] In a Jamesian spirit, I shall propose a common-sense test of saintliness based on the body and its inherent potential for disability and death, or the body in decline and dying. This test will be *self-sacrifice*, and how lives 'exalt' this *bodily* to one degree or another. But first, it is important to set up James's view of saintliness for the purpose of seeing exactly what he thinks it is as well as all it is not, and then developing our own thought from there.

James on the saintly character

The 'ripe fruits of religion' James calls 'Saintliness,' or that character for which 'spiritual emotions' are the 'habitual centre of the personal energy.'[33] Two matters arise. On the one hand, James identifies and describes at length those 'ripe fruits,' or outgrowths of 'spiritual emotions.' Intellectually, these were associated with his father and with his father's imminent death. James called him 'ripe,' this being a tribute to his 'sacred old Father.'[34] At first sight, we are led to believe that if a person can be said to evidence all of the spiritual emotions most of the time, then *ipso facto* saintliness is present in that life.[35] One could read James as a member of a group of thinkers who constitute a major lineage of American Puritan thought. For instance, one could well associate James's list of spiritual emotions with Benjamin Franklin's 'little book of virtues,' in terms of which Franklin assessed his daily success or failure at character building.[36]

On the other hand, however, James falls short of suggesting just how people might establish such an 'habitual centre of the personal energy.' This methodological shortfall is perhaps characteristic of James's iconoclastic intellectual style and resistance to functional explanations, in favor of the personal autobiographical testimonial and phenomenological descriptions of lived experience. James suggests that the 'fruits' of religion appear on the vine of life of certain individuals, but he says little about the dynamic 'ripening' of such fruits. Perhaps by failing to take up this matter of the formation of the saintly character, James sustains vicariously (and happily) an aura of mystery about the religious experience beneath the surface of his father's intellectual life. Thus, the process of the 'ripening' of the saintly character needs to be addressed lest we end up only with (say) 'sour grapes' about religious commitments that may fail, or fruit that 'rots on the vine,' never finding suitable expression. (Such 'rot' is not without spiritual bearing, as the final chapter of this book (Chapter 10) will suggest.) After all, James's discussion of saintliness, as one major commentator has put it, is 'not to describe or endorse' any particular and exclusive *list* of fruits of religion, so much as it is to insist that it is 'to the fruits, the pragmatic outcome, that we must look for validation' of an inner process of growth, come what may.[37] However, unripened fruit is of little use.[38]

What is saintliness, variously ripened in the lives of individuals, for James? The Jamesian view is twofold, with what he calls (1) 'fundamental inner conditions' that override in importance what he suggests are (2) 'characteristic practical consequences' that grow from them.[39] Of the former, (1) 'fundamental inner conditions,' which pertains to the 'habitual centre' of a person's self-understanding, four 'spiritual emotions,' or archetypal affects, are mentioned: (i) 'A feeling of being in a wider life than that of this world's selfish little interests; and a conviction, not merely intellectual, but as it were sensible, of the existence of an Ideal Power';[40] (ii) 'A sense of the friendly continuity of the ideal power with our own life, and a willing self-surrender to its control';[41] (iii) 'An immense elation and freedom, as the outlines of the confining selfhood melt down';[42] and (iv) 'A shifting of the emotional centre towards loving and harmonious affectations, towards "yes, yes," and away from "no," where the claims of the non-ego are concerned.'[43] These four internal spiritual emotions constitute the 'fundamental mystery of religious experience.'[44] They yield the more formulaic view, as James put it in his famous definition, that religion is the sum total of 'the feelings, acts, and experiences of individual men in their solitude, so far as they apprehend themselves to stand in relation to whatever they may consider the divine.'[45]

Of the latter, (2) 'characteristic practical consequences' of saintliness, or the 'ripe fruits' of religion that are said to follow from well-established 'fundamental inner conditions,' James cites four specific lifestyle features that arise and shape the saintly character. Each is an aspect of the overall shift of the emotional center of the self to the 'fundamental mystery of religious experience,' the central axis of *homo religiosus*: (i) 'Asceticism,' which is an idiom of 'sacrifice' and a measure of 'loyalty to the higher power';[46] (ii) 'Strength of Soul,' or a sense of 'enlargement of life,' one so uplifting that the power of self-interest is denied and 'new reaches of patience and fortitude open out';[47] (iii) 'Purity,' or an enhancement of sensitivity to 'spiritual discords' and an imperative to cleanse from existence 'brutal and sensual elements';[48] and (iv) 'Charity,' or 'tenderness for fellow-creatures,' which inhibits 'ordinary motives to antipathy' and makes the saint love his enemies and treat 'loathsome beggars as his brothers.'[49] The laudatory nature of James's list loses its otherwise compelling force with the realization that in time it could appear to be dated and neglected, much as Franklin's list of virtues is today. What counts most for James 'as a good outcome' of cultivating spiritual emotions depends in large measure 'on the culture and expectations and values within which the outcome occurs.'[50]

However, although such 'characteristic practical consequences' may possibly vary from context to context, presumably the 'fundamental inner conditions,' or one's 'spiritual emotions,' do not. Quite apart from 'asceticism,' 'strength of soul,' 'purity,' and 'charity,' the inner 'spiritual emotions' specify a self-conscious engagement by an individual, as James puts it, in the 'fundamental mystery of religious experience,' or that basic emotional center of the self as essentially religious, or dialectically related to 'Otherness' as a quality of lived experience. But James never goes into these emotions. The process that ties together the 'fundamental inner conditions' remains unelaborated. But this is precisely where the 'common-sense' test of self-sacrifice and its bodily exaltation in lives come into play.

I shall argue that an elaboration of the 'fundamental inner conditions' of a person's self-understanding will readily be served by focusing on the *human body*, and on the ways in which the body, by necessity, engages in a *sacrificial cycle of life*. Cultivating an awareness of this natural process, not resisting it, is to engender 'spiritual emotions.' Certain elements to which the body is responsive during living occasion the 'fundamental inner conditions' of the individual. James only partially took up this consideration, and it needs to be developed beyond what he offers.

The 'human standards,' or 'human working principles,' soon to be described, form what James profiled as the saintly person, who is beckoned on by the pursuit of an ideal social self that is 'at least *worthy* of approving recognition by the highest *possible* judging companion.'[51] This 'sense of an ideal spectator' is an inner tribunal that most men 'carry in their breast ... (and) ... those who have *most* of it are possibly the most *religious* men.'[52] Here possibly is stated James's understanding of the conscience as a visual modality, based not on a sense of punishment, but literally on *facing* disability and death, or the body in decline and dying, and bearing witness to this, or seeing all of one's life from such an angle of vision. Both William James and Erik Erikson share a visual perceptual relatedness to the world.

Each searches for an original relation with the universe in which retrospection is rejected. The point is that James himself 'embodied' such witness. For example, his style of embodying mortality made a lasting impression on Sigmund Freud when they met at Clark University in 1909:

> I shall never forget one little scene that occurred as we were on a walk together. He (James) stopped suddenly, handed me a bag he was carrying and asked me to walk on, saying that he would catch me up as soon as he had got through an attack of angina pectoris which was just coming on. He died of that disease a year later; and I have always wished that I might be as fearless as he was in the face of approaching death.[53]

Thus, it is not sufficient to react to terminal illness only as James suggested it should best be met, namely, by 'gentlemanly levity, by high-minded stoicism, or by religious enthusiasm ... taking each in turn *pro re nata*.'[54] How, by facing disability and death, or the body in decline and dying, a list of cultural and/or social values or virtues arises, is not my specific task here.

'There was such a horror of him'

An unconscious conspiracy with the force of evil, in which one unknowingly turns a blind eye toward disability and death, or bodily decline and dying, gives rise to 'healthy-mindedness' and the 'once-born' type of consciousness, which, says James, bears 'no element of morbid compunction or crisis.'[55] For the 'Sick Soul,' evil has become a conscious recognition, one that can be evoked repeatedly and thereby it becomes a valuable standpoint for strenuous and robust living. When one surveys contemporary culture, a preponderance of the former kind of personality is evident. 'Healthy-mindedness' implies an attitude of denial towards death; the 'Sick Soul' suggests an obsession with dying.

Two principles contribute to the formation of saintliness as a process of *ongoing human sacrifice*, itself based on a need to embody thought. The two principles to abide if thought is to become embodied and if a lifestyle of self-sacrifice is to command allegiance, are what I have called (1) the *turnover/succession of generations*, that we live not just 'now,' but also out of past generations and into future ones; and (2) *biological/gender complementarity*, that males and females, not just males and not just females, together create generational turnover. Although these two principles are downplayed in many contemporary religious outlooks, increased attention to them will be the foundation on which an expanded worldview, itself based on a new 'historical horizon,' namely, the *'death event,'* can be established.[56] Like James, who was haunted by the prospect of bodily disability and decline, so too we are invited to think under the specter of an awareness framed by dying and death. Being human is represented by the body as a biological entity, with an ecological integrity and inherent principles all of its own, ones beyond our control. Humans forget that they are another species of animal. Such a primordial recognition of who we are collectively is a point of entry into knowing about James's 'fundamental mystery of religious experience.' Our knowledge may compel us to present our bodies as living sacrifices to life.

The 'mystery of religious experience,' by means of an emphasis on the body, can be recovered just as James gathered himself together after his nervous collapse of 1869 and amidst his grief over the death of Minny Temple a year later. James embodied the 'mystery of religious experience' by means of his 'panic fear' vision that is recounted in *The Varieties of Religious Experience* in 1901–2. In his vision, evil was banished and death squarely faced in bodily form, right on down to the 'pit' of his stomach:

> a black-haired youth with greenish skin, entirely idiotic ... looking absolutely non-human. ... *That shape am I*, I felt, potentially. ... There was such a horror of him ... I became a mass of quivering fear ... I awoke morning after morning with a horrible dread at the pit of my stomach, and with a sense of the insecurity of life ... (that) has made me sympathetic with the morbid feelings of others ever since.[57]

James's 'panic fear' vision is a virtual orchestration of the two principles that contribute to the formation of saintliness as a process of ongoing human sacrifice.

Thus, feeling panic and fear in the 'pit of my stomach' leads the 'French sufferer' (i.e. James) to think that most people are 'unconscious of that pit of insecurity beneath the surface of life' – a 'revelation' from which, curiously, the sufferer sought to shield his 'mother,' in spite of the 'religious bearing' of that insight and his own personal tactic of taking refuge in 'scripture texts' that invoked 'God.'[58] Generations mix in the scenario, along with male and female associations. James then draws out a lesson of disability and death, or bodily decline and dying, from the sufferer's 'fear of the universe,' namely, 'it always is that man's original optimism and self-satisfaction get levelled with the dust.'[59] Here James implies that the human body is the basis of religious thought. Such thought embodies life-giving death, or generational turnover/succession, and shared sexuality, or biological/gender complementarity.

An adherence to such principles of embodied thought leads to primordial associations with the symbolic infrastructure of the world's religions. With regard to the first principle of the turnover of generations, symbolic associations, or traditions of 'wisdom' have always been passed down through generations, usually by moral exemplars like respected 'tribal elders.' 'Apostolic succession' and other 'lineages' of highly developed individuals in a number of the religions of the world are examples of this. Primordial symbolic associations that flow from the second principle of biological/gender complementarity link women with the earth, the waxing and waning moon, and fertility; and men have been traditionally linked with the sky, the fire of the sun, and tool usage. Such symbolic associations represent life sacrificed, or less than sanguine prospects in the cultural and religious repertoire of humankind for accessing, retrieving, and cultivating human meaning, belonging, and a sense of personal empowerment. James was clearly on to this.

He thought that the 'completest religions' of the world were those in which the 'pessimistic elements are best developed,' and he cited Christianity and Buddhism as the best known examples.[60] The motif of the sacrificed life is pointedly illustrated in Christianity by the figure of Jesus (not yet the Christ, the Savior) being crucified on the cross, and in Buddhism by the emaciated Siddhartha Gautama (not yet the Buddha, the Enlightend One) surrendering his quest for enlightenment beneath the Bo Tree. Both images portend a 'sacred marriage' (*hieragamos*), where the sky (male) and the earth (female) are joined by means of axial 'trees of life,' this connection made available to us as the 'birth' of the 'wisdom' of the Christ's and Buddha's acts and teachings. Such cultural imagery constitutes an unending reverie that exists as an actuality beneath the moral reflection according to which the human species aims to survive and thrive into the future, and it is linked to nature and to the human body in a principled fashion.[61] In such a spirit, I shall now embody my own thought and become autobiographical, pursuing as far as possible a trajectory of personal realization as a reader and writer of the life of William James. I see myself 'mirrored' by James when I engage him empathically in a process of constructing him biographically as a 'text.' I then use the process introspectively as an occasion for comparative autobiographical reflection — how are I and James both different and similar? How might each of us be located on the trajectory of personal realization?

Stopped dead in my tracks: a lesson

The central Jamesian question throughout *The Varieties of Religious Experience* is: How might one secure an integrated worldview, and then live it out, from moment to moment, always on the brink of a fundamental disintegration and the possibility of death? The process of affirming our 'common humanity,' its joys but especially its sorrows and horrors, even as we are biologically similar, is for me the source of the saint's 'fundamental inner conditions' or 'spiritual emotions.' Living out this process, which is both moral and biological, engages us in what Christian theologians call 'incarnation,' the inseparable unity of 'flesh' and 'spirit,' where disintegration and death are more commanding than is the integrated worldview and life itself. As a reader and writer of lives, an approach of 'empathic introspection' is invited, a strategy in which a perceptual and emotional relatedness to a subject also becomes an introspective pathway into oneself, at least insofar as human similarity or sameness are sought.

My conviction about the importance of this derives mainly from my spiritual mentor, Martin Luther King, Jr. I volunteered to work in King's American Civil Rights movement during summers early in the 1960s. Besides advocating political enfranchisement for southern blacks in a segregated (and still racist) society, the movement also represented a spiritual and moral force not seen in the United States since the end of the Civil War in 1865. During my time in the Deep South, I was nearly killed twice by gunfire and once badly assaulted, wounded, and hospitalized due to the hostility of my fellow white Americans, albeit southern 'rednecks.'

This historical engagement with forces beyond my control subsequently had a psychological expression. When King was assassinated in 1968 an acute grief reaction overcame me, one that links me intimately with William James and his own critical personal juncture of 1869–70. My experience involved a visionary episode, or a temporary psychotic break with reality, in which my body discorporated (horribly) and was then reincorporated (profoundly peacefully). Since becoming an Australian citizen, I look back on this episode and offer the following testimony on behalf of that 'American sufferer,' who was a person who consciously recognized evil in a way that was similar to James's own 'nervous collapse' and devastation over Minny Temple's death:

> News of the assassination came on the radio, and I fell back on my bed listening in disbelief late into the afternoon. But things soon grew strange and began to change horribly. There I stretched out on my bed – no, what?! – a slab of slate on the floor of a desert canyon that was encircled by low rolling hills. Stars in the night sky twinkled overhead. A green/yellow light enveloped my body, at first emanating from my heart, and pulsated from head to toe. Fear overcame me. Then I was seized by panic. It was the *horror* of observing my body fall apart, seeing bones protrude through my flesh and blood vessels spurt like leaking hoses, and then witnessing my body decay into a puddle of putrid matter and gore. 'Dead,' I said to myself. However, suddenly I was caught by the realization that it was I myself who was watching my discorporation from above, and reassurance seemed to emanate from the stars overhead. Calmness took hold and I felt a profound trust in the universe, as if my body no longer was needed, as if a lesson was being learned. Nonetheless, the scene then slowly reversed itself: my body reincorporated, the pulsating light diminished, and I found myself back on my bed in the middle of the night with the radio

still on, though the station was now off the air. Neither before nor since that day has anything else so powerfully moved me, causing me to doubt all security and trust in the universe, and thereafter shaping my life personally and professionally. You could say that my historical and psychological engagement with Martin Luther King, Jr., truly a religious leader in a worldly sense, continues to fuel most of my vocational activities and preoccupations in one way or another, even to this day. I never mentioned any of it to my parents. It is an understatement for me to say that I can relate personally to the 'panic fear' vision of William James, which he presented surreptitiously as the testimony of the 'French sufferer' in the *Varieties of Religious Experience*.

Always pursuing a liberating historical cause I, none the less, continue to walk through the 'valley of the shadow of death,' so to speak, itself a powerful and ever-present psychological actuality. But I cannot say comfortably the line that follows (Psalms 23: 4), namely, 'I fear no evil.' More of the evil and horror than the goodness and peace of that powerful personal event remain a memory that has impact on my life each day.

Back then in 1964–68 I found, and today I keep on finding, myself propelled into a hallucinatory scenario that resolves itself in a most powerful conviction that violence must always precede nonviolence, that spiritual wholeness comes about only by means of the *bodily expenditure of life*, and that 'wholeness' comes in only second to 'falling apart.' Continuing to haunt me from my youth, now for very different reasons, is not only the Old Testament imagery of the 'valley of dry bones' (Ezekiel 37: 1–14), itself also an uncanny representation of my more recent experience of the Australian Outback. But also premonitory and haunting is the New Testament injunction, 'I appeal to you brethren, by the mercies of God, to present your bodies as a living sacrifice, holy and acceptable to God, which is your spiritual worship' (Romans 12: 1). Perhaps needless to say, this injunction also resonates within the Four Noble Truths of Buddhism, which imply that extinguishing the human desire to make all things permanent (including the body and its extension, the self) is the central soteriological task of the *arhat*, or saint. An implicit theology of lived experience becomes evident, one that suggests to me now, as James had sought for himself in his Gifford Lecture on 'Saintliness,' accredited theological beliefs that are based on my own (in James's words) 'religious life.'[62]

Such now accredited theological beliefs can be stated. They are extensions of the truth discovered by being 'stopped dead in my tracks,' so to speak. Thus, what I now call the 'god of death,' who exacts humility, is more important than the 'god of life,' who supports human pride, at least when we claim to reckon with saintliness and saintly formation, whatever tradition of explicit religion may from time to time command our interest and personal commitment. All this has propelled me into a life of religious preoccupation and, at the same time, has set me thinking, as academics must, about 'human standards' of the 'religious life' based on my experience.[63] While most people are familiar with the 'god of life,' I argue that, in the end, it is the 'god of death,' or the harbinger of all sorrow, horror, disintegration, and annihilation, with whom we must become acquainted if Jamesian saintliness is to become a living actuality in our lives. Together, both of these gods can be combined and called the *god of destruction*, whose lure is inescapable for those who would seriously engage in saintly formation. It was the god of destruction who touched James irreversibly in 1869–70, and who remained a powerful influence even into his last decade of life. My own historical engagement with Martin Luther King, Jr, and his movement during the summers of 1964 and 1965 drew my intuition to the god of destruction, and laid the foundation for my 'vision' of 1968, itself of continuing influence decades later.

James tried to reckon with this god within his inner sense of himself. 'I am getting really anxious lest I be cut off in the bud,' he wrote in 1903.[64] Although he wanted to write 'a general system of metaphysics,' James embodied his project and called the task of formulating truths a 'virulent disease' that he had recently contracted:[65]

> I actually dread to die until I have settled the Universe's hash in one more book, which shall be *epoch-machend* at last, and a title of honor to my children! Childish idiot – as if formulas about the Universe could ruffle its majesty, and as if the common-sense world and its duties were not eternally the really real![66]

Throughout all of James's works, the never-ending dramatic convergence of forces of destruction in the individual is a dominant motif.

Childish vanities though he resists, such motives have driven other people to create other-worldly images by which an individual might feign saintliness. Even though we can all be 'cut off in the bud' and may 'dread to die,' our anxiety can volatize into images of attaining an afterlife, the final human actuality of disability and death, or bodily decline and dying, notwithstanding. James himself occasionally submitted to such vanity:

> I never felt the *rational* need of immortality ... but as I grow older I confess that I feel the practical need of it much more than I ever did before; and that combines with reasons ... to give me a growing faith in its reality.[67]

Like James alive, but now in death's tightening grip, the urge toward creativity was heightened.

Enjoying spiritual solace was never a Jamesian activity, though seeking it was. He often sifted through the Christian tradition for spiritual mentors, individuals who might appear to vent his hagiographical impulse. When his sister, Alice, died in 1892, a grief-stricken James selected a passage from Dante's *Divine Comedy* (1300) to be inscribed on her urn: 'After long exile and martyrdom comes to this peace.'[68] From Dante, James turned to a Protestant for consolation when he cited John Bunyan's *The Pilgrim's Progress* (1678 and 1684). Although James refers to John Bunyan as 'Poor patient Bunyan,' a typical case of the 'psychopathic temperament' and sensitive of conscience 'to a diseased degree,' he uses Bunyan's testimony as confirmation of his own 'sense of the insecurity of life,' the absolute and horrible nadir of his 'panic fear' vision.[69] It may be unusual that James relies very little on Augustine's autobiography in the *Varieties of Religious Experience*. He does say, however, that Augustine illustrated a 'discordant personality,' in which having a 'divided self' continued to be a nagging emotional problem for at least four years after his conversion episode of 386 CE.[70] But James himself was not palliated by sifting through the works of would-be spiritual mentors, though his impulse to hagiography was great. By being 'otherworldly,' they were too sanguine; the human potential for devastation, horror, and death were neglected. This James realized bodily, deep in the 'pit' of his stomach.

To my mind, James's preoccupation with disability and death, or bodily decline and dying, at every turn of thought makes him more responsive to the 'god of death' than to the 'god of life.' While I had a sense of *walking* in the 'valley of the shadow of death' during my Civil Rights engagement in the early 1960s, it was the actual sense of dying during my visionary episode of 1968 that literally 'stopped me in my tracks.' As James himself realized, the likes of Dante, Bunyan, Augustine, and others may offer only limited insight into the necessary connections between saintliness and the mortal body. In other words, James remained more 'incarnational' in his views on such matters, perhaps, than did his well-known Christian theological predecessors, which I myself can well appreciate.

Movement through imagined time and space, perhaps journeying even to heavens, hells, and within reincarnational cycles of rebirth, characterizes the religion of 'healthy-mindedness,' where growth, personal development, and self-actualization are emphasized. But typical of the religion of the 'sick soul' is a cessation of movement, a recognition of things at an end. The spiritual journey *as journey* is nothing more than, as Ralph Waldo Emerson once put it about global travel, a 'fool's paradise.'[71] However, for those travelers who would not finally be fooled, it is a matter of recognizing that the end of life and a cessation of 'traveling' count most toward saintliness, or that which stops us, so to say, 'dead in our tracks' during the course of living. The realization of cessation constitutes the final phase of a trajectory of personal realization for the reader and writer of lives who would embark on a 'spiritual quest.'

A 'common-sense' test of saintliness: life sacrificed

A *sacrificed life* (to death) model of religious experience is proposed as an elaboration of what James had in mind when he wrote about 'human standards,' or 'human working principles,' that lie at the heart of saintliness. The human community itself, *not* individual selves, looms into prominence. The sacrificed life (to death) model accomplishes three things: it allows us to (1) take disability and death, or bodily decline and dying, on board; (2) raise high the body itself (not just thoughts or symbols of the body) as our natural sacrifice ('human sacrifice') to the future (generational turnover/ succession); and (3) affirm the inclusivity of the human community (biological/gender complementarity). This leads to a pervasive sense of global human solidarity and to moral vision based on a desire to repeat affirmations of such solidarity wherever and whenever this may be possible. Sacrifice in such a sense is actually a communication system that binds people together.

However, let life sacrificed not be taken naively. The predatory design of nature by which our bodies are determined presents a radical evil the minute our eyes are closed to it. Writes James,

> The lunatic's visions of horror are all drawn from the material of daily fact. ... To believe in the carnivorous reptile of geologic time, is hard for our imagination. ... Yet there is no tooth in any one of those museum-skulls that did not daily ... hold fast to the body struggling in despair as some fated living victim. Forms of horror just as dreadful to their victims, if on a smaller spatial scale, fill the world about us today. ... Crocodiles and rattlesnakes and pythons are at this moment vessels of life just as real as we are ... and whenever they or other wild beasts clutch their living prey, the deadly horror which an agitated melancholic feels is the literally right reaction on the situation.[72]

It is not only a 'literally right reaction' for the melancholic, but also an appropriate reaction that may contribute to building up a 'moral community' in the sense described by Emile Durkheim and, more importantly, by his nephew and most distinguished pupil, Marcel Mauss.[73] Mauss concluded that human exchange as a system of reciprocal communication between participants was a key to moral empowerment: a 'wise precept' that is evident in 'human evolution' and valuable as an action plan for living, he writes, is that 'we should come out of ourselves and regard the duty of giving as a liberty, for in it there lies no risk.'[74] I suggest that a human 'moral community' would be one supported by a vision of an *exchange of bodies* through death, sexuality, and birth, a vision that is based on the two principles identified above. Each principle works in concert to foster such an exchange of bodies. Together the principles develop James's thought. My suggestion is that they are elaborations of the 'fundamental inner conditions' by which, says James, the 'spiritual emotions' of saintliness are formed.

The first principle of the sacrificed life model, as we said, is the turnover or succession of generations. It is activated by what I have called the 'god of death.' Lived experience becomes moral insofar as present self-understanding is framed by awareness of one's ancestral past as it converges on the present, and how this gives rise to progeny and a future. Generational turnover is marked best by taking seriously the possible role played by mortality in one's life. It is difficult in living to 'learn to die,' or to give way to the next generation, and obedience to this first standard requires unusual moral courage. French thinker, Georges Bataille, suggests that religious experience is an exercise in cultivating 'animality,' this being an inner sense of 'immediacy and immanence.'[75] Animality is the unbroken, unselfconscious continuity between an individual being and its environment. Emblematic of this is that instant, writes Bataille, in which *one animal eats another*.'[76] Thus, the oneness of the animal world is such that violence and death are no disruption to it, but simply stages through which all life passes. Such a view represents the predatory design of nature to which James himself pointed.

The standard of this design is the 'sacrificed life,' in which death of the body and an annihilation of the self are, at bottom, fundamentals of living. Involved here is a process of exchanging bodies — those of the older generation, albeit ones that do not in themselves get returned, for those of the new generation. In Christianity, it is the metaphor of 'crucifixion' writ large, and in Buddhism it is the metaphor of the 'extinguished flame' of the human desire for permanence. The prospect of exchanging bodies sets in motion a series of challenging personal interrogations: Are we 'death-aware'? Do we look for signs of death-awareness in others? Thus, when I read stories of lives like that of the 'French sufferer' and others with mortality management in mind, or tell my own personal story as the 'American sufferer,' do I find useful instruction in *ars moriendi*, the 'art of dying,' as a lifestyle amidst my ordinary suffering?[77] One hopes so.[78]

The second principle of the sacrificed life model, also foreshadowed above, is biological/gender complementarity. It is activated by what I have called the 'god of life,' but who is obedient at all times to the first god. Biological production of the future requires women and men to behave sexually. Here sexuality leads to natality, but also may lead to horrific sexual perversity and violence, as nature's predatory design implies and as Georges Bataille underscores.[79] But reproduction must also occur socially and culturally. This process would include not only the 'front line,' so to speak, of heterosexual practice, but also a homosexuality that is responsive to intergenerational realities and responsibilities. Any creative effort on behalf of the future in the face of the god of destruction must take into account not gender exclusivity, but inclusivity – that men and women reproduce the best of themselves together, as they also die together as members of their generation.[80] Learning to be biologically (as well as socially and culturally) inclusive, perhaps by gaining an initial awareness of this through sensuality and eroticism, implies a moral stance for life. Sexuality in practice, of course, usually implies a pleasurable exchange of bodies, albeit ones that ordinarily get returned after sexual activity, at least short of any possible 'fatal attraction' involving sadomasochistic excess.

However, there is a downside to this sanguine view of sensuality and eroticism. Sexual activity partakes of the idiom of mortality: the self loses, or temporarily 'sacrifices' itself to the partner in an exchange process. Nevertheless, in Christianity the metaphor of 'resurrection' expresses this second principle of biological/gender complementarity on the basis of an erotic and sensual dimension, and this is also played out in some Buddhist traditions (*Tantra*) where erotic and sexual practices become means to 'enlightenment.' Here, too, challenging personal interrogations arise: Do we embrace inclusive sensuality/sexuality as an idiom of self-understanding, even by means of empathy, perhaps as James approximated in his relationships with Minny Temple and Eliza Putnam Gibbens? Do we view others not only with their sex lives in mind, but also with a view to the biologically procreative and culturally creative implications of sexuality? (One could well wonder whether James's Gifford Lectures would ever have eventuated had he not received pampered personal indulgence from his wife in Europe, and professional support by means of correspondence from his mother-in-law at the time.) Thus, when I read stories of lives like that of the 'French sufferer' and others with inclusive sensuality/sexuality appreciation in mind, or tell my own story as an 'American sufferer' of decades ago and even to this day, do I find useful instruction in how to seek extension and completion of myself while affirming the 'Other,' this on the backdrop of my biologically evident incompleteness, as I am obviously not a woman? One hopes so.

In other words, what I call the god of destruction, or that combination of the 'god of death' and the 'god of life,' with the latter always obedient to the former, has three faces – mortality, sexuality, and natality. These biological forces constitute what can be abstracted and called 'Otherness.' This collective force is inherent in each of our bodies. Like a spreading malignancy, it annihilates us in the end, often horribly, as James himself well realized from his personal trials of 1869–70. A sacrificed life is a *pre-emptive style of life* that is congruent with disability and death, or bodily decline and dying. A realistic lifestyle strategy would include as a central preoccupation an ongoing consideration of the role played by this force in a life. Such, then, is a lifestyle of saintliness. James, I trust, would be sympathetic to such a view.

It is the nature of the universe, says James, that everyone is 'drawn and pressed' into 'sacrifices and surrenders of some sort' as 'permanent positions of repose.'[81] Unlike non-religious sacrifices, which are viewed as necessary, in the saintly life, on the contrary, 'surrender and sacrifice are positively espoused.'[82] James concludes, '*Religion thus makes easy and felicitous what in any case is necessary.*'[83] Inseparable from the body, selfhood is a continuously revised narrative of reckonings with the predatory design of nature. Eyes must open to see the 'material daily fact' of evil, James wrote; and life must be lived facing the reality that 'forms of horror ... fill the world about us today.'[84] Glimmers of insight come particularly when each and every one of the three faces of the god of destruction gains recognition in a life. Saintly formation, as a constructive means of mortality management — one that affirms disability and death, or bodily decline and dying, and does not deny it — will develop insofar as generational turnover/succession and biological/gender complementarity lend order to living.[85]

The question of whether these two general principles are affirmed together in a life, even deliberately cultivated by means of some kind of disciplined spiritual practice, provides us with a 'common-sense' test of saintliness. This test specifies and elaborates upon what James called the 'human standards,' or 'human working principles,' by which saintliness can be recognized. The test permits us to understand the connection between the 'fundamental inner conditions' of saintliness in individuals, and how these might be said, as James put it, to undergo 'ripening' into identifiable 'spiritual emotions' that mark the saintly character the world over. The test is based on 'common sense,' namely, that we are born and die and rehearse each of these dramas together under the banner, 'LIFE.' However, though it is in that way a 'common-sense' test of saintliness, the sense of cultivating a saintly character is far from common.

Introspection has allowed me to know the test from experience, or from that uncanny inner connection I continue to feel between James's 'French sufferer,' my own 'American sufferer,' and our shared compliance with the exacting demands of the god of destruction. Perhaps specifically because of our similar adversities, known empathically — James's of 1869–70 and mine of 1964–68 — this god would propel us both on a road in life that slowly becomes a shared realization of sainthood. For me, the ripening of saintliness takes place only 'over my dead body,' so to speak. Or, at least, with reference to the daily actuality of disability and death, or the body in decline and dying, within the lived experience that holds me, as it clearly held William James, in its ever tightening grip.

9 Magical deification of a convulsing body

Let us begin by noting the fine line between biography and autobiography, because this chapter tells the story of one man's life. He used magic while being held in captivity by Muslim terrorists in Lebanon in the 1980s and developed a 'mystical' sense of self which led to 'deification' of the body insofar as magical practice was used. We shall sense, perhaps, our own implication in the man's human struggles, and join vicariously in an exercise of survival that was based on magical performances. This means that when the line between a sense of self and a social context of other people blurs, a psychology of narcissism is invoked as an inner tactic of survival. This sets a stage for magical performances: a person literally comes 'face-to-face' with oneself 'mirrored' in the story of a life, especially with the inevitabilities of living. The goal becomes to sustain the 'illusion' of the self in spite of life-threatening circumstances, like torture and the deprivation of means for survival by a person's captors. Implied in this is an invitation to reckon with dying and death in all experiences of the self, and to gain a modicum of procreative purchase on them. This serves to foster the 'spiritual quest,' or an outlook based on human mortality as a central existential fact, and also as a locus of magical practice that itself may eventuate in a 'mystical' sense of self and 'deification' of one's body. Reckoning with dying and death, these being forces that hold all of us captive, is a psychological engine driving the construction and destruction of world religions.

Magic as bodily performance

Such reckonings imply spontaneous *magical practice*, or actions by which marvelous results are produced by compelling the aid of an unseen 'Other' – spirits or secret forces of nature – to conspire in bringing about such results, including a heightened sense of self, if not actual eternal life. Magic is a proactive endeavor born out of a sense of helplessness. It aims to control largely uncontrollable circumstances. This is done on the basis of a psychology of crisis, in which narcissistic self-inflation serves as a *modus operandi* for confirming ongoing selfhood and bodily integrity. While it is possible to control many aspects of living, and to 'get back in control,' so to speak, magic goes to the core of uncontrollable things, to the incorrigible aspects of existence, the chief of which are dying and death. The analogy of 'human captivity' is apt: we are all captives of a sort, prisoners of existence; and this leads many of us into an unwitting practice of magic. Studying the lives of others can be an extension of such activity. This occurs on the backdrop of taking dying and death as a protracted crisis of living. One could respond with a psychology of narcissistic self-inflation and its practical outcropping, namely, magical attempts to manipulate critical circumstances with a view to ensuring the survival of 'body and soul,' so to speak.

According to the philosopher of religion, Peter Donovan, 'magic, like luck, fortune, or even fun, is a concept transcending cultural differences, and bridging vast social and ideological gulfs.'[1] Most recent studies of magic emphasize what is called its performative character. Contemporary discussion is steered away from magical rites as invoking the mysterious causal efficacy of personal occult desires and secret supernatural powers. Magic involves the manipulation of a social situation.[2] Anthropological thinker, Daniel O'Keefe, draws on the philosophy of language of Ludwig Wittgenstein when he suggests that magic is a communication system based on 'agreeing to agree':

> We can borrow this powerful concept and use it to explain how strange experiences that erupt when the cognitive frame weakens are patterned. They are patterned, defined, institutionalised and overhauled − by agreement. The experiences are so varied and subjective that we have to agree that we are agreeing. We even have to agree that anything at all has happened. That is basically how magic works; it systematically weakens the frame to produce some vague experience, and then the small experimental act-as-if magical group agrees to define this experience as significant and momentous.[3]

Thus, magic operates socially, based on pre-existing public conventions. The relationship between *captors and captives*, or predators and those preyed upon, is one such public convention, as we shall soon see. The use of techniques for creating effective illusions is permitted by such shared conventions. Magic works like rhetoric, salesmanship, or media 'hype.' It produces an appearance of agreement which is in fact functional, even though not requiring a generally shared conviction or in itself necessarily creating any actual consensus.[4] Captives remain at the will of their captors; the existence of predators keeps prey vigilant.

The psychological locale or 'space' in which such magic is practiced can be plotted between our outward empathic skills and our inward introspective capacities, themselves requisites for embracing human lives effectively. When the life of another person is investigated, perhaps we realize the potential to be changed ourselves simply by studying the life and letting it impact upon us. Thus, we begin by 'agreeing to agree' that engaging a life can be 'significant' or 'momentous.' Sacred biographies (even hagiographies) have been compelling forces in the lives of religious people the world over. An empathic capacity in particular carries with it an implied affirmation of the solidarity of the human species, this at primordial biological, ethological, and symbolic levels. Introspection punctuates individuality amidst a realization of basic human sameness.

Thus, we may concern ourselves with narrations about the *body*, the locus of existentiality, of birth, sexuality, and mortality (to name but three possible dimensions). The body is taken to be a specific and major instance of a shared humanity in an evolutionary context. Narrations about bodies can become 'magical' extensions of the self. Such embodied stories represent experiences of the self as a nexus of personal realization, even mystical insight, in a soteriological key.[5] The body, and uses of it in captivity, is central to a psychology of crisis that leads to personal religious realization. Captives, especially those subjected to torture, indicate that they become preoccupied with how the physical integrity of the body might be maintained. They speak of thoughts they have had about how the body might also undergo transformation into something 'incorruptible,' in which is potent a sense of being an everlasting physical presence wherein a feeling of rebirth or 'resurrection' seems imminent.[6]

Transgression of bodily limits and spirituality

The work of the French thinker, Georges Bataille, is instructive on how the body can undergo 'deification,' and become a basis for a mystical sense of self.[7] Bataille's intellectual project is aligned with a Nietzschean worldview in which desires for pleasure fuse with pain and come under powerful subjugation. Bataille's interests begin in an appreciation of the writings of Marquis de Sade, and his subjects include analyses of eroticism, sexuality, violence, and pornography. In general, his potential for understanding the self *as* body, or as an idiom of personal deification owing to implicit religion or the 'spiritual quest,' has been largely untapped by thinkers in religion and the human sciences. It has been said that it 'neither designates objects, nor signifies ideas ... rather it charts the limit experience.'[8] *Thought at the limit is entirely visceral.* In the experience of extremes, such as excruciating pain or orgasmic pleasure, the convulsing body is quite simply the beginning and the end of expression. Interior experience in such instances is irreducible; in its immediacy it neither begins nor ends in language, as it evokes ineffability.[9]

Similarly, the body itself is the locus of mystical experience. As philosopher Alexander Irwin notes, the experience of the convulsing body itself is for Bataille a criterion of spiritual process.[10] A failure to recognize the immediacy of such experience in general leads to a deferment of full existence: actions become not experiences with intrinsic value, but are subjugated and turned towards a purpose or project in life. Existence 'at the limit' is continually 'put-off.'[11] Thus, Bataille saw dogmatic or doctrinal religion as functioning to subvert the very *experiential immediacy* that lay at the basis of its own implicit religion or 'spirituality.' Ironically, such a project brings into being biological and ethological discontinuity, or 'separation' from the 'state of nature.' At the same time, the drive of the religious life paradoxically seeks an end to separation by affirming continuity between the individual 'at the limit' of lived experience and the wider world of nature with its predatory design: Bataille says that the purest spiritual impulse desires 'the undifferentiated flow of animal interaction, the ... cycle of devouring and being devoured.'[12] As a captive of Muslim terrorists, Brian Keenan's story depicts this struggle for survival when surviving requires the magical illusion of safety, as we shall note.

Experience 'at the limit' of visceral extremes, with the *convulsing body* clearly in the mind's eye, constitutes the relationship between captors and captives, predators and those preyed upon. Abolished are all projects (such as obtaining the 'sacred') which are ordinarily thought to be the goals of explicit ('institutionalized') religion. The only means to the end of a deified body or a mystical sense of self is to surrender 'means/ends' thinking. And so Bataille ultimately rejects the notion of a division between the sacred and the profane. Both must be read together because they are linked at the level of language.[13] The zenith of inner experience was achievable by means of 'communication,' which Irwin describes as 'the ecstatic state in which the boundaries of selfhood dissolve and the individual communicates in fusional unity with the world.'[14] Mysticism is the result, based on transgressing bodily limits. Julian Pefanis notes that involved is a certain 'method of obstinacy,' a 'will to self-loss,' and this is performed in intense experiences of pain, torture, terror, and disgust.[15] (One could venture to say here that such was the 'method in the madness' of Marquis de Sade's lifestyle as a libertine, and a spiritual dynamic at work in sadomasochistic sexuality.) An illustrative image that comes to mind is that of the early Christian martyrs who in their pain experienced Christ and, often with it, powerful and convulsive orgasms.

Paradoxically, the self experiences itself most when narcissistic inflation becomes a counterpoint to severe self-loss. Although selfhood is achieved, the victory is pyrrhic: only as the limits of the body, language, and culture are transgressed does the embodied self come into being. Explains philosopher Carolyn Dean, 'the loss of the self is experienced as the constituent moment of selfhood.'[16] Magical practice is analogous. Just when an act of prestidigitation appears impossible and about to fall apart, an agreement is struck with an audience, who agree that a 'rabbit' is, indeed, pulled marvelously 'out of a hat,' so to speak. Sustained is the shared communication that the 'illusion' is not an illusion at all. Or that even if reality (of the embodied self) has been 'lost' (or could be lost at any second), none the less, we shall all act as if the reality of our awareness of the ongoing integrity of the physical body has been confirmed yet again!

Here in Bataille's thought, then, is an understanding of the 'spiritual quest' that is grounded in the immediacy of bodily extremes. The distinction between body and self dissolves, and they become one – an agreement to agree that a magical illusion is greater than the sum of its parts, or that there is 'more to it' than meets the eye. Clearly the body functions as the starting point and continuing locus of magically induced spiritual experience. Given this, one might expect it to be reflected in certain kinds of religious life-writing, autobiography in particular. Brian Keenan's book, *An Evil Cradling* (1992), illustrates all this. It is a biographical construction that describes his most lucid autobiographical reflection about his body 'at the limit.' A reader engages in agreeing to agree with Keenan that his efforts to survive actually 'did the trick.' Although it probably could be said that Keenan suffered from extreme psychological depersonalization during his captivity, it was precisely this state of mind that propelled the 'convulsing body' to the forefront of his awareness. In this sense, what would ordinarily be thought to be a pathological psychiatric condition actually led to a personal realization event that achieved its highest pitch in Keenan's sense that his own body became, indeed, deified, or part of the body of God. This god, I might suggest here, has the appearance of the *god of destruction*, which in Chapter 8 was identified in the context of my own lived experience and sense of persistent bodily jeopardy and survival.

Keenan's story

An Evil Cradling is an enthralling book in which Irishman Brian Keenan tells of his experiences as a hostage who was held for over four-and-a-half years during the late 1980s by Muslim political extremists in Beirut. What results is a compelling and stirring revelation of one man's self-discovery under barbarous extremes, a revelation in which an experience of the body *as* self becomes an apotheosis. Compelling theoretical grounds exist for making this suggestion. Mark Johnson, a well-known philosopher of metaphor and the body, contends that all experience relies for its description on image schemes and metaphors whose meanings are ultimately grounded in the body, and his contention helps to capture this view of the bodily basis of inner experience.[17]

The title of the book reflects the paradox in which Keenan's brutal confinement nurtured a new sense of self. As he put it, 'I do not wish to tell the whole of life, but only of an incident: an episode in time, a short sequence, yet one that seems dreadfully long and meaningful to me.'[18] Keenan regards the impulse to write the work as a call to come to terms with what happened to him in Lebanon, and to direct his thoughts and actions to desired results, including magical healing. His cell of torture would be converted into a place where his body would eventually 'cradle' new outlooks. Keenan's narration itself suggests a psychology of magical thought and practice, one that is based on narcissistic self-inflation with its illusory sense of mastery over captivity. In the process of readjustment, writes Keenan, 'we are our own self-healers. The writing of this book has been part of that healing.'[19] The desire to share his story with others appears integral to the restoration of health. That the physical act of writing should be associated with magical healing begins to reflect the degree to which the book itself is a receptacle of corporeality. Like early Christian and medieval reliquaries in which the mortal remains of saints were kept and venerated by the faithful, the book contains Keenan's sense of self as a physical reality, a body being tortured to death. Sharing his story itself implies a wider generative function, one which summons unseen powers, relatives, and other ancestors. These become props that support the illusion of safety.

Keenan begins with his decision to leave Northern Ireland to take up a teaching post at the American University in Beirut. In this beginning, the issue of mortality figures prominently. He confides that he is still not sure what finally convinced him to go, but he remembers a conversation with a friend some months before: 'we talked of ageing ... I suddenly felt myself becoming afraid of not going anywhere, afraid of the challenge that life itself presents.'[20] Armed with an awareness of his mortal body, he inscribes a temporal truth: 'We come to an age when choice is forced upon us ... knowing that ... it will be the last and final change we might comfortably make.'[21] Keenan's physical translocation to Lebanon represented the body in process, or as he put it, an 'inner compulsion to change.'[22] This bore a conscious decision, an attempt, he wrote, to 'remould or remake myself' in the face of morbidity, or in other words, to act magically in order to bring about his desired results.[23]

Keenan indicates at the outset that one of the few recurring memories of his student days during his confinement was that of his first confrontation with death. The following anecdote was, for Keenan, magical activity designed to achieve a step on his long road to healing and recovery from his trauma. As a boarder in a house run by an elderly couple, a Mr and Mrs Paul, he had returned one evening to find the woman sitting quietly by herself. Apparently in a state of shock, she calmly told him that her husband had just died. Keenan was left to inform the couple's sons and daughters, but the aspect which memory preserved for him the most was the sight of the dead man lying alone in the room. As a hostage, Keenan tried to recall poetry that he had written at the time. The attempt, he wrote, 'became for me a mental exercise to overcome my own pathetic condition, reaching back to what I had originally written as a memorial to this old [man] and to my first confrontation with death.'[24] Keenan believed this exercise was part of the process of escaping the immobility that affects the hostage. Immobility is simultaneously physical and mental, but 'the feeling of total constriction ... demands of us some kind of survival strategy. We must look within to find it.'[25] His virtual 'ancestral' connection to the dead old man was not only empathic, but also patently introspective. He was 'mirrored' by the dead old man, face-to-face with himself, agreeing to agree with himself that he would somehow remain unimplicated in death's finality.

The bulk of *An Evil Cradling* in fact covers the story of how Keenan survived. Survival involved both conscious action, as well as a kind of instinctual mechanism about which French thinker Georges Bataille is most instructive: in Bataille's thought, no distinction between body and self exists, and this is evident in Keenan's text; the story of one is the story of the other. Keenan's story of 'self-confrontation' involves the gradual stripping away of the conditioned elements of self, or the external cultural accretions of time that signify personal identity. This culminates in deeper awareness that itself resides in the immediacy of his raw bodily experience while in a state of extreme physical deprivation, pain, and ever-present bodily jeopardy. Let us now consider these magical moments when Keenan tacitly agrees with himself to sustain the paradox of magically deifying his body in spite of his life-threatening captivity.

Magical moments

It was only three weeks after arriving in Beirut that Keenan was kidnapped, and to this day he does not know which Muslim political faction held him hostage. His account of the actual kidnapping 'captures well' the somatic reality of the event — mental shock, use of magical activity such as compliant posturing and body language to avoid harm, and his reluctance to lose cherished items of clothing. For example, he wore his father's shirt:

> What would these men want with my father's shirt? With slow deliberation I removed [it] and handed it at full arms' length to this man, looking always into his eyes and smiling at him ... I believe to this day that that sardonic smile, and my staring him full in the face restrained him from whatever violence he was prepared to offer.'[26]

Shirtless, body revealed, Keenan became all the more vulnerable to unprovoked violence. The externals of his identity were literally stripped off, but his magical efforts to control events seemed to be working.

Keenan's initial confinement rapidly influenced his senses and overall perception: 'The food was tasteless ... though it was heavily spiced and flavoured. [There] was just a blandness in my mouth. I thought that the shock of what had happened was finally ebbing slowly into me, dulling the faculties of taste and perception with tension, and an unacknowledged fear.'[27] Thus, Keenan's sense of bodily coherence was assaulted by a change of diet. However, his experience of having many personal possessions removed from him was more troublesome: 'They had taken my watch, my ring, a necklace a friend had given me ... leaving me only what I stood up in: my father's shirt, a pair of grey trousers, socks and a pair of shoes ... I dreaded the loss of those shoes ... Perhaps as long as I had my shoes I had some dignity.'[28] An unknown number of days later, when Keenan saw one of his captors wearing his sunglasses, he became angry and upset: 'Insignificant and inexpensive things had now become ... vitally important to me. Parts of me had become parts of someone else.'[29] Keenan's clothing represents a symbolic extension of his body. Thus, he was 'cannibalized' by his captors. Items such as shirts, necklaces, shoes, and sunglasses become foci of magical manipulation, and the newly intensified view of the relationship with one's captors that follows makes such objects commodities of ritualized exchange. Keenan's description of the need for physical exercise can be cited as a further and even more embodied example of this.[30]

Notably, the need to demonstrate routine control of one's body is a fundamental means of maintaining self-identity, albeit magically. According to sociologist Anthony Giddens,

> Regularised control of the body is a fundamental means whereby a biography of self-identity is maintained; yet at the same time the self is also more or less constantly 'on display' to others in terms of its embodiment. The need to handle both of these aspects of the body simultaneously, which originated in the early experiences of the infant, is the main reason why a feeling of bodily integrity – of the self being safely 'in' the body – is so closely tied to the regular appraisal of others.[31]

The management of 'illusion' for his captors as well as for himself was a magical hedge against psychological 'disillusionment.' Keenan's demand for exercise was an effort to maintain a sense of the equation, 'my body equals my self' in the face of increased social isolation. Part of the trauma of being a hostage results from losing control, because routines of exercise, ablutions, and so forth are determined not by oneself but by others.

Keenan's account of his hunger strike, which occurred some weeks after being kidnapped, therefore conveys a stronger sense of ritualized control. His persistent requests for the reason for his kidnapping remained unanswered. And so he decided to take, in his words, 'a door which was always to remain with each hostage, and which we alone could open and go through.'[32] Keenan located the magical activity of the hunger strike in his 'Irishness':

> Hunger strike is a powerful weapon in the Irish psyche. ... It removes and makes negligible the threat of punishment. It powerfully commits back into the hunger striker's hands the full sanction of his own life and his own will. I was desperate for information. I needed to know something, anything ... something on which my mind could fix and cling to for survival. I simply stopped eating. ... So each morning as breakfast arrived I would simply consign it to a corner and forget about it.[33]
> I was committed to confrontation. But the days of hunger, or rather the indifference to hunger, had steeled my purpose. I remember as I refused to eat each meal feeling myself grow stronger.[34]
> For the next few days nothing happened and I ate nothing. ... Things would come flying through the grille. A piece of cheese, and different pieces of food ... I laughed and laughed. Here was a game I was winning; I was in control and control could not be taken away from me.[35]

Conveyed is the sense of an empowered self generated by a mastery (of a sort) over the body. Noticeably, however, the body is not being treated with disdain here, as if it was merely an obstacle to insight and growth as, perhaps, it has been in traditional religious autobiographies, for example, in Augustine's *Confessions*. Instead, the body becomes for Keenan a positive presence and an idiom of identity, a locus of magical control. His hunger strike amounts to a somatic declaration of selfhood amidst powers he aims to propitiate. Soon afterwards, however, he endured experiences of physical transgression which took him well beyond the limits of his body.

The hunger strike ended when he was told the alleged reason for his captivity, namely, the American bombing of Libya: 'I had become a tiny insignificant pawn in a global game over which I had no control.'[36] Thus begins his account of 'disillusionment,' or psychological dissolution in which the body *as* self participated. It culminated in an awareness of 'God,' this being an event of magic transmuted into intense personal experience. Keenan spent at least one year in solitary confinement in a small drab cell with no natural light or ventilation. The routine imposed by his captors was unchanged, and due to the barrier of language he remained a virtual isolate. Taken together, Keenan's somatic descriptions of his experience of captivity imply a 'limit experience' (as Bataille describes it) – immediate and ultimately ineffable. Nevertheless, the 'limit experience' itself was grounded, as Bataille would put it, in the organic 'animality' of the body. Writes Keenan,

> I am back from my daily ablutions ... I set down my plastic bottle of drinking water and the other empty bottle. From bottle to bottle, through me, this fluid will daily run ... I pace my four paces backwards and forwards, slowly feeling my mind empty, wondering where it will go today. Will I go with it or will I try to hold it back. ... There is a greasy patch on the wall where I lay my head. Like a dog I sniff it.[37]
> I squat and rock backwards and forwards reciting a half-remembered rhyme like a religious mantra. I am determined I will make myself more mad than my mind.[38]
> Always in the morning I see the marks of the night's battle. Red lumps like chicken pox, all raging to be itched and scratched. ... The more I try to resist the more difficult it becomes and the more demanding is my body for the exquisite pain of my nails tearing my own flesh.[39]
> I have been impotent for weeks. I am reduced to this animal thing, to this failure of my genitals to come alive in me. What have they done to me, this final insult and indignity. That most primitive and animal part of me has been ripped from me ... I might never be a father, might never hold a child.[40]

The graphic physicality of these and other such images are the most engaging feature of Keenan's work.

Such physicality builds to a crescendo as a transgression of Keenan's conventional norms and bodily limits is described. Writes Keenan,

> I take up one of the magazines, *Time* or *Newsweek* ... I defecate on the reason why I am being held in this asylum of a place and then carefully wrap my excrement in a parcel. ... Tomorrow I will lift this piece of myself and cast it into that cockroach filled hole in the ground. ... Excrement, sweat, the perspiration of a body and a mind passing through waves of desperation ... I am breaking out of myself, urges, ideas, emotions in turmoil are wrenched up and out from me. ... In a half-blissful state my mind caresses and delights me and I am content with all that is about me and do not want to leave it. I am reaching out and feeling an ecstatic embrace enfold me. Now I am thrust into agonizing torrents of tears. I am weeping not knowing from where the tears come ... I am weeping and weeping is all I am ... I cannot stop it, though I crush myself against the wall to assure myself I have a body, I cannot quell the grief ... I am full of nothing ... I am a bag of flesh and scrape, a heap of offal tossed unwanted in the corner of this filthy room.[41]

Animality and inner religious experience become linked. Because of their governance by ritual prohibition through religious practice, the organic elements expelled from the body (for example, excrement, urine, tears, blood, semen, and so forth) represent zones of ultimate reference between the sacred and the profane.[42] (Think also of human hearts offered up to the Sun God of the Aztecs of Mesoamerica.) The zones are also elements that can be magically manipulated and exchanged with captors.

Bataille used the example of the sexual act to suggest that the organic necessity for 'communication' entailed a posture of vulnerability and the loss of material substance, these being linked to self-attenuation and self-extinction. His idea was extended into the domain of religion and spiritual formation.[43] Two beings communicate through vulnerability and loss of their very substances, especially within a structure of domination and subjugation (a Sadean, or sadomasochistic scene, perhaps not unlike a crucifixion) and, for an instant, the two beings dissolve into a unity after which they each experience a greater clarity of self. For Bataille, rituals, sacrifices, and festivals in religion evidence a will to 'lose excess,' and cause a similar dissolution of the individual into the group. This carries forward the tradition of thought about ritualized magic initiated by Marcel Mauss in his study of the forms and functions of exchange in archaic societies, with the *potlatch* of the Tlingit and Haida tribes of northwest Canada being his central example.[44] In such a sense, Bataille suggested that 'the 'sacred' is communication between things.'[45] Thus, the loss of material (bodily) elements, on the backdrop of vulnerability, can represent a concrete expression of a religious encounter with embodied power in one's midst. A narcissistic inflation of such encounters profoundly affects self-under-standing, even the course of a life. For Keenan, his sense of himself in such encounters represented a moral subversion of the politics of extremism – the magical deification of his own physically deprived and tortured convulsing body.

Keenan states that he had an experience of 'God,' and clearly this encounter was mediated through his body, I dare say, made 'incarnate.' The dissolution he experienced culminated with the introduction into his cell of a bowl of fruit. The reintroduction of colour, smell, and form caused him to be transported beyond his circumstances, carried away: 'I am drunk with something that I understand but cannot explain. I am filled with a sense of love. I am filled and satiated by it.'[46] However, just as Bataille suggests, the event is fleeting. Keenan describes the decline of the moment: 'I cannot hold the ecstasy of the moment and its passionate intensity. It seems to drift slowly from me as the place in which I am being held comes back to remind me of where I am and my condition.'[47] Here is evident a form of perceptual relatedness to the sensory world that is akin to an infant's style of perception and cognition.

That Keenan's experience was beyond language and, yet, that its starting point was in the body in which he cradled himself is clear. By trying to explain to a guard his rationale for not eating the fruit he realized the inadequacy of words to describe, as he put it, 'what is only understood in my senses and not in my mind.'[48] The bond that he described is one of perceptual relatedness, with its grounding in the bodily senses, themselves channels of physicality and awareness. Thus, in accord with Bataille's idea of the sacrifice of the body as the means of achieving inner religious experience, Keenan appears to have generated magically a dissolution through self-loss that involved life-threatening vulnerability and a loss of 'bodily substance,' all this being followed by moments of extreme lucidity.

Periods of intensity with feelings of closeness to God were to return unexpectedly over the next four-and-a-half years of Keenan's captivity, especially during the time he spent with fellow hostage, John McCarthy. Keenan sensitively describes his relationship with McCarthy and the bond of love that grew between them and which, at times, was expressed in anger and confrontation. Their common experience allowed them to talk openly not only about each others' fears and weaknesses, but also about the personal world of things religious: 'In its own way our isolation had expanded the heart, not to reach out to a detached God but to find and become part of whatever 'God' might be.'[49] Companionship was a result of Keenan's magical activities, and it affected his outlook profoundly, now as a shared moral and communal force.

Keenan said that the physical presence of another was comforting: 'my whole body seemed relaxed, and the anxiety and tension melted away.'[50] What was to make the bond between McCarthy and Keenan particularly strong was their being forced to witness each other *in extremis* and completely devoid of privacy. In having openly to defecate in front of one another, especially during agonizing bouts of acute diarrhoea, for example, cultural taboos surrounding intimate zones of the body were necessarily broken down. Being in a body entailed living an 'animal' reality, and frequently living it intimately with another person in a 'caged' situation, just like animals in a zoo. (Keenan's reports of their obsessive routines together, including endless chess-like games, remind one of the magical 'pacings' of caged wild animals.)

The ultimate transgression of bodily limits, as well as the limits of language (and therefore culture), figured in the physical torture Keenan endured. Understandably, he does not provide the reader with extensive accounts of the painful events themselves, these being virtually ineffable. In his beatings though, he notes that the mind 'fused with something previously unknown.'[51] According to philosopher Elaine Scarry, the effect of such pain is not without description: 'Physical pain ... obliterates all psychological content, painful, pleasurable, and neutral. ... Our recognition of its power to end madness is one of the ways ... we acknowledge its power to end all aspects of self and world.'[52] This remains the nearest one can get to the bodily experience of torture. In the way objects of the everyday are used in the act, the world becomes magically 'unmade,' its normal order and meaning overturned. As Bataille notes, the boundary between extreme pain and pleasure is diffuse, in both 'one is occupied by an alien force and in both a strange event explodes over the established order of things.'[53] The magical 'illusion' of the ordinary world is thereby posed. One enters into new time, 'primordial time,' when the generations fuse, in which individual awareness merges with the past and future, with remembered ancestors and anticipated progeny presenting themselves as powerful images that extend who one thinks he or she is. For this reason the 'force' which takes over the body, and the proximity of death in the experience of torture, may engender an a posteriori sense of 'Otherness,' or 'Thou,' for the captive subject in pain. This is a borderline psychotic condition, or a critically involuted form of acute narcissism – the psychological basis of magical practice. Constructive personal, and sometimes positive political effects, may result.

That Keenan reached these boundaries is attested to by the 'short sequence' which is itself the story contained in *An Evil Cradling*.[54] He makes its conclusion simply with a chapter entitled, 'Back to the Beginning' in which he describes the rapid and unexpected manner of his release. Told to shower, he was shaved, dressed, blindfolded, and driven to an intersection where he was dropped on the street. Keenan is not involved in a simple reversion to his former life. The very act of writing *An Evil Cradling* is itself testimony to how transformed he had become. Writing his autobiography was the bodily expression of a self seeking health through a personal disclosure of how he stood outside of himself, witnessed his 'mortal body' on the brink of dissolution, and then went on to wrest meaning and purpose for living from that now physically embodied vantage point. He was a witness to the divine drama of transgressing the limits of bodily existence, a witness to the specter that would force upon awareness the tricks of magic behind the 'illusion' of ordinary living. Keenan's text itself is both a treatise on and an exercise of magic as a springboard to the lived experience of a religious life, an incipient hagiography with compelling moral impact.

Thus, we see the body *as* self in Keenan's religious autobiography. That the document shows an awareness of the 'warp and woof' of mortality and sexuality on the 'loom' of natality, appears self-evident, and that the reader gains much from Keenan's report of his body at the limit is beyond question. It is an experience which truly only Keenan endured but we would agree that it is one, as he himself concludes, 'in which so much more of what we are as human beings was revealed.'[55] That this revelation itself is a treasuring, a valuing which can be communally shared, is established by means of embracing the body not only as a biological fact, but also as an existential presence.[56]

Finally, it can be said that the human body can be seen to extend narcissistically (in an idiom of heightened self-esteem) beyond the notion of cultural construction, or beyond the realm of the 'illusions' of ordinary magic. The body is also the locus of spiritual formation, or 'mystical selfhood' that possesses moral power to subvert even the politics of extremism and the violent captivity which extremism may exact. We have seen throughout how a psychology of magical practice based on acute narcissism brought about by 'captivity' can unlock the religious meaning of lives. Such a psychology invites those of us who think we are 'free' to rethink the matter, and perhaps to see just how illusory such freedom may be. This, I believe, is the calling to which Keenan and other fellow-hostages so compellingly testify. Magic is practiced not by default, but because we would aspire to be gods in flesh and blood.

10 A foretaste of the world to come

Not until the twentieth century have people enjoyed a significant increase in human longevity. Medical science has made considerable leaps that have surpassed efforts of the past to bring about a long, healthy life for a majority of people, especially in Western societies. Knowledge of antiseptics, immunology, advanced surgical techniques, a vast range of drugs, and other factors have made possible such modern leaps into longevity.[1] In addition, many people are taking seriously priorities for health promotion such as smoking cessation, physical exercise, nutrition and weight control, stress management, and the appropriate use of alcohol and other drugs.[2] To be 'health-conscious' is a value most people would espouse these days. A glass of red wine, perhaps a foretaste of the future, is said to be good for lowering the blood fat levels and for the overall management of average blood pressure ranges.

Curiously, however, accompanying all this has been a pervasive amnesia about human mortality, a social psychology of forgetting. A repression of our intellectual past, in which dying and the death of the body counted as part of the fullness of life, has occurred.[3] When human longevity was on average much shorter than it is for most today, death was ever palpable, the object of a vital awareness. Dying was constantly forced upon the senses; it was evident daily – the dead were seen, touched, smelled, and so forth.[4] Dying bodies grew heavy, and also heavy on the mind. However, with the advent of increased longevity, dying and death have been gradually removed from living. They no longer concentrate the mind as much as they once did. This is accompanied by apathy and an attenuation of community morality, against which the contemporary 'death awareness movement' has usually fought.[5] Mostly 'out of sight,' the human face of dying appears largely 'out of mind,' perhaps so much so that even our grandparents' generation would view us sadly as being woefully naive about life. And so I suggest we are. Generally, human mortality now is less palpably evident as a sensuous bodily feeling than it once was. In effect, the body has become 'disembodied.' Not only is this astonishing in itself, but it also implies that we have forgotten war in our century, and the 'life and death' struggle that it has forced upon many of us, even as recently as during the Vietnam War. Biographical constructions of individuals as 'texts' and our own autobiographical reflections on how best to live are perilous endeavors if they do not take into account the *extension of bodies beyond life*, or bodies, as Brian Keenan implied, that are 'deified' precisely because they have gone beyond 'convulsion.'

Thus, it is habitual to think of the body in Western thought as 'in flight,' or as an idea alone, an abstract concept usually considered only in isolation from other things: the reactionary 'body on the slab' view I am always surprised by how biographers and autobiographers feel bound automatically to organize their writings and readings of lives according to the 'birth and death' of their subjects, as if no other presentation is possible. Unfortunately, the chronicle style of biography (and autobiography) continues to dominate the life-writing/reading scene. However, the body and how to narrate its story ought to be thought about differently. Narrations of lives that would claim to be 'spiritual operations,' in which the *simulated life* is the key, should take seriously the body of the person studied in terms of the wider context of bodily existence, or what can be called 'embodied living.'[6] When we think of the body we should assume not that it is discarnate, or an abstraction that is separated from a person's living awareness of bodily existence. Instead, the body should be considered to be incarnate, where it is taken to be synonymous with our awareness of embodied living as a flesh-and-blood activity involving being born, growing up, being sexual, aging, dying, and even putrefying. The body is flesh potent with 'resurrection.'[7]

It is this incarnational view of the body that needs to be restated anew in contemporary times. After all, bodies may be portrayed as existing not only between birth and death, but also as links in an unbroken chain of generations. Generations stretch from the distant, largely unknown past into an uncertain future, which itself invites writing and reading lives that are larger than any one life itself. In this sense, all of us can be said to outlive ourselves. Eastern Orthodox Christianity has pressed this idea, namely, that the 'spirit' is non-existent except insofar as it is 'enfleshed,' and carried over through the generations. Enfleshment is usually called *theosis*, deification, or 'oneself becoming God,' which eventuates from a soteriological partnership between a person and God.[8] A restatement of an incarnational view of the body depends on highlighting a prevailing understanding of the body in Christian mythology. By a prevailing understanding of the body, I do not mean the popular theological understanding of a conjoined 'body and soul' package, which itself has suggested for many Christians that the soul is capable of leaving the body at death and going to reside eternally in heaven or hell, with the body 'on hold,' awaiting the end of history, or Christ's return to earth and his 'resurrection' of the faithful.[9]

Although you may not at first believe it, the 'body and soul' idea is not a dominant expression of the historical understanding of the body in Western culture. The 'body and soul' idea is only that view of the medieval Catholic theologian, Thomas Aquinas, who appropriated Greek philosophical ideas from Plato and Aristotle and applied them to Christianity. He was a rationalist theological thinker, and not particularly given to entering into the imaginative reverie of Christian mythology. Aquinas was not really responsive to the deeper theological currents that remain intrinsic to the Christian tradition, and which stemmed especially from its creation myth in which stories of the creation of human bodies are told. Aquinas's view, although intellectually interesting for some, has been shown to have been a minority theological position about the body in Western thought.[10] As sociologist Anthony Giddens suggests,

> The existential question of self-identity is bound up with the fragile nature of the biography which the individual 'supplies' about herself. A person's identity is not to be found in behaviour, nor – important thought it is – in the reactions of others, but in the capacity *to keep a particular narrative going*. The individual's biography, if she is to maintain regular interaction with others in the day-to-day world, cannot be wholly fictive. It must continually integrate events which occur in the external world, and sort them into the ongoing 'story' about the self.[11]

The 'particular narrative' to keep going here is not that of the 'body and soul' package. Rather, it is one based on the mythological foundations that give rise to an understanding of human nature in Western civilization. I refer to the myth of creation as it is written in the Old Testament Book of Genesis, and to the narratives about Adam and Eve and the Garden of Eden. With this particular focus, a narrative of the body may lend weight and proper perspective to biographical constructions of individuals as 'texts,' and also to our autobiographical reflections on how, in comparison with others, we might best live out the remainder of our days.

The prevailing majority theological position on the question of the body has been curiously suppressed since the late medieval period. This suppression, perhaps, may have resulted from but clearly coincides with the attenuation of the influence of the patristic theology of Eastern Orthodoxy on Western European Christianity, and with the rise of Protestantism in the sixteenth century, which virtually turned its back on the thought of the early church fathers. At any rate, the majority view of the body in Western culture involves two issues.[12] On the one hand, involved is a mixture of the possible, perhaps improbable, biological process and certain cultural/symbolic constructions of 'death and resurrection.' On the other hand, Christian mythology also involves faith in bodily continuity after death, this being a basis for creating a secure selfhood for the individual in the present. These aspects of our understanding of Christian mythology, as drawing our attention to embodied living, beginning and ending in the mythological relationship between Adam and Christ amidst the drama of the creation of the world, including the world to come, clearly appear first in the medieval period in Europe where the body, according to Piero Camporesi, was treated not as a 'body and soul' package but, rather, primarily as a 'great distillery.'[13]

The idea was (and remains) that the human body produced a range of valuable fluids, exudations, essences, and excreta that served as medicinal substances as well as magical and practical ones: saliva, urine, sperm, feces, milk, blood. Moreover, the body was an instrument particularly well suited to absorb the powers of the sensuous world. Thus, 'the nose was the channel through which the mysterious and divine sneeze was transmitted: a sensitive and refined conduit up which aromatic messages made their way, ascending finally to the brain, the presumed seat of human reason.'[14] One would be advised to absorb only beneficial powers conducive to good health, and to avoid situations and practices that led to the absorption of debilitating forces. These understandings are at the basis of many liturgical, magical, and hygienic practices. Such realizations flow from an awareness of embodied living. Who among us has never entertained the embodied thought that sandalwood incense is, somehow, 'good' for us?! Or that a whiff of salt air at the beach can 'cure' what ails us?! Besides, sneezing gets rid of potentially harmful agents that get stuck to the mucus membranes inside the nasal cavity. And is it not true that most of us like to 'nose around' in other people's business?

Viewing the body as a process of distillation is inherently spiritual ('implicit religion'), and such a process signals bodily continuity, or 'resurrection,' after death. The 'great distillery' of the human body links death as the spontaneous fermentation of organic matter with the idea of birth *ex putri*. Distillation is inherent in all of creation. Camporesi notes how images of paradise are filled with exotic fluids: streams, perfumes, unguents, balms, saps, resins, and potable springs. (A contemporary nostalgia for a rain-forested world and all things 'natural' are instances of such a psychology of paradise that is linked to the body. This also has an affinity with the mirror-like pond into which Narcissus stared entranced for the remainder of his days.) The fluids bring forth the lush life of barely imaginable herbs and fruits dripping with vitality. Thus, the sweet smells of the Garden of Eden stand in stark contrast to the deathly stench of the rotting cadaver and its moldering juices, or 'Life, a rotting filth; and death, the embodiment of decay.'[15] Insofar as human mortals remain in contact with the revitalizing fluids of paradise, their flesh became 'incorruptible,' a sign of divine immortality for medieval theologians. According to Camporesi,

It was said that from the dead bodies of God's virgins and the buried flesh of his saints there gushed forth a healing sap, a wondrous balm. A 'most gentle odour,' a 'marvelous odour' were unmistakable signs of the thaumaturgical presence of a saintly corpse, the aromatic liberator from 'all manner of sickness.'[16]

How was such a view of the body discerned by contemporary researchers of the past? By sifting through the minutiae found in cookbooks, court records, incantatory formulae, exorcism, and the practices of alchemy, pharmacy, surgery, and medicine, vivid detail about some shocking practices and viewpoints associated with the body in medieval Europe were found.[17] Camporesi, for one, used studies of the medieval carnival as a guide. The associated array of bodily images, smells, sounds, tastes, postures, and ministrations he discovered is nearly overwhelming — all things sensuous, body-based. The goal of decoding the incorruptibility of the moist, fragrant flesh of saints is also pursued. We discover to what extent science, asceticism, torture, emotional life, and social relations were governed by a religious understanding that harked back to the creation myth of Jews, Christians (and Muslims), and to mortality in the violent expulsion of human beings, Adam and Eve, from the redolent Garden of Eden. Trees, fruit, and foods figure in the myth of the Fall and in the economy of salvation (*theosis*) from the Fall, which constitutes subsequent history.

Central, of course, is the fact that the primal garden of delights contained the Tree of Life. The *arbor vitae* exfoliated from the center of paradise and connected all life in the world. If human frailty had separated human flesh from the organically connected channels of flowing juices that stream from creation into all of history (that is, when Eve gave the 'apple' to Adam, and he ate it), then the coming of Christ regrafted human life onto the Tree of Life. From Christ's crucified side, speared on the cross, gushed the newly flowing waters of life. Falling to the ground, these precious, immortal fluids caused paradisical plants to sprout. Those herbs had medicinal and magical properties that restored vital fluid, health, and life, like good sex. Thus, the wooden cross of Christ reconnected human mortality to the sap flowing through the Edenic Tree of Life. Christ himself served as the vessel of newly flowing fluids of divine life and became the model for all other forms of revitalization stemming from the life in the garden of paradise. Writes Camporesi,

The Garden of Eden was above all an orchard of health, a mild place sheltered from illness and decay, a general clinic in the open air, an aromatic apothecary's shop oozing with dew, elixirs, balms, oils, gums, dripping with miraculous resins, rarefied honeys, where the air exudes aromas of delicate unguents, precious woods exhale vegetable inebriants which prepare the body for beatitude, soft fattiness, and the total amnesia of the ecstatic condition ... a place immune to putrefaction, where neither human beings nor the fruits of the earth suffer degeneration. ... Both body and fruit are as though 'fixed' in eternity, time stands still for ever. Dewy, honeyed and redolent with aromatic balms, the saint was equipped to survive, mummy-like, in a timeless world.[18]

Christ's body had distilled the precious waters of salvation, in which all could be reimmersed through baptism, the eating of his incorruptible flesh, and the drinking of his blood.

The soteriological promise of bodily incorruptibility, or resurrection and eternal life, not only stems from theological ramifications of the sensuous, bodily basis of the story of the Garden of Eden in Western culture. Also, the worst and repugnant aspects of the body were spiritually glorified. The Garden of Eden, this mythical *hortus deliciarum*, writes Camporesi, 'was a place immune from putrefaction, where neither human beings nor the fruits of the earth suffered degeneration. It was rather like a warm refrigerator or an enchanted embalming laboratory, where matter that would normally perish, survived intact from year to year.'[19] Such an astonishing promise, namely, that the corruptible processes intrinsic to dying and putrefying flesh can be halted, even reversed and made incorruptible, is supported by a prevalent medieval anthropology. This anthropology held that the human being was a worm, spontaneously arising out of the putrefying chaos that forms the universe. The presence of such worms gave new life to the fermenting cosmos, much as they do to the compost heap in my backyard.

Moreover, *fermentation* always precedes *distillation*. Distillation has a spiritual analogue: it may become an internalized process of realization that is enfleshed by the aging, sick, dying, and putrefying body, which is (literally) a 'foretaste,' so to speak, of the *life of the world to come*. The Dominican Friar Tommaso Campanella, for example, held such a view. He drew attention to the lice and worms that infested the human body and digestive tract because, as Camporesi puts it, 'the world was seen in terms of an entomic, or insect-related, ratio: the worm is to man's belly, as man the worm is to the belly of the world.'[20] For the good Friar Campanella, mankind, 'like the worm in our stomachs,' lives inside the belly of the world and stands in relation 'to the earth as lice do to our heads; and we do not know that the world has a soul and love, as worms and lice do not know by reason of their smallness of our soul and intelligence.'[21] The exuded juice of worms was synonymous with the creation of the world, or the vitalization of the dead who can be said to bring about the 'life of the world to come,' as the Christian Nicene Creed puts it.

This matter of life-giving worms which ferment putrefying flesh does not merely end with an anthropology, but also carries over into Christian theology and soteriology. Out of the wormy juice of fermentation arises bodily activity, or 'di[s]-stilled' embodied living. As worms crawl in and out of corpses on slime trails they point the way toward the eternal life of the body. According to Friar Campanella, 'God is a worm because he is not born of copulation, man, too, is a worm because worms are born, again, not from copulation, but from the putrefaction and decomposition of his flesh.'[22] Thus, meat was put on the bones of the passage from 1 Corinthians 15: 22: 'For as in Adam all die, so also in Christ shall all be made alive.' A paraphrase of this would be something like, 'I am a worm, the son of man, and not a man: which is to say, I am Christ who breathes life into all; not Adam in whom all dies' (for example, see Psalm 22: 6, 'But I am a worm, and no man; scorned by men, and despised by the people'). Worms provide the living link between Adam and Christ, between the dead and those arising again. The image of bringing life out of death was taken from Psalm 6 and developed by other Christian writers in different ways, even by Augustine. In a contemporary vein, where youthful looks and physical fitness are highly sought-after qualities, the medieval view is most congruent, even instructive: 'The most striking feature of medieval fantasies about paradise,' writes Camporesi, 'was their desperate fixation with good health, their striving for beatitude (particularly physical), unobtainable on earth.'[23] Perhaps we are more medieval in outlook than we think we are, especially those rigorous high-achievers for whom low-fat eating and regular aerobic exercise have (unwittingly) replaced the rigors of archaic religious practice, and where the de-wormers are readily available in the pharmacopia at the chemist's shop.

Thus, finally, we can briefly note that it was Augustine who himself, we recall, perhaps represents the minority theological position about the body in Western culture. His autobiography, *Confessions*, is a testimony to his repugnance toward his own bodily nature (especially his sexuality), and his flight from embodiment in lives, including his own, of the *god of destruction*, which we encountered for the first time several chapters ago. Augustine hardly held that the body was a 'great distillery' created in the beginning of all time and modeled on the sensuous mythological imagery of the Garden of Eden. Augustine would be the last person to revere saints' bodies, after death, as a source of life, health, and curative power. Instead he turned away from such an embodied mythology and drew from the abstract philosophical discussions of Plato and Aristotle, who held that human beings were composed, instead, of two parts, namely, a corruptible 'body,' which was of little consequence, and an incorruptible 'soul,' which could last for eternity. Thus, the groundwork was laid in the history of Christianity for a theological assault on the body ever afterward by a minority of powerful churchmen who followed the Augustinian line, an assault that, as we may now realize, is actually at odds with the symbolic infrastructure (that is, the mythic reverie that gives rise to theological thought) of a Christian (Jewish and, perhaps, Muslim) mythology of the body in Western culture.[24] Such deeper (perhaps unconscious) and compelling reverie about the body as a 'great distillery,' refining the human spirit, has for centuries, even up to the present, fired the imagination of the public, or those people who continue to appreciate embodied living more than a disembodied rejection of a life of the flesh. Is it not the case that from flesh and blood life arises, and resurrection is at hand?

Conclusion

This book has shown how reading and writing lives involve both a scholar's interest and a preoccupation of people who seek fuller lives, lives to be lived with greater social bearing and personal moral integrity. The final result is intelligent self-reliance. This is not a matter of skills or technical mastery of everyday life by the individual, but of confident humility. Such an attitude, or bearing in the world, is engendered by viewing living as an experience of a dying body. Valuing others insofar as such a view is shaped is a social outcropping of this inner state of awareness. The literary genre of life-writing, in particular biography and autobiography (self-biography), is a point of entry into reading and writing lives for achieving both intellectual understanding and religious insight. These achievements result from what throughout the book is referred to as the 'spiritual quest.'

Noted first in the book was how the study of life-writing and reading lives contribute bridges from biography and autobiography to scholarly work in religion and the human sciences. From the outset, the reader was encouraged to be open to personal change, at least to the possibility of reframing outlooks. Life-writing and reading lives were considered to be at their best when what was called soteriological biography prevailed. This type of life-writing, along with its specific agenda for reading lives, aims to articulate a subject's inner 'excellence' (*arete*) which, itself, reflects the way a person responds to the 'human,' especially to the biological conditions of existence that bind readers and writers of lives to their subjects in a shared physical ('embodied') and ethological ('species-specific') condition. This binding together of individuals during the process of life-writing and reading lives was said to result from 'empathic introspection,' which much of the book has explored.

Moreover, we noted two genre-specific requisites of biography, itself the dominant form of life-writing and reading lives (but not forgetting autobiography). These two structural characteristics of the genre of biography were churned up by the history of biography in the West, and they are also evident in modern psychological and psychobiographical concerns. The two requisites are a search for the 'coherent character' and a sense of the 'fateful irony' of a life. On the one hand, James Stanfield, Gamaliel Bradford, and Henry Murray and, on the other hand, James Boswell, Sigmund Freud, and Lytton Strachey represent, among others who have worked the field of biography, a dialectic of endeavor in which each party is faithful to their respective requisite. Within this same endeavor, and acceding to the structure of the genre of biography, readers and writers of lives construct narrative configurations of their subjects. This has been called the biographical construction of individuals as 'texts.' The process of reading and writing lives is played by such rules, which the tradition of professional literary biography in particular sets out like a board game.

Such construction is guided by paying attention to empathy and introspection. Questions about the nature of the relationship between readers and writers of lives and their subjects come quickly to the foreground. Must the investigator be only objective, or is subjective involvement an idiom of understanding another person? Who exactly the investigator is, and who exactly the individual who is investigated is, are questions that require introspection on the part of the reader and writer of lives, as well as historical narration about a subject's 'life and times.' Once differences are noted between oneself and a biographical subject, an empathic grasp of an individual invites an investigator to seek ways in which similarities to his or her own life might appear and be appreciated. This may occur, if only initially, by the simple recognition that as human beings both readers and writers of lives and their subjects share bodies of flesh and blood, cultural differences notwithstanding. Empathy, on the backdrop of introspective skill, travels along tracks of perceptual and emotional relatedness to others. As Erik Erikson, Ernest Schachtel, and others have shown, the fundamental physicality of perception and emotion connects a subject who is read or written about bodily to the investigator, at least at the investigator's behest: '*That shape am I,*' as we noted William James once put it, to his own astonishment. This particular process has been called autobiographical reflection on how best to live, compared with the lives studied. Drawing a life together into a narrative configuration is the point of embarkation from which the reader/writer of lives begins to grow aware of being on a fundamental formative path. Throughout the book this path has been called a *trajectory of personal realization,* or 'spiritual quest.'

The religious nature of such an inner experience of realization, or a transforming consciousness amidst the phenomenal world of the senses, propels the reader and writer of lives into an orbit fraught with the potential of existential dread. The body itself becomes the focal point of reflection, the body that is born and dies helplessly, and in between is sexual but only with help from others. The reader and writer of lives must face natality, sexuality, and mortality time and again in the lives of the individuals who are scrutinized, who, one could hope, have themselves given deliberate thought to such matters and might thereby be taken to be oracles of sage advice. Wisdom might first interrogate how individuality is understood: how is it possible to shape an outlook in which one is thought of as an individual not in isolation but, instead, conceived within a succession of people linked together in a process of generational turnover, itself an ethological cycle and a major dimension of our animality or sense of being part of an animal species? The challenge is not to be taken lightly, as it requires embracing our physical nature as a force that flies in the face of human will. For those who hold firmly to the Cartesian maxim, *cogito, ergo sum,* 'I think, therefore I am,' recognizing the daunting power of human physicality is indeed difficult to swallow.

The force of an ever-mortal body binds us in obedience to the law of dying and death, as those who venerate 'mortal remains' contained in reliquaries understand and, of course, William James himself and others like Robert Murphy and John Updike, we read, well realized. Yet, women and men complement each other's bodies, with female bodies and male bodies going together and making 'whole' the bifurcated body of humankind as it evolves, or as Erikson put it, 'speciates' through time and space. Readers and writers of lives remain open for instruction from their subjects about sexuality, and how to 'pass up' much of the moment for the sake of 'passing on' a future to the next generation, a bodily future, and a foretaste of ever-renewed physicality imbued with personal realization and supported by a nurturing (even sensual) culture. Perhaps worms, after all, portend the nature of life in the world to come. Life exacts a surrender of individuality as such, and realizing this is the moral imperative that undergirds authentic self-reliance.

An illustration helps to summarize what is at stake. There is a story of an only child who, like us all, though closer to the end than most, is dying. The child is put to bed one night and is given the usual comfort and assurance that most children and parents expect of each other as a matter of course. In so many words, the indication is that all is well for now and that tomorrow will come. However, the child senses within his own rudimentary internal grasp of things, an introspection of a sort, that these night-time ministrations, themselves so well intended by caring parents, go only so far. Intuition tells the child that all is not quite as usual, but exactly how this is so is unclear; perhaps the child is further along the path of realization than his parents could know. The child's heart may even go out to those parents amidst their anguish and grief-filled anticipation of such a great loss. In not too long a time the house that was a home will be only a house. The door to the bedroom is about to be closed, as worried parents slowly make their exit. 'Mummy?' says the child softly, 'Leave the door open.' Of course, mother does so, but then asks, 'Why do you want me to leave the door open — in order to let in the light?' The child pauses and then answers, perhaps with a wisdom born of recent albeit inchoate personal realization, 'No, Mummy. I want the door open to let out the darkness.' Well, such darkness may never leave a life, in fact it inhabits each of us. However, from within such a changed kind of reality that had possessed that child, in which self-reliance is played out differently from how others claim to master their lives daily, a statement of integrity that stops the flow of time and commands the moment had been made. One is startled and stopped in one's tracks by it.

Søren Kierkegaard may have sensed, as he put it, that 'in the proper sense of the word I had not lived,' and, as we know, he entertained thoughts of suicide as a result of his awareness. However, others have pressed this Kierkegaardian edge even further along their own trajectories of personal realization, beyond discarnate reflection and through bodies under great stress and physical threat. William James, we noted, suffered from chronic frailty and sickness of one sort or another throughout his life, and he came close to insanity several times. Brian Keenan, we saw, underwent torture and not merely bouts of existential anxiety but many mixed messages, violent caprice, and threats of death from his captors. For these two individuals, life-writers and readers of lives both, the body itself made real and actual the task of realizing personally that life exacts from us our individuality as such. This is not to say that we become less self-reliant as individuals. Rather, we learn to respond to necessity, or to living in a mortal body over which control is but a moderately comforting illusion. Violence that is not allowed to volatize into philosophical thought alone but which is brought to bear on the body can be paradoxically 're-creational' in the best sense, even as Georges Bataille and the much-maligned Marquis de Sade before him suggest.

A spiritual quest is not a flight from the world of violence, birth, sex, and death (or from what James called the 'predatory design of nature'), but an outcome of facing up to horror and to those exquisite configurations of pleasure and pain by which we habitually draft and sign contracts with reality. Reckoning with the natal, sexual, and mortal body, at least to a degree greater than was possible 'just a moment ago,' impels one to live from the 'inside out' of a new awareness about a non-reactive self-reliance that attends such experience. The body is willingly presented as a sacrifice that is made on the path toward a higher realization than we underwent 'just a moment ago,' or toward insight into exactly who one now is. Reading and writing lives while pressing the edge of personal realization with this in mind becomes a compelling soteriological exercise, or a process of 'spiritual formation' guided by the moral imperative of bodily and physical sacrifice.

What is achieved in the end if such an overall strategy for reading and writing lives from the point of view of a trajectory of personal realization is adopted? Perhaps nothing, but the promise of doing so elicits a new awareness of a moral strength that accompanies sacrificing our bodies to what toward the end of the book was called the *god of destruction*, an imperative to act in living with dying in mind. Only by means of avoiding being dissuaded from this primordial ritualization of human experience, however horrible or however ecstatic it may be from time to time, is 'more life,' as a readiness for qualitative self-reliant experiencing, indeed possible. The form taken by this surfeit of life is twofold. There is, first, a revalorized outlook that is based on confident humility; and, second, an increased capacity to value others in the immediacy of the present, all this as one lives inhaling the breath of death and exhaling the breath of life — or is it the other way around? It hardly matters. Most people will agree that they are, so to say, 'dying to live' better and richer lives, but few, I believe, would readily see the wisdom in 'living to die,' which, paradoxically, and as this book has suggested, is the same thing for those with enough insight, personal realization, and gumption to stand their ground on the matter and silently witness those not yet so far along the path, hopefully, also gradually coming to their senses.

Notes

Preface

1. Paul Murray Kendall, *The Art of Biography* (New York: W.W. Norton, 1985).
2. *Ibid.*, pp. 147–8.

1 Biography and religious life

1. As quoted in Walter Lowrie, *A Short Life of Kierkegaard* (Princeton: Princeton University Press, 1946), p. 107.
2. *Ibid.*
3. The evolution of individuality in the West is documented in fine detail by Karl Weintraub, *The Value of the Individual* (Chicago: University of Chicago Press, 1978); and briefly in 'Autobiography and historical consciousness,' *Critical Inquiry*, **1** (4) (June 1975): 821–48.
4. See especially, Frank Reynolds and Donald Capps (eds), *The Biographical Process: Studies in the History and Psychology of Religion* (The Hague: Mouton, 1976). Also representative is Michael A. Williams (ed.), *Charisma and Sacred Biography* (Journal of the American Academy of Religion Thematic Studies), **48** (3 and 4) (Atlanta: Scholars Press, 1982).
5. See Paul Murray Kendall, *The Art of Biography* (New York: W.W. Norton, 1985).
6. On the popularity of biography in contemporary society, see Richard A. Hutch, 'Reading lives to live: mortality, introspection, and the soteriological impulse,' *Biography: An Interdisciplinary Quarterly*, **17** (2) (1994): 125–43; 1.
7. A definitive text on reader-response criticism in literary theory is Stanley Fish, *Is There a Text in This Class? The Authority of Interpretive Communities* (Cambridge, MA: Harvard University Press, 1980). Within religious studies scholarship, such criticism has appeared in biblical studies in which a leading theoretical statement is Edgar V. McKnight, *The Bible and the Reader: An Introduction to Literary Criticism* (Philadelphia: Fortress Press, 1985).

8. For examples of this, see Richard A. Hutch, 'Writing lives in psychoanalytic silence,' *Religious Studies Review*, **22** (2) (April 1996): 114–18.

9. Richard Holmes, *Footsteps: Adventures of a Romantic Biographer* (London: Hodder & Stoughton, 1985), p. 27.

10. *Ibid.*

11. *Ibid.*

12. *Ibid.*

13. *Ibid.*

14. *Ibid.*

15. See relevant section on method in James Boswell, *Life of Johnson*, ed. George Birkbeck Hill and revised L.F. Powell (Oxford: The Clarendon Press, 1934–50), vol. I, pp. 29–33; 30.

16. *Ibid.*

17. *Ibid.*

18. See Paul Murray Kendall, *The Art of Biography*.

19. *Ibid.*

20. James Stanfield, *An Essay on the Study and Composition of Biography* (Sunderland: George Garbutt, 1813). The quotation from Stanfield's book is in Richard D. Altick, *Lives and Letters: A History of Literary Biography in England and America* (New York: Alfred A. Knopf, 1965), p. 81.

21. Quoted in Altick, p. 383.

22. Leon Edel, *Writing Lives: Principia Biographica* (New York: W.W. Norton, 1984), p. 45. Typological ranges of biographical texts that demonstrate the 'bridging' nature of biography are described in James Clifford, *From Puzzles to Portraits* (Chapel Hill: University of North Carolina Press, 1970), Leon Edel, *Literary Biography* (London: Rupert Hart-Davis, 1957), Paul Murray Kendall, *The Art of Biography* (New York: W.W. Norton, 1985), and Stephen B. Oates (ed.), *Biography as High Adventure: Life-Writers Speak on Their Art* (Amherst: University of Massachusetts Press, 1986).

23. A neglected and hardly dated introduction to the study of religion that is based on life-writing, and autobiography in particular, is Michael Novak, *Ascent of the Mountain, Flight of the Dove: An Invitation to Religious Studies* (New York: Harper & Row, 1971).

24. The use of the label 'psychohistorian' by scholars in the humanities in general was inspired during the late 1960s and early 1970s by the work of the psychoanalytic and social thinker Erik Erikson. See Erik H. Erikson, *Young Man Luther: A Study in Psychoanalysis and History* (New York: W.W. Norton, 1958) and *Gandhi's Truth: On the Origins of Militant Nonviolence* (New York: W.W. Norton, 1969). The first compilation of work that intended to launch a discipline of

psychohistory in the humanities was Bruce Mazlish (ed.), *Psychoanalysis and History* (New York: The Universal Library, Grosset & Dunlap, 1963; revised 1971). See also William Runyan, *Life Histories and Psychobiography: Explorations in Theory and Method* (New York: Oxford University Press, 1982).

25. For example, see Reynolds and Capps (eds), *The Biographical Process*.

26. For example, Richard A. Hutch, *Religious Leadership: Personality, History and Sacred Authority*, Vol. 10, Toronto Studies in Religion Series (New York: Peter Lang Publishing, Inc., 1991).

27. On the former track, see E.R. Dodds, *Pagan and Christian in an Age of Anxiety* (New York: W.W. Norton, 1965), and Zevedei Barbu, *Problems of Historical Psychology* (New York: Grove Press, 1960); on the latter emphasis, see Donald Capps and Walter Capps (eds), *The Religious Personality* (Belmont, CA: Wadsworth Publishing Company, Inc., 1970).

28. Richard A. Hutch, 'A psychology of religious devotion: Thomas à Kempis at prayer,' *Journal of Psychology and Christianity*, **4** (1985): 82–93; 'Elizabeth Kübler-Ross as a religious leader,' *Omega: Journal of Death and Dying*, **16** (1985): 89–109 (co-authored with Dennis Klass); 'Helena Blavatsky unveiled,' *Journal of Religious History*, **11** (1980): 320–41; 'Jonathan Edwards' analysis of religious experience,' *Journal of Psychology and Theology*, **6** (1978): 123–31; 'Here today, gone tomorrow: Jemima Wilkinson as a religious leader,' in E.W. Conrad and T.G. Newing (eds), *Perspectives on Language and Texts: Essays in Honor of Francis I. Andersen's Sixtieth Birthday July 28, 1985* (Winona Lake, IN: Eisenbrauns, 1986), pp. 314–23; 'Emerson and incest,' *The Psychoanalytic Review*, **62** (1975): 320–32.

29. Nietzsche's hostility toward his sister and the lifelong torment that anger caused him are vividly portrayed in Ronald Hayman, *Nietzsche: A Critical Life* (Harmondsworth: Penguin, 1982).

30. See Erikson, *Young Man Luther* and *Gandhi's Truth*. See also Jacques Barzun, *Clio and the Doctors: Psycho-History, Quanto-History & History* (Chicago and London: University of Chicago Press, 1974) for a definitive critique of Erikson's and others' similar academic endeavors.

31. Hutch, 'Helena Blavatsky unveiled.'

32. On the idea of *homo religiosus*, or the essential religious (implicit) nature of the individual, as a working concept in the history and phenomenology of religion, see Mircea Eliade, *The Sacred and The Profane: The Nature of Religion*, trans. William R. Trask (New York: Harcourt, Brace & World, Inc., 1959), especially pp. 162–213 ('Human existence and sanctified life').

33. Harold Lasswell, *Power and Personality* (New York: W.W. Norton, 1948).

34. Interesting are developments in the psychology of religion, a field of

study akin to biographical and autobiographical studies. Prior to the 1980s, motivation to practice religion was thought to be either 'extrinsic' (socially useful) or 'intrinsic' (personally meaningful). See this discussion that was initiated by the work of Gordon Allport, *The Individual and His Religion* (New York: Macmillan, 1950), and Gordon Allport and J.M. Ross, 'Personal religious orientation and prejudice,' *Journal of Personality and Social Psychology*, **5** (1967): 432–43. Recently, researchers have posited a third motive which they have called 'quest.' It represents a less static appreciation of how explicit religion is managed by the individual, and aims to articulate the ongoing, open-ended dynamism of implicit religion. While this book turns on the difference between explicit and implicit religion, with the latter ('spirituality') being emphasized throughout, the early development of 'intrinsic' motivation falls short. The new 'quest' motivation expresses better what is being called here implicit religion, that is, the 'spiritual quest.' On this important recent discussion in the psychology of religion, see C. Daniel Batson, Patricia Schoenrade, and W. Larry Ventis, *Religion and the Individual: A Social-Psychological Perspective* (New York and Oxford: Oxford University Press, 1993).

35. For details of Buber's life and work, see Maurice Friedman, *Martin Buber's Life and Work: The Early Years, 1878-1923* (London: Search Press, 1982), pp. 3–25.
36. Quoted in Friedman, p. 5.
37. *Ibid.*, p. 7.
38. *Ibid.*, p. 6.
39. See Martin Buber, *I and Thou* (Edinburgh: T. & T. Clark, 1970).
40. William James, *The Varieties of Religious Experience: A Study in Human Nature* (London: Crowell-Collier, 1961), p. 42.
41. See, for example, Richard A. Hutch, 'Mircea Eliade and orthodoxy,' *Phronema*, **2** (1987): 55–67.
42. An example is Hutch, *Religious Leadership: Personality, History and Sacred Authority.*
43. See Richard A. Hutch, 'Biographies of the Buddha,' *Asia Journal of Theology*, **2** (1988): 440–9.
44. Examples of studies along this line are several articles contained in the volume on religious biography edited by Reynolds and Capps (1976): Richard A. Hutch, 'Ralph Waldo Emerson: the birth of a seer'; Victor Turner, 'Religious paradigms and political action: "The Murder in the Cathedral" of Thomas Becket'; William LaFleur, 'The death and "lives" of the poet Monk Saigyo'; and Frank Reynolds, 'The many lives of the Buddha: A study of sacred biography and Theravada tradition.'
45. For example, see Joanne Puzo Waghorne, 'The case of the missing autobiography,' *Journal of the American Academy of Religion*, **44**(4)

(December, 1981): 589–603; and Richard Howard, 'Modern Chinese biographical writing,' *Journal of Asian Studies*, **21** (4) (1962): 465–75.

46. Ernst Kris, *Psychoanalytic Explorations in Art* (New York: International Universities Press, 1952).

47. This task has been set by the historian and phenomenologist of religion, Mircea Eliade, 'New humanism,' in *The Quest: History and Meaning in Religion* (Chicago: University of Chicago Press, 1969), pp. 1–11. It has been augmented by Wilfred Cantwell Smith, *Towards a World Theology* (Philadelphia: Westminster, 1981). The task is creatively carried forward in N. Ross Reat and Edmund Perry, *A World Theology: The Central Spiritual Reality of Humankind* (New York: Cambridge University Press, 1991).

48. Capps and Capps (eds), *The Religious Personality*.

49. Richard A. Hutch, 'Types of women religious leaders,' *Religion*, **14** (1984): 155–73; and *Religious Leadership: Personality, History and Sacred Authority*.

50. See Henry Pommer, *Emerson's First Marriage* (Carbondale, IL: Southern Illinois University Press, 1967); Joel Porte, *Representative Man: Ralph Waldo Emerson in His Time* (New York: Oxford University Press, 1979); Ralph Rusk, *The Life of Ralph Waldo Emerson* (New York: Columbia University Press, 1949); Edward Wagenknecht, *Ralph Waldo Emerson: Portrait of a Balanced Soul* (New York: Oxford University Press, 1974). More 'psychological' biographies that approximate the ideal being suggested are Gay Wilson Allen, *Waldo Emerson: A Biography* (New York: Viking Press, 1981); and Richard A. Hutch, *Emerson's Optics: Biographical Process and the Dawn of Religious Leadership* (Washington, DC: University Press of America, 1983).

51. See, for example, Hutch, *Emerson's Optics*.

52. See Richard A. Hutch, 'Ralph Waldo Emerson: the birth of a seer,' in Reynolds and Capps (eds), *The Religious Personality*, pp. 187–200; 'Emerson and incest,' *The Psychoanalytic Review*, **62** (1975): 320–32. The famous quotation, 'faith is a telescope,' is from W.H. Gilman *et al.* (eds), *The Journals and Miscellaneous Notebooks of Ralph Waldo Emerson*, Vols I–V (Cambridge, MA: The Belknap Press of the Harvard University Press, 1961), Vol. II, p. 308.

53. Edel, *Writing Lives*. This is the general theme of Edel's book.

54. Erik H. Erikson, *Gandhi's Truth*, p. 11; also see Erik H. Erikson, 'On the nature of psychohistorical evidence: in search of Gandhi,' in Dankwart Rustow (ed.), *Philosophers and Kings: Studies in Leadership* (New York: George Braziller, 1970), pp. 33–68.

2   Searching for coherent character

1. See James Stanfield, *An Essay on the Study and Composition of Biography* (Sunderland: George Garbutt, 1813).
2. Henry A. Murray, *Explorations in Personality* (New York: Oxford University Press, 1938), dedication frontispiece.
3. Gamaliel Bradford, *The Journal of Gamaliel Bradford 1883–1932*, ed. Van Wyck Brooks (Boston: Houghton Mifflin, 1933), p. vii.
4. Gamaliel Bradford, *Types of American Character* (New York: Macmillan, 1895), pp. vii–ix.
5. Henry A. Murray, 'What should psychologists do about psychoanalysis?', *Journal of Abnormal and Social Psychology*, **35** (1940): 152–3.
6. *Ibid.*
7. *Ibid.*
8. *Ibid.*
9. Gamaliel Bradford, *A Naturalist of Souls* (New York: Dodd, Mead & Co., 1917), pp. 8–9.
10. *Ibid.*
11. *Ibid.*, pp. 4–5.
12. Gamaliel Bradford, *American Portraits* (Boston: Houghton Mifflin, 1922), p. 28.
13. Mark Twain, *Complete Works* (Hillcrest, 5th edn) (New York: Harper, 1913), p. 19. Quoted in Bradford, *American Portraits*, pp. 12–13.
14. Murray, *Explorations in Personality*, p. 605.
15. *Ibid.*
16. *Ibid.*
17. *Ibid.*, pp. 605–6.
18. *Ibid.*, p. 609.
19. *Ibid.*, p. 4.
20. Henry A. Murray and C. Kluckhohn, 'Outline of a conception of personality,' in H.A. Murray, D. Schneider, and C. Kluckhohn (eds), *Personality in Nature, Society, and Culture* (New York: Knopf, 1953), p. 30.
21. Havelock Ellis, *Views and Reasons* (London: Harmswork, 1932), pp. 96–7.
22. Sigmund Freud, *Leonardo da Vinci: A Study in Psychosexuality*, trans. A.A. Brill (New York: Vintage, 1916; 1947).
23. John Garraty, 'The interrelations of psychology and biography,' *Psychological Bulletin*, **51** (6) (1954): 569–82, 571.
24. Murray, *Explorations in Personality*, p. 123.
25. Erik H. Erikson, *Young Man Luther, A Study in Psychoanalysis and History* (New York: W.W. Norton, 1958), pp. 251–67.
26. Murray, *Explorations in Personality*, pp. 604–5.

27. See Erikson. Bradford's and Murray's approaches to establishing coherent character are illustrated by Erikson's cogent suggestion that Luther's 'fit in the choir could well have happened' (p. 37).
28. Gamaliel Bradford, *The Journal of Gamaliel Bradford*, p. 270.
29. Quoted in Dana K. Merrill, *American Biography: Its Theory and Practice* (Portland, ME: The Bowker Press, 1957), p. 92.
30. On the typology of biography at work here, see Paul Murray Kendall, *The Art of Biography* (New York: W.W. Norton, 1985) Although he traces the development of the 'scientific' chronicle and 'literary' critical types of biography, he advocates the centrality of biography as 'life simulation.'
31. Gamaliel Bradford, *Biography and the Human Heart* (Boston: Houghton Mifflin, 1932), p. 239.
32. Richard Altick, *Lives and Letters: A History of Literary Biography in England and America* (New York: Alfred A. Knopf, 1965), p. 225.
33. Murray is recognized in the field of psycho-diagnostics for his pioneering work on the study of the psychoanalytic dynamic of projection. He and an associate developed the Thematic Apperception Test (TAT) to study the phenomenon. See Henry A. Murray, *Manual of the Thematic Apperception Test* (Cambridge, MA: Harvard University Press, 1943).
34. Carlyle is quoted in Altick, p. 226.
35. Murray, *Explorations in Personality*, p. 609.
36. Garraty, 'The interrelations of psychology and biography,' p. 580.

3 Sensing fateful irony

1. Louise E. Hoffman, 'Psychobiography, 1900-1930: some reconsiderations,' *Biography: An Interdisciplinary Quarterly*, 7 (4) (1984): 341–51.
2. John Garraty, 'The interrelations of psychology and biography,' *Psychological Bulletin*, 51 (6) (1954): 569–82; and Leon Edel, *Writing Lives: Principia Biographica* (New York: W.W. Norton, 1984), and 'Transference: the biographer's dilemma,' *Biography: An Interdisciplinary Quarterly*, 7 (4) (1984): 283–91.
3. In psychoanalytic traditions, hostility and the successful repression and sublimation of hostility are the source of all forms of humor, not the least of which is irony. Freud cites irony as a sophisticated form of hostility, which he calls 'representation by the opposite.' See Sigmund Freud, *Jokes and Their Relation to the Unconscious*, trans. and ed. James Strachey (New York: W.W. Norton, 1963), pp. 73f. (The 'hostile purpose' of humor is considered in detail by Freud on pages 102–16.) For Freud's own venture into biography according to a multi-dimensional (but, perhaps, constructionist) approach, see Sigmund

Freud, *Leonardo da Vinci: A Study in Psychosexuality*, trans. A.A. Brill (New York: Random House, Vintage Books, 1947). Fateful irony is evident throughout the biography, for example, when Freud points out that da Vinci's 'effeminate delicacy of feeling did not prevent him from accompanying condemned criminals on their way to execution in order to study and sketch in his notebook their features, distorted by fear' (p. 14). Starkly put, Freud said that da Vinci presented 'unusual traits and apparent contradictions' (p. 13). Freud explained these according to his psychoanalysis, mainly in terms of the unitary pattern of unconscious oedipal conflict. In this sense, although one could argue that Freud represents a multidimensional approach to the study of the individual in the history of psychology in the early part of the twentieth century, one would be hard pressed to say that Freud was a deconstructionist. He maintains a constructionist stance when he reduces the facts of a life to unitary characterizations. Compared to Freud, Strachey can be said to shift Freud's multidimensional approach from the reductionism of the constructionist stance to a non-reductionistic, incipient deconstructionist approach. Thus, Strachey the biographer was able to manage the transference relationship between biographers and their subjects more effectively than did Freud the psychoanalyst. The pretense of authority was not as evident in Strachey's biographical narratives as it was in Freud's case studies. Here, then, one could easily argue that Strachey, in successfully managing the transference relationship, was more 'Freudian' than Freud. It was all a result of irony being deployed strategically as a sophisticated form of hostility in a deconstructionist manner, this without any pretense of the clinical detachment of an orthodox psychoanalyst. Freud was obliged to view lives only through the lens of the theory of personality that he himself had constructed.

4. See Paul Murray Kendall, *The Art of Biography* (New York: W.W. Norton, 1985).

5. Leon Edel, 'Biographer and subject: Lytton Strachey and Van Wyck Brooks,' in *Prose Studies*, Special Issue on Biography (Leicester, 1982), pp. 281–308. The phrase 'fateful irony' is mine, not Edel's. It is used to suggest the method developed and used by Strachey as a biographical style. With this slant on lives, he paved the way in the history of twentieth-century biography for biographical writing that takes seriously modern psychological science and discourse. This kind of biography, especially as it attends to psychoanalytic insights, is what Edel calls the 'New Biography.' See Edel, *Writing Lives: Principia Biographica*, pp. 19–32; 248. Also noteworthy is the tribute written after Strachey's death by Leonard Woolf: 'I think that the most significant thing about Lytton Strachey both as a person and as a

writer is that his writings came so directly from himself, from the very core of his character.' See Leonard Woolf, 'Lytton Strachey,' *The Bloomsbury Group: A Collection of Memoirs, Commentary, and Criticism,* ed. S.P. Rosenbaum (Toronto: University of Toronto Press, 1975), p. 178. The subtle connection between transference and the emergence of verbal irony is described in Martin Stein, 'Irony in psychoanalysis,' *Journal of the American Psychoanalytic Association,* **33** (1) (1985): 37–57. Particularly apt is Stein's use of Henry Fowler's understanding of irony as being tied to an *alter ego*: 'The word *irony*, which in its more general sense may be defined as the use of words intended to convey one meaning to the uninitiated part of the audience and another to the initiated, the delight of it lying in the secret intimacy set up between the latter and the speaker; it should be added, however, that there are dealers in irony for who [*sic*] the initiated circle is not of outside hearers, but is an *alter ego* dwelling in their own hearts' (p. 36). My point is that Strachey's technique of sensing fateful irony in a subject emerged in his writings against the foil of his own *alter ego*, itself expressed in terms of the figures that he selected to 'work through,' so to speak, as he wrote about them. See Henry Fowler, *A Dictionary of Modern English Usage* (London: Oxford University Press, 1954), p. 296. Similar understandings of this latter, transference-based variety of fateful irony are offered by literary critics like Wayne Booth, *A Rhetoric of Irony* (Chicago: University of Chicago Press, 1974); Norman Knox, *The Word Irony and Its Context* (Durham, NC: Duke University Press, 1961); Douglas Muecke, *The Compass of Irony* (London: Methuen, 1969), *Irony: The Critical Idiom* (London: Methuen, 1970), and *Irony and the Ironic: The Critical Idiom* (London: Methuen, 1982).

6. See A.R. Buss, 'The emerging field of the sociology of psychological knowledge,' *American Psychologist,* **30** (1975): 988–1022. The suggestion of this line of thought is to say that Strachey, unlike so many others, was the right person in the right place at the right time, and that he internalized it all.

7. Eileen Overend, 'Attitude, drama, and role in Strachey's *Elizabeth and Essex,' Biography: An Interdisciplinary Quarterly,* **7** (2) (1984): 158–68, 159.

8. Henry A. Murray, *Explorations in Personality* (New York: Oxford University Press, 1938), p. 715.

9. See examples in Frank E. Reynolds and Donald E. Capps (eds), *The Biographical Process: Studies in the History and Psychology of Religion* (The Hague: Mouton Press, 1976); Michael Williams (ed.), *Charisma and Sacred Biography* (Journal of the American Academy of Religion Thematic Studies), **48** (3 and 4) (Atlanta: Scholars Press, 1982).

10. James Stanfield, *An Essay on the Study and Composition of Biography* (Sunderland: George Garbutt, 1813).

11. Stanfield is quoted in Richard Altick, *Lives and Letters: A History of Literary Biography in England and America* (New York: Alfred A. Knopf, 1965), p. 81.
12. Kendall, *The Art of Biography*.
13. Murray, *Explorations in Personality*, p. 715.
14. Wilson is quoted in Edel, *Writing Lives: Principia Biographica*, p. 182.
15. James Boswell, *The Life of Johnson*, ed. George Birkbeck Hill and revised L.F. Powell (Oxford: The Clarendon Press, 1934–50), vol. I, pp. 29–31.
16. *Ibid.*
17. On rudiments of these basic attitudes in the disciplines of the humanities, see Harold Bloom (ed.), *Deconstruction and Criticism* (New York: Seabury Press, 1979) and *Agon: Towards a Theory of Revisionism* (Oxford: Oxford University Press, 1982); Jacques Derrida, *Of Grammatology* (Baltimore: Johns Hopkins University Press, 1976); Christopher Norris, *Deconstructionism: Theory and Practice* (London: Methuen, 1982); Mark Taylor, 'Deconstruction: what's the difference?', *Soundings*, **65** (4) (1983): 387–403; David L. Smith, 'Emerson and deconstruction: the end(s) of scholarship,' *Soundings*, **67** (4) (1984): 379–98. Also, a good example of unidimensional construction in biography studies is Stephen Hay, 'Digging up Gandhi's psychological roots,' *Biography: An Interdisciplinary Quarterly*, **6** (3) (1983): 209–19. Offered together as what Hay calls Gandhi's 'traits of character' (p. 209) are the following: 'devotion to serving others when they are in difficulty'; 'skill in mediating among conflicting parties'; and 'readiness steadfastly to refuse to obey a law or command repugnant to his conscience' (pp. 209–10). Thus, Gandhi's life is circumscribed and, perhaps, reduced to a short-list of motivational values or 'constructions.' The emergence of 'model free' life-writing in the allied genre of autobiography is carefully described by Karl Weintraub, *The Value of the Individual: Self and Circumstance in Autobiography* (Chicago: University of Chicago Press, 1978); see also his 'Autobiography and historical consciousness,' *Critical Inquiry*, **1** (4) (1975): 821–48.
18. Leon Edel, *Literary Biography* (London: Rupert Hart-Davis, 1957), p. 88. Also in *Writing Lives: Principia Biographica*, p. 182.
19. Lytton Strachey, 'Froude,' in *Biographical Essays* (New York: Harcourt, Brace, 1969), pp. 257–63.
20. Martin Kallich, 'Psychoanalysis, sexuality, and Lytton Strachey's theory of biography,' *American Imago*, **15** (1958): 368, n. 16. A thorough study of the influence of psychology on Strachey is Martin Kallich, *The Psychological Milieu of Lytton Strachey* (New York: Bookman Associates, 1961).
21. Kallich, 'Psychoanalysis, sexuality, and Lytton Strachey's theory of biography,' p. 368.

22. Biographical information about Strachey can be found in two major sources: Michael Holroyd, *Lytton Strachey: A Biography* (Baltimore: Penguin Books, 1971); Michael Holroyd (ed.), *Lytton Strachey by Himself: A Self-Portrait* (New York: Holt, Rinehart and Winston, 1971). The note at hand is from Holroyd (ed.), p. 118.
23. Holroyd (ed.), *Lytton Strachey by Himself*, p. 127.
24. *Ibid.*, p. 79.
25. Quoted in Altick, *Lives and Letters*, p. 234.
26. *Ibid.*
27. Strachey, 'Froude,' p. 257.
28. *Ibid.*
29. *Ibid.*
30. *Ibid.*
31. *Ibid.*, p. 258.
32. *Ibid.*
33. *Ibid.*
34. *Ibid.*, p. 263.
35. Kendall, *The Art of Biography*, pp. 147–8.

4 Erik Erikson as a life-writer/reader

1. For a recent review of the status of Erikson's work during the 1990s after his death (1993), see 'Special issue: Erik H. Erikson,' *The Psychohistory Review: Studies of Motivation in History and Culture*, **22** (1) (Fall 1993). In this issue it is noted that 'Unlike seventeen years ago [i.e., in a comparable 1976 volume of the same periodical about Erikson's work], most of our current contributors are at least somewhat concerned with how Erikson's life impacted his texts' (p. 5).
2. Erik H. Erikson, *Young Man Luther: A Study in Psychoanalysis and History* (New York: W.W. Norton, 1958), p. 16.
3. Erik H. Erikson, *Gandhi's Truth: On the Origins of Militant Nonviolence* (New York: W.W. Norton, 1969), p. 9.
4. This proposal is a form of what biographer Stephen B. Oates, following the lead of Paul Murray Kendall, calls 'pure biography,' which he himself embraces. It is the kind of biography which 'employs fictional techniques without resorting to fiction itself,' and it aims at a simulation, in words, of a person's life, from all that is known about that person. Two other types of biography are specified, namely, the 'critical study' and the 'scholarly chronicle.' The former is solely an intellectual project of the biographer, often comprised of psychoanalytic insight into the subject, which serves the author's purposes. The latter is simply a recitation of the facts of a life, nothing more and nothing less. See Stephen B. Oates (ed.), *Biography as High Adventure:*

Life-Writers Speak on Their Art (Amherst: University of Massachusetts Press, 1986), pp. ix–x. Also, Paul Murray Kendall, *The Art of Biography* (New York: W.W. Norton, 1985), pp. ix, 13–14, 28.

5. On the psychology of imagination and its bodily basis, see Mark Johnson, *Moral Imagination: Implications of Cognitive Science for Ethics* (Chicago: University of Chicago Press, 1993); *The Body in the Mind: The Bodily Basis of Meaning, Imagination, and Reason* (Chicago and London: University of Chicago Press, 1987); George Lakoff and Mark Johnson, *Metaphors We Live By* (Chicago: University of Chicago Press, 1980).

6. 'Mythic reverie' gives rise to conceptual thought. This particular methodological assumption is articulated by Gaston Bachelard, *The Poetics of Reverie: Childhood, Language, and the Cosmos*, trans. Daniel Russell (Paris: Presses Universitaires de France, 1960; Boston: Beacon, 1971).

7. Oates (ed.), *Biography as High Adventure*, pp. ix, 13–14, 28.

8. Erikson, *Gandhi's Truth*, p. 5.

9. *Ibid.*, p. 99.

10. Erikson, *Young Man Luther*, pp. 176–7, 252, 210. The 'meaning of meaning it' was expressed by Luther in his insistence that his effects be tamed and his speech be restrained until he was 'convinced,' or 'meant it'; this was a conviction because of the closeness of the fit between 'intellectual meaning' and an 'inner sense of meaning it.' Luther's identity, insofar as it depended on an adequate ideology, rose above religious dogmas of his day for reasons related to factors of his early psychological preparation to take the whole issue of 'meaning it' or 'not meaning it' literally as a matter of 'life or death.' In this he surpassed the awareness of most of his peers.

11. Erikson, *Gandhi's Truth*, p. 433. See also Roger Mucchielli, *An Introduction to Structural Psychology* (New York: Funk & Wagnalls, 1970) for an analysis of animals' rituals which emphasize the behavioral patterns involved, doing so on the basis of a cybernetic model of information gathering and modifying.

12. Erikson, *Gandhi's Truth*, p. 435.

13. *Ibid.*, p. 448.

14. Erikson, *Young Man Luther*, p. 9.

15. Erikson, *Gandhi's Truth*, p. 229.

16. *Ibid.*, p. 231.

17. *Ibid.*, p. 436.

18. *Ibid.*, p. 438.

19. *Ibid.*, p. 439.

20. *Ibid.*

21. *Ibid.*

22. Mircea Eliade, *Cosmos and History: The Myth of the Eternal Return* (New York: Harper and Row, 1959). History is regenerated insofar as humankind expresses an impulse to reverse historical 'terror' or *dureé*. This, Eliade suggests, is the basic nature of spiritual experience in the world's religions.

23. Erik H. Erikson, 'Jefferson Lectures, 1973,' as reported in *The Congressional Record*, 2 May 1973, p. S8122. Erikson ties his work on identity formation to American national identity, but identity formation itself remains the central point to be noted here.

24. Roland Bainton, 'Psychiatry and history: an examination of Erikson's *Young Man Luther*,' *Religion in Life* (Winter 1971), pp. 450–78.

25. Jacques Barzun, 'History: Her muse and her doctors,' *Journal of History*, 77: 36–64.

26. Kendall, *The Art of Biography*, pp. 147–8.

27. Erik H. Erikson, 'Human strength and the cycle of generations,' *Insight and Responsibility* (New York: W.W. Norton, 1964), pp. 111–57.

28. Quoted in Wilhelm Dilthey, *Pattern and Meaning in History*, ed. H.P. Rickman (New York: Harper and Row, 1961), p. 89.

29. *Ibid.*, p. 91.

30. *Ibid.*

31. *Ibid.*

32. *Ibid.*, p. 94.

33. James Olney, *Metaphors of Self: The Meaning of Autobiography* (Princeton: Princeton University Press, 1972), p. 32.

34. Erikson, *Young Man Luther*, p. 254.

35. *Ibid.*, pp. 251–67. Much of the 'earlier Erikson' is contained in Erik H. Erikson, *Childhood and Society* (New York: W.W. Norton, 1963).

36. See Erikson, *Gandhi's Truth*, pp. 128f, 42f. On the one hand, Erikson talks about the 'curse' felt by Gandhi after he paused from nursing his ailing father in order to be alone with his wife and, while he was doing so, his father died. On the other hand, there are indications that considerations of classical Gestalt theory are on Erikson's mind as well, at a perceptual level in his surmise of Gandhi's life.

37. Erikson, *Young Man Luther*, p. 13.

38. Erikson, *Gandhi's Truth*, p. 19.

39. See *Gandhi's Truth*, pp. 68–79. It is distinctive that Erikson considered his own meeting with the mill owner, Ambalal Sarabhai, to be something of an experience which bore similarities to Gandhi's own encounters with the man in 1918. This subjective experience is thus taken as data in its own right for the kind of study Erikson then goes on to write. The biographical introspection as careful self-conscious-ness in the study of Gandhi by Erikson is hardly as evident in *Young Man Luther*.

40. *Ibid.*, p. 33.
41. *Ibid.*, p. 39. Play performances of American children are exemplified in *Childhood and Society*, pp. 202–38. Here one child at a time is confronted with an empty table ('stage') and series of toys ('cast') and asked to construct a 'scene.'
42. *Ibid.*, p. 40.
43. *Ibid.*
44. Ernest G. Schachtel, *Metamorphosis* (New York: Basic Books, 1959), pp. 81–4; Erikson, *Childhood and Society*, pp. 257f, 63f, 67, 176. Mutuality is usually related to the crisis of 'intimacy versus isolation' when sexual intimacy requires reciprocity of meaningfulness. But mutuality has its epigenetic roots in the first crisis of 'basic trust versus basic mistrust.' Here the value of hope is engendered to the degree that the infant is adequately nurtured by his mother and senses, in return, that she herself is satisfied by doing so.
45. Schachtel, *Metamorphosis*, p. 83.
46. *Ibid.*, p. 83.
47. *Ibid.*
48. See Zevedei Barbu, *Problems of Historical Psychology* (New York: Grove Press, 1960). This non-psychoanalytic psychohistorical approach is built upon an understanding of the vicissitudes of human 'perception.' It has as its aim an understanding of the 'character' of various cultures, for example, the 'character' of the English people. It is Barbu's work which first suggested to the author the possibility that Erikson himself was engaged implicitly in a similar project. At least, that perception played as much a role in Erikson's psychohistorical work as Barbu avowed it did in his. The study at hand seeks a *rapprochement* between the Eriksonian and the Barbuian approaches. This is intended in two ways: first, by suggesting that reading/writing lives is a meeting ground that each approach must come to grips with; second, by suggesting that each approach, in having to do with perceptual factors, touches base with a kind of psychology which has classical Gestalt theory at its base.
49. Schachtel, *Metamorphosis*, pp. 83–4.
50. *Ibid.*, pp. 85–90.
51. Reference is made to the typology of biography specified by Paul Murray Kendall and Stephen B. Oates. See n. 4 above.
52. See Rudolf Arnheim, *Art and Visual Perception* (Berkeley: University of California Press, 1971); and Arnheim, *Visual Thinking* (Berkeley: University of California Press, 1969). The use of Gestalt theory has also been evident in musicology. See Leonard Meyer, *Emotion and Meaning in Music* (Chicago: University of Chicago Press, 1956).

5   Biography, empathy, and introspection

1. Samuel Johnson, *Idler*, No. 84, 24 November 1795. Quoted in James L. Clifford, *Biography as an Art* (New York: Oxford University Press, 1962), p. 43.

2. A more detailed rendition of Dilthey's notion can be found in H.A. Hodges, *The Philosophy of Wilhelm Dilthey* (London: Routledge Kegan Paul, 1952), p. 38f. Also, one line of thought exists which suggests that Dilthey's notion serves as a basis upon which an ontology can be elaborated with the facilitation of psychological ideas drawn directly from classical Gestalt theory. Here *Erlebnis* forms one of three notions basic to literary art; the others being *Zeitgeist* and *Weltanschauung*. For this line of thought, see Kurt Muller-Vollmer, *Towards a Phenomenological Theory of Literature: A Study of Wilhelm Dilthey's 'Poetik'* (The Hague: Mouton Press, 1963), pp. 33–8.

3. James Boswell, *Life of Johnson*, ed. George Birkbeck Hill and revised L.F. Powell (Oxford: The Clarendon Press, 1934–50), vol. I, pp. 29–33. Quoted in James Clifford, *Biography as an Art*, p. 53.

4. James Stanfield, *An Essay on the Study and Composition of Biography* (Sunderland: George Garbutt, 1813). Quoted in Clifford, *Biography as an Art*, pp. 66, 62–3.

5. See John A. Garraty, 'The interrelationships of psychology and biography,' *Psychological Bulletin*, **51** (6) (1954): 569–82. Although his article begins with the statement, 'the best biographers, like the best novelists, have always been students of human psychology, and the development of psychological science has tended to confirm insights long ago achieved' (p. 569), Garraty chooses to move quickly into what might be called a consideration of how each discipline can share 'techniques.' Most of his emphasis is on psychoanalysis and the uses that might be made of some of its experimental findings. He fails to note several highlights in combining psychology and biography (James Stanfield is not even mentioned in the article) and therefore seems more concerned with the present than with tracing historically the tradition of biographical interrelationships.

6. Richard D. Altick, *Lives and Letters: A History of Literary Biography in England and America* (New York: Alfred Knopf, 1965), p. 80. Stanfield's remark is quoted.

7. *Ibid.*, p. 81. Quoted by Altick.

8. *Ibid.*, p. 383. Quoted by Altick.

9. *Ibid.*, p. 185.

10. Carlyle contributed the point of view that biography was about 'Great Men' of history. Boswell and Stanfield are regarded as the earliest formulators of theories about the 'techniques' available to the working

biographer; thus, Carlyle's work during the nineteenth century can be viewed as building on elements of those theories. The work of Carlyle itself will be more thoroughly mentioned later.

11. Leon Edel, *Literary Biography* (London: Rupert Hart-Davis, 1957), p. 82. See updated version of the same concern in Leon Edel, *Writing Lives: Principia Biographica* (New York: W.W. Norton, 1984). Also of interest for its concern to apply psychological sensitivities to biography is Leon Edel, *Stuff of Sleep and Dreams: Experiments in Literary Psychology* (London: Chatto & Windus, 1982).
12. Edel, *Literary Biography*, pp. 82–3.
13. *Ibid.*, p. 83.
14. *Ibid.*
15. *Ibid.*, p. 84.
16. *Ibid.*, p. 83. This is similar to Stephen B. Oates's 'pure biography,' following Paul Murray Kendall. See Stephen B. Oates, *Biography as High Adventure: Life-Writers Speak on Their Art* (Amherst: University of Massachusetts Press, 1986).
17. Edel, *Literary Biography*, p. 87.
18. *Ibid.*, p. 88.
19. *Ibid.*
20. Quoted in Altick, p. 294. From Herbert Gorman, *A Victorian American: Henry Wadsworth Longfellow* (New York: George Doran, 1926).
21. Edel, *Literary Biography*, p. 88.
22. See James L. Clifford, *From Puzzles to Portraits* (Chapel Hill: University of North Carolina Press, 1970), pp. 83–9. This book elaborates on the typology. All quotations are taken from the pages listed.
23. S.B. Oates (ed.), *Biography as High Adventure*, Prologue, pp. ix–xiii.
24. Edel, *Literary Biography*, p. 1.
25. *Ibid.*, p. 60.
26. Richard Holmes, *Footsteps: Adventures of a Romantic Biographer* (London: Hodder and Stoughton, 1985), p. 27.
27. In addition to Erikson's work, a practical, step-by-step approach to the subjective dimension, or the inner flow of experience, of lives can be found in the work of James F.T. Bugental. See in particular his *The Art of the Psychotherapist* (New York: W.W. Norton, 1987).
28. Erik H. Erikson, 'The nature of clinical evidence,' in *Insight and Responsibility* (New York: W.W. Norton, 1964), pp. 47–80. Previously published in Daniel Lerner (ed.), *Evidence and Inference* (Glencoe, IL: Free Press, 1959).
29. *Ibid.*, p. 80.
30. *Ibid.*, p. 52.
31. *Ibid.*, p. 59.
32. *Ibid.*

33. *Ibid.*, p. 58.
34. *Ibid.*, p. 72.
35. *Ibid.*, p. 77.
36. *Ibid.*, p. 79.
37. Erik H. Erikson, *Young Man Luther* (New York: W.W. Norton, 1958), p. 259.
38. *Ibid.*, p. 115.
39. *Ibid.*, p. 117.
40. *Ibid.*, p. 119.
41. *Ibid.*
42. *Ibid.*, pp. 117–19.
43. Erik H. Erikson, *Gandhi's Truth* (New York: W.W. Norton, 1969), p. 395.
44. *Ibid.*, p. 129.
45. *Ibid.*
46. See Norman Mailer, *Marilyn: A Biography* (New York: Grosset & Dunlap, 1973).
47. Ralph L. Rusk, *The Life of Ralph Waldo Emerson* (New York: Columbia University Press, 1949), p. 85. Rusk's entire treatment of the Emerson–Gay relationship is contained in the paragraph mentioned from page 85. Subsequent quotations are taken from that paragraph.
48. *Ibid.*, p. 84. Emerson graduated 'number thirty' in a class of fifty-nine. It is reasonable to assume that, at the outside, a total of about 250 students were enrolled at Harvard College at the time.
49. See Rudolf Otto, *The Idea of the Holy*, trans. John W. Harvey (New York: Oxford University Press, 1923). Traditions of reflection in the phenomenology and history of religions offer ways of understanding psychological ambivalence as a variation of a numinous religious experience, in which the 'self' and the 'other,' not losing separate identities by means of a mystical merger with each other, stand out as 'figure' and 'ground' respectively in powerful moments of lived experience. Phenomenologists of religion, especially, have developed the method of *Verstehen* in their comparative work on world religions and the human nature of religious experience.

6 Soteriological biography

1. J.Y. Cole, 'Biography: a symposium at the Library of Congress,' *Library of Congress Information Bulletin*, **43** (9 April 1984), 116–20, 116.
2. See Stephen B. Oates (ed.), *Biography as High Adventure: Life-Writers Speak on Their Art* (Amherst: University of Massachusetts Press, 1986), Prologue, pp. ix–xiii.

3. See L.A. Wood, 'Biographies, autobiographies growing in popularity,' *Publishers' Weekly*, **226** (5 October 1984): 34. Charts of statistics are included.

4. *Ibid.*

5. *Ibid.*

6. R.W. White, 'The case of Earnst,' in Henry A. Murray (ed.), *Explorations in Personality* (New York: Oxford University Press, 1938), pp. 604–702, 605.

7. Henry A. Murray, *Explorations in Personality*, pp. 605, 607.

8. In the biographical spirit of Murray is the volume of essays presented to Murray on his seventieth birthday, 16 May 1963, by R.W. White (ed.), *The Study of Lives: Essays on Personality in Honor of Henry A. Murray* (Chicago and New York: Aldine/Atherton, 1963). White says that the spirit of Murray's work was that 'significant things about personality' are actually part of the 'whole enterprise of living' (p. xiii). Recent biographical studies have mainly ignored such a phenomenological spirit.

9. The most significant so-called 'manifesto' of postmodernism is F. Lyotard, *The Postmodern Condition: A Report on Knowledge*, trans. G. Bennington (Minneapolis: University of Minnesota Press, 1984).

10. Meredith McGuire, 'Religion and the body: rematerializing the human body in the social sciences,' *Journal for the Scientific Study of Religion*, **29** (1990): 283–96.

11. See thematic issue 'The Body,' *History of Religions*, **30** (1990).

12. Edith Wyschogrod, 'Man-made mass death: shifting concepts of community,' *Journal of the American Academy of Religion*, **58** (1990): 165–76, 173.

13. Erik H. Erikson, 'Human strength and the cycle of generations,' in *Insight and Responsibility* (New York: W.W. Norton, 1964), pp. 109–57, 133. Lest one believes that 'wisdom' is a natural culmination of the values of orientation of people living in modern industrialized contexts, the critical study by Neil Postman, *The Disappearance of Childhood* (New York: Vintage Books, 1982; 1994), can be cited as cutting against the grain of generational turnover which, it can be added, is much to Postman's dismay.

14. The emphasis on a feminist appreciation of the power of reproduction broadly conceived is at its clearest in the work of Julia Kristeva, *The Kristeva Reader*, ed. T. Moi (New York: Columbia University Press, 1986); *Desire in Language: A Semiotic Approach to Literature and Art*, ed. T. Gora *et al.*, trans. L.S. Roudiez (Oxford: Basil Blackwell, 1980).

15. See Sarah Ruddick, *Maternal Thinking: Toward a Politics of Peace* (Boston: Beacon, 1989).

16. See the example identified in Erik H. Erikson, 'The golden rule and the cycle of life,' in R.W. White (ed.), *The Study of Lives* (New York and Chicago: Aldine/Atherton, 1963), pp. 413–28.

17. The intellectual background of such a methodological discussion in studies in religion scholarship is found in Donald Wiebe, 'The failure of nerve in the academic study of religion,' *Studies in Religion/Sciences Religieuses*, **13** (1984): 401–22.

18. Broadside criticisms of humanistic psychology and its applicability to scholarship in the humanities, including biographical studies, include Maurice Friedman, 'Aiming at the self: the paradox of encounter and the human potential movement,' *Journal of Humanistic Psychology*, **16** (1976): 5–34; Volney Gay, 'Against wholeness: the ego's complicity in religion,' *Journal of the American Academy of Religion*, **47** (1979): 539–55.

19. David L. Norton, *Personal Destinies* (Princeton: Princeton University Press, 1976).

20. *Ibid.*, p. ix.

21. See Wyschogrod, 'Man-made mass death.'

22. An excellent critical study of the technological forces that militate against an individual's sense of self-worth in community groups is Neil Postman, *Technopoly* (New York: Vintage Books, 1992).

23. Bruno Bettelheim, *Freud and Man's Soul* (London: Fontana/Flamingo, 1985; original work published 1982), p. 77.

24. Norton, *Personal Destinies*, p. x.

25. J. Brooks Bouson, *The Empathic Reader* (Amherst: University of Massachusetts Press, 1989), p. 3.

26. *Ibid.*, p. 13.

27. *Ibid.*, p. 22.

28. Heinz Kohut, 'The psychoanalyst in the community of scholars,' in P.H. Ornstein (ed.), *The Search for the Self* (New York: International Universities Press, 1978), pp. 685–724, 712.

29. Heinz Kohut, *How Does Analysis Cure?* (Chicago: University of Chicago Press, 1984), pp. 82, 175.

30. Kohut, 'The psychoanalyst in the community of scholars,' p. 712. See also D.S. Jaffe, 'Empathy, counteridentification, countertransference: a review, with some personal perspectives on the "analytic instrument,"' *Psychoanalytic Quarterly*, **55** (1986): 215–43.

31. See Gelya Frank, 'Becoming the Other: empathy and biographical interpretation,' *Biography: An Interdisciplinary Quarterly*, **55** (1985): 189–210; L.L. Langness and Gelya Frank, *Lives: An Anthropological Approach to Biography* (Novato, CA: Chandler & Sharp, 1981).

32. See David Bleich, *Subjective Criticism* (Baltimore: Johns Hopkins University Press, 1978); Stanley Fish, *Is there a Text in this Class?* (Cambridge, MA: Harvard University Press, 1980); Wolfgang Iser, *The*

Act of Reading: A Theory of Aesthetic Response (Baltimore: Johns Hopkins University Press, 1980); Michael Riffaterre, *Text Production*, trans. T. Lyons (New York: Columbia University Press, 1983).

33. Jonathan Culler, *On Deconstruction: Theory and Criticism after Structuralism* (Ithaca, NY: Cornell University Press, 1982), p. 70.
34. *Ibid.*, p. 76.
35. Robert Alter, *Motives for Fiction* (Cambridge, MA: Harvard University Press, 1984), p. 21.
36. Bouson, *The Empathic Reader*, p. 280.
37. Heinz Kohut, 'Introspection, empathy, and the semicircle of mental health,' *International Journal of Psychoanalysis*, **63** (1982): 395–408, 395.
38. See Erikson, 'Human strength and the cycle of generations.'
39. For this general and representative typology of biography see Oates (ed.), *Biography as High Adventure*, Prologue, pp. ix–xiii.
40. This line of thought is taken from Robert F. Murphy, *The Body Silent* (London and New York: W.W. Norton, 1990), pp. 226–7.
41. Wyschogrod, 'Man-made mass death,' pp. 173–4.
42. Jacques Lacan, *Écrits: A Selection* (London: Tavistock, 1977; original work published 1966), pp. 146–7.
43. Richard Holmes, *Footsteps: Adventures of a Romantic Biographer* (New York: Viking, 1985).
44. See the discussion on the ritualization of human biology with a view to raising children and the turnover of generations in Erik H. Erikson, 'Reflection on ethics and war,' *Yale Review* (Summer 1984): 481–6; 'Pseudospeciation and the nuclear age,' *Political Psychology*, **6** (1985): 213–7; Stephen Jay Gould, 'A biological comment on Erikson's notion of pseudospeciation,' *Yale Review* (Summer 1984): 487–90.
45. Lesser known aspects of the psychohistorical work of Erik Erikson are currently receiving renewed interest from life-writers because of the eudaimonism implied in his work. This is reflected in Erikson's emphasis on the biology of *communitas*, or the overall genetic integrity of *Homo sapiens*. He calls the material dynamic of shared lives 'speciation,' and this serves as a *telos* for structuring human strengths, or 'virtues,' according to democratic social and institutional life.
46. On the themes of character and irony, out of which personality is constructed in biographical narratives, see Richard A. Hutch, 'Explorations in character: Gamaliel Bradford and Henry Murray as psychobiographers,' *Biography: An Interdisciplinary Quarterly*, **4** (1981): 312–25; 'Strategic irony and Lytton Strachey's contribution to biography,' *Biography: An Interdisciplinary Quarterly*, **2** (1988): 1–15. Revised portions of these articles form the basis of Chapters 2 and 3.
47. See Oliver Sacks, *The Man Who Mistook His Wife for a Hat and Other Clinical Tales* (New York: Summit Books, 1985), pp. 42–52, for a lucid

description of proprioception and its interruption. In general, Sacks's work on neuroscience has popularized the lived experience of the body, in its best and worst clinical conditions. This parallels the popularity of biography, at its best and worst, in contemporary culture.

48. Oates (ed.), *Biography as High Adventure*, Prologue, pp. ix–xiii. Oates's work on biographical method derives from an appreciation of the work of Paul Murray Kendall. See Paul Murray Kendall, *The Art of Biography*, with a new introduction by Stephen D. Oates (New York: W.W. Norton, 1985). Without empathy based on body-awareness, or proprioception, biography remains of either the 'Scholarly Chronicle' or the 'Critical Biography' types in Oates's typology. Oates advocates 'Pure Biography' (Kendall's terms), for which empathy is an essential tool of research. This type of biography aims at 'simulating lives' in narrative form.

49. Kendall, *The Art of Biography*, pp. 147–8.

50. A good recent example of an embodied life, or one written up with *bios* clearly and centrally in mind, is the self-biography, or autobiography, of John Updike, *Self-Consciousness* (New York: Fawcett Crest, 1989). The formative affect of psoriasis and poor dental health on his self-understanding and work as a writer is painfully explored. How mortality itself affects his self-consciousness is superbly described in the final chapter, 'On being a self forever.' Whether the book is actually an autobiography or a biography written by the subject himself demonstrates biographical introspection at work, namely, an experiential process which breaks down the traditional divide between those two literary genres.

51. This theme is explored in Western culture and Christianity in the exemplary work of Caroline Walker Bynum, especially in 'Material continuity, personal survival, and the resurrection of the body: a scholastic discussion,' *History of Religions*, **30** (1990): 51–85. See also Lawrence E. Sullivan, 'Bodyworks: knowledge of the body in the study of religion,' *History of Religions*, **30** (1990): 86–99.

52. See Ruddick, *Maternal Thinking*; and Elaine Scarry, *The Body in Pain* (New York and Oxford: Oxford University Press, 1985). Scarry recognizes the body – bodily injury – as a locus for the destruction and reconstruction of worldviews. For example, during war 'injuring ... provides, by its massive opening of human bodies, a way of reconnecting the derealized and disembodied beliefs [worldviews] with the force and power of the material world' (p. 128). A material dynamic similar to war occurs during childbirth. See N. Huston, 'The matrix of war: mothers and heroes,' in S.R. Suleiman (ed.), *The Female Body in Western Culture: Contemporary Perspectives* (Cambridge and London: Harvard University Press, 1986), pp. 119–36.

53. Ruddick, *Maternal Thinking*, p. 82.
54. See Wyschogrod, 'Man-made mass death.'
55. A theologically attuned approach to narrations of embodied lives, especially in regard to the first law of the mortal body (turnover of generations, and implied dying and death), is Lucy Bregman and Sara Thiermann, *First Person Mortal* (New York: Paragon House, 1995).

7 Impulse to hagiography

1. This project is one of moral reflection, which must usually account for three things, or the three sub-disciplines of ethics: (1) principles or rules of right and wrong (deontology); (2) a vision of the good end and thus the need to cultivate those virtues and practices that enhance good ends and avoid evil and vice (teleology); and (3) a way of reading the concrete contexts of life wherein the issues of right and wrong, good and evil find embodiment (ethology). This project stands in debt to the work of Alasdair MacIntyre, whose distinctive emphasis is to recover and reestablish a classical eudaimonistic view of teleological ethics and to link it with an historicist ethological account of human behavior. See, for example, Alasdair MacIntyre, *After Virtue: A Study in Moral Philosophy* (South Bend: University of Notre Dame Press, 1981); *Whose Justice? Which Rationality?* (South Bend: University of Notre Dame Press, 1988); *Three Rival Versions of Moral Philosophy* (South Bend: University of Notre Dame Press, 1990). Helpful in the study of MacIntyre's work is Max L. Stackhouse, 'Alasdair MacIntyre: an overview and evaluation,' *Religious Studies Review*, **3** (1992): 203–8.
2. See Erik H. Erikson, 'Human strength and the cycle of generations,' in *Insight and Responsibility* (New York: W.W. Norton, 1964), pp. 109–58.
3. A provocative call to such a concern is sounded in Robert Kastenbaum, 'The age of saints and the saintliness of age,' *International Journal of Aging and Human Development*, **2** (1990): 95–118.
4. For context, see Richard A. Hutch, 'Memory: grist of the spiritual life,' *St. Vladimir's Theological Quarterly*, **3** (1988): 223–32. Useful for determining the accuracy of personal memories is Bruce M. Ross, *Remembering the Personal Past: Descriptions of Autobiographical Memory* (New York and Oxford: Oxford University Press, 1991).
5. Implied is 'somatic style' as a factor of personality. I am indebted to the careful and provocative work of Joseph Lyons on the body and styles of human behavior. Lyons develops the work of fellow psychological researcher, William Sheldon, whose theory of 'somatotypes' (endomorph, mesomorph, ectomorph) has drawn considerable criticism and raised controversy in the field of personality theory since it was first proposed during the 1940s. See Joseph Lyons, *Ecology of the Body:*

Styles of Behavior in Human Life (Durham, NC: Duke University Press, 1987). In his chapter, 'Somatic style and art,' Lyons takes up the question of how saints' bodies have been depicted in the history of Christianity, and also the depiction of bodily form in modern art (for example, Caravaggio, Arp, Giacometti).

6. This intermingling of different kinds of 'time and space' in regard to reliquaries and their impact on reverent individuals is identified and described in terms of an 'emotional inversion of suffering' by Peter Brown, *The Cult of the Saints: Its Rise and Function in Latin Christianity* (Chicago: University of Chicago Press, 1981), pp. 50–68 ('The invisible companion'), and 84–5.

7. Such a call in studies in religion has been sounded by Lawrence E. Sullivan, 'Body works: knowledge of the body in the study of religion,' (entire issue) *History of Religions*, **30** (1990): 1. That the body has been neglected in historical studies is identified, and ways in which it might be studied in the future are pointed out, including a brief section on religion, by R. Porter, 'History of the body,' in P. Burke (ed.), *New Perspectives on Historical Writing* (Cambridge: Polity Press in association with Basil Blackwell, 1991), pp. 206–32.

8. This line of research is evident in the important work being conducted at the Washington Singer Laboratories, University of Exeter, UK, by M.J.A. Howe, 'Biographical evidence and the development of outstanding individuals,' *American Psychologist*, **37** (1982): 1071–81. Whereas Howe and his colleagues are concerned about intellectual achievements, the effort at hand is about religious achievements.

9. What several important existential psychological thinkers call 'personality hardiness,' defined as a combination of 'commitment, control, and challenge,' results. See Salvatore R. Maddi, 'On the problem of accepting facticity and pursuing possibility,' in S.B. Messer, L.A. Sass, and R.L. Woolfolk (eds), *Hermeneutics and Psychological Theory: Interpretive Perspectives on Personality, Psychotherapy, and Psychopathology* (New Brunswick and London: Rutgers University Press, 1988), pp. 182–209, 197. See also S.C. Kobasa, 'Stressful life events, personality, and health: an inquiry into hardiness,' *Journal of Personality and Social Psychology*, **42** (1979): 707–17; and 'The hardy personality: toward a social psychology of stress and health,' in G.S. Sanders and J. Suls (eds), *The Social Psychology of Health and Illness* (Hillsdale, NJ: Lawrence Erlbaum, 1982). A recent call to restore the body to thought in studies in religion and the human sciences is Philip A. Mellor and Chris Shilling, 'Reflexive modernity and the religious body,' *Religion*, **24** (1994): 23–42; and 'Modernity, self-identity and the sequestration of death,' *Sociology*, **27** (3) (1993): 411–31. The same call is made more generally for studies in the social sciences and humanities

in Chris Shilling, *The Body and Social Theory* (London: Sage/Theory, Culture and Society, 1993).

10. I am indebted to the style of discourse in Carol P. Christ, *Diving Deep and Surfacing: Women Writers on Spiritual Quest* (2nd edn) (Boston: Beacon, 1986). Purportedly a 'feminist' style, I urge its consideration in the struggle of those men who seek to make their own distinctive work morally acceptable to women.

11. Two works that illustrate attempts to unmask the counterproductive strategy of cultural studies as dispassionate research and scholarship are Bruno Bettelheim, *Freud and Man's Soul* (London: Chatto & Windus, 1982; Flamingo Edition, 1985) and Clifford Geertz, *Works and Lives: The Anthropologist as Author* (Stanford: Stanford University Press, 1988). Bettelheim suggests that the English translation of Freud's works by William and Alix Strachey misled the medical establishment in Britain and America into assuming that psychoanalysis was not as Freud intended it, namely, a technique by which analyst and analysand discovered what was most valuable in human life while one was alive (*psyche*, or soul), but a dispassionate scientific method of therapy. Geertz shows how he and other well-known twentieth-century anthropologists, namely, Lévi-Strauss, Evans-Pritchard, Malinowski, and Benedict, were purportedly scientifically studying other cultures ('being there'), but in fact projected their own interests and sense of what counted into them ('being here'). Clearly evident is the incipiently biographical nature of these kinds of illustrations.

12. This issue arises in discussions of the place of truth within postmodern thought. In the first instance, preference could be assigned here to Richard Rorty's view that 'truth' can be identified with human 'solidarity,' or the capacity to suffer and to feel pain. See Richard Rorty, *Contingency, Irony, and Solidarity* (Cambridge: Cambridge University Press, 1989). Upon further consideration, Donald Davidson's view that 'truth' involves the 'capacity to engage with one another' (see Malpas below, page 300), and then together to recognize other human capacities, would be commanding. See Donald Davidson, *Inquiries into Truth and Interpretation* (Oxford: Clarendon Press, 1984). This general discussion is summarized in Jeff Malpas, 'Retrieving truth: modernism, post-modernism and the problem of truth,' *Soundings: An Interdisciplinary Journal*, **2-3** (1992): 287–306. Biography can be a prime focus of the place of truth within postmodern thought, itself a curiously avoided topic amongst most postmodern thinkers.

13. Of course, such marks of human biology become socially and culturally encoded. Reading the codes embedded in a life story is less a matter of literary deconstruction criticism and more about structural hermeneutics. For examples, see Piero Camporesi, *The Incorruptible Flesh: Bodily*

Mutation and Mortification in Religion and Folklore, trans. T. Croft-Murray (Cambridge: Cambridge University Press, 1988); M. Featherstone, 'The body in consumer culture,' *Theory, Culture & Society*, **1** (1982): 18–33.

14. For the link between introspection, empathy, and human change, see R.L. Randall, 'Soteriological dimensions in the work of Heinz Kohut,' *Journal of Religion and Health*, **2** (1980): 83–91. Of interest in regard to the 'bodily' basis of empathy, especially in relation to people born without limbs or who have become paraplegics or quadriplegics, see Gelya Frank, 'Becoming the Other: empathy and biographical interpretation,' *Biography: An Interdisciplinary Quarterly*, **8** (1985): 189–210.

15. Useful studies of 'wisdom' in western and eastern religions respectively are W. Andrew Achenbaum and Lucinda Orwoll, 'Becoming wise: a psycho-gerontological interpretation of the *Book of Job*,' *International Journal of Aging and Human Development*, **1** (1991): 21–39; L. Eugene Thoman, 'Dialogues with three religious renunciates and reflections on wisdom and maturity,' *International Journal of Aging and Human Development*, **3** (1991): 211–27. A general psychological approach that defines wisdom as the 'recognition of and response to human limitation' (p. 1) is Maria A. Taranto, 'Facets of wisdom: a theoretical synthesis,' *International Journal of Aging and Human Development*, **1** (1989): 1–21. Aspects of gender and wisdom are biographically illustrated in Natalie Rosel, 'Clarification and application of Erik Erikson's eighth stage of man,' *International Journal of Aging and Human Development*, **1** (1988): 11–23.

16. Suffering is a readily available idiom of human mortality. It is an experiential point of embarkation to an understanding of systems of soteriology (transformation of the self) evident in the history of religions. See the important comparative work on this in Philip A. Mellor, 'Self and suffering: deconstruction and reflexive definition in Buddhism and Christianity,' *Religious Studies*, **27** (1991): 51–63.

17. For example, the 'monastic community' implies neither a primary nor an exclusive form of religious vocational commitment amongst many Christian groups. That a 'nuptial community' predominates in historical Christianity suggests that gender complementarity, especially the biology inherent in it, forms the basis of a religious vocational commitment that is at least on a par with taking monastic vows. See C. Stevens, 'The trinitarian roots of the nuptial community,' *St. Vladimir's Theological Quarterly*, **4** (1991): 351–8.

18. Homosexuality is a cultural epiphenomenon with a biological appearance. It is not directly engaged in biological reproduction but may, of course, contribute a 'sensuality of care' that supports the rearing of children and, more broadly, constructively contributes to the

future of the species. (The responsible management of HIV infection by means of insisting on 'safe sex' and the compassionate regard and care of AIDS sufferers are examples of this. Not only is this strictly a short-term private matter, but it may also become the basis for long-term political activism and social policy formation.) In effect, the exclusivity evident in gay and lesbian communities must in the end bow to a species-specific awareness of the necessity of inclusivity, or the requirement to pass up self-autonomy and to foster a sensuality of care that favors the future, cultural gender issues notwithstanding. Views contrary to this are put in D. Fernbach, *The Spiral Path: A Gay Contribution to Human Survival* (London: Gay Men's Press, 1981) and H. Hay, 'A separate people whose time is come', in M. Thompson (ed.), *Gay Spirit: Myth and Meaning* (New York: St Martin's Press, 1987), pp. 279–91.

19. Useful contextual material for this consideration is found in J. Kotarba and A. Fontana (eds), *The Existential Self in Society* (Chicago: University of Chicago Press, 1984).

20. See n. 12 above.

21. The linkage between biography, narratology, and morality is clearly made in recent sociological literature. See Anthony Giddens, *Modernity and Self-Identity: Self and Society in the Late Modern Age* (Cambridge: Polity Press, with Basil Blackwell, 1991), pp. 5, 54–5, 57-9, 60, 65–6, 85. See the general introduction to the field in D.E. Polkinghorne, *Narrative Knowing and the Human Sciences* (New York: State University of New York Press, 1988). Also of interest in regard to mortality and narration is A. Kleinman, *The Illness Narratives: Suffering, Healing and the Human Condition* (New York: Basic Books, 1988). General orientation to psychology and life-writing is easily gained from D.P. McAdams, 'Biography, narrative, and lives: an introduction,' *Journal of Personality*, 1 (1988): 1–18. Finally, see the most interesting text, Lucy Bregman and Sara Thiermann, *First Person Mortal: Personal Narratives of Illness, Dying and Grief* (New York: Paragon House, 1995).

22. See n. 14 (above) on Randall, 'Soteriological dimensions in the work of Heinz Kohut.' Also, typologies of the literary genre of biography include those types of life-writing that allow sufficient latitude for this sort of 'vicarious personal development.' See Stephen B. Oates (ed.), *Biography as High Adventure: Life-Writers Speak on Their Art* (Amherst: University of Massachusetts Press, 1986).

23. On the 'morality' encoded in 'speciation' see Erik H. Erikson, 'Reflections on ethics and war,' *Yale Review* (Summer 1984): 481–6; 'Pseudospeciation and the nuclear age,' *Political Psychology*, 6 (2) (1985): 213–17; Stephen Jay Gould, 'A biological comment on Erikson's notion of pseudospeciation,' *Yale Review* (Summer 1984): 487–90.

24. On the one hand, conventional narratologists seek to discover, describe, and explain the mechanics of narrative, or the elements responsible for its form and functioning. This is the view taken by the well-known narratologist G. Prince, in *Narratology: The Form and Functioning of Narrative* (Amsterdam: Mouton Publishers, 1982). On the other hand, others hold that narratology should go beyond studying a mechanical system composed of such elements as the narrator, the narratee, and the narration; its presentation, temporal/spatial relationships, grammar, and the reader. Rather, they believe that narratology is an act of communication. A narrative act of communication occurs, according to one narratologist, 'whenever and only when imparting a transitive view of the world is the effect of the message produced.' This less conventional view is represented by D. Coste, *Narrative as Communication* (Minneapolis: University of Minnesota Press, 1989), and the previous quotation is his (p. 4). Moreover, Coste specifically addresses the narrative nature of hagiography in terms of 'demonstrative didacticism' (pp. 303–4). This accords with the aspect of change ('transitive view') that is evident in what is being suggested about self-consciously appropriating the *bios* by means of identifying with and rehearsing others' life stories as if they were one's own.

25. The relationship of narrative to moral practice is understood to go beyond a simplistic application of moral theory to specific ethical issues and uncertain or ambiguous situations. The 'narrativity' of moral practice is taken up in recent discussions on moral philosophy, and done so in the context of 'saintly lives' made, such as a result of relating to the 'Other,' by Edith Wyschogrod, *Saints and Postmodernism: Revisioning Moral Philosophy* (Chicago and London: University of Chicago Press, 1990), pp. xxii, 10–11, 29, 121, 160, 162. Also, Coste (see n. 24 above) distinguishes 'deliberative' and 'exemplary' didacticism, and these correlate with *graphos* and *bios* as sources of hagiographical ideals of selfhood. Says Coste, 'In deliberative didacticism the addressee is placed in the scope under the umbrella of the rule; in exemplary didacticism, he himself becomes a necessary part of the construction of rule, a *piece of evidence*: imitation itself is proof of the validity of the *imitandum*' (pp. 303–4, his emphasis). For good examples of studies of saints from the world's religions, see Richard Kieckhefer and George D. Bond (eds), *Sainthood: Its Manifestations in World Religions* (Berkeley: University of California Press, 1988).

26. Although considerations of the biology of value have suffered, unfairly or fairly, from their association with what has in the past been called 'sociobiology,' a useful summary worthy of consideration is G.E. Pugh, *The Biological Origin of Human Values* (London and Henley: Routledge & Kegan Paul, 1978).

27. See, for example, Caroline Walker Bynum, *The Resurrection of the Body in Western Christianity, 200–1336* (New York: Columbia University Press, 1995).

28. See Robert F. Murphy, *The Body Silent* (New York: W.W. Norton, 1990). Another recent example along lines similar to Murphy's book is Arthur Frank's *At the Will of the Body* (New York: Houghton Mifflin, 1992). Frank decries any objectifying of critical illness or death that reduces them to mere objects of investigation, management, or control. He invites conversation with one's bodily life, its wonder, pain, and eventual death. A reader becomes engaged in an intimate conversation with the text. At first, the reader of Frank's biographical vignettes experiences vicariously but then existentially the wonder of the human body (whether healthy or ill), in spite of the privacy of pain and grief. Insights do not disintegrate into wooden advice; personal testimony never becomes a recipe for a conquest of death. Struggle becomes worthwhile as an internal recognition of life's tragedy occurs, and tragedy that is taken on board rather than exorcised. The theoretical study by Elaine Scarry, *The Body in Pain: The Making and Unmaking of the World* (New York: Oxford University Press, 1986), is also relevant to these examples of physical deterioration and to the discursive connections between natality, sexuality, and mortality.

29. Murphy, *The Body Silent*, p. 3.

30. *Ibid.*, p. 36.

31. *Ibid.*, p. 38.

32. *Ibid.*, p. 96. Murphy comments insightfully about paralysis and sexuality especially on pp. 95–9. Noteworthy is a French idiomatic expression for sexual intercourse, *petit mort*, or 'little death.' This expression underscores the predominance of the linkage between sexuality and mortality over the connection of sexuality to idioms of natality like personal sexual gratification, relational sensuality, pregnancy, and the birth of children. The existential balance tips in the direction of learning to be still and silent, which are clearly emblematic of human existence in paralysis. These are idioms of dying, of giving way to the next generation.

33. *Ibid.*, p. 221.

34. *Ibid.*

35. Murphy includes in his story references to Samuel Beckett's novel *Murphy* (New York: Grove Press, 1957). The novel is a parable of the human condition and an epitaph for the Irish, in which the protagonist, like Murphy the anthropologist, engages in a search for the self, and for a prolongation and enlargement of life. To accomplish this, his days are spent sitting naked in a rocking chair, where he rocks hard at first but gradually slows down until all movement stops; 'with his body so

negated, his mind can wander free, seeking oneness within himself' (Murphy, p. 228). This occurred continually in the context of his relationship with his lady friend, Celia, a streetwalker by profession, who was anxious that Murphy 'get up and about and doing' (*ibid.*). Thus, the hero of Beckett's novel tried to 'stay the leakage of life' by naked immobility – a paralysis by choice – a technique later used by the soldier in the novel by Joseph Heller, *Catch-22* (London: Corgi Books, 1964), who sat still and naked in darkness as a way of slowing time, and thus prolonging his life, while escaping the carnage of war.

36. John Updike, *Self-Consciousness: Memoirs* (New York: Fawcett Crest, 1989).
37. *Ibid.*, p. 33.
38. *Ibid.*, pp. 33–4.
39. Alice Hamilton and Kenneth Hamilton, *The Elements of John Updike* (Grand Rapids, MI: William B. Eerdmans Publishing Company, 1970), p. 35.
40. Quoted by Jane Howard, 'Can the nice novelist finish first?', *Life* (4 November 1966): 74–82; 80.
41. Suzanne H. Uphaus, *John Updike* (New York: Frederick Ungar Publishing Company, 1980), pp. 5–6.
42. Hamilton and Hamilton, *The Elements of John Updike*, p. 249.
43. John Updike, *The Poorhouse Fair* (New York: Alfred A. Knopf, 1959).
44. Uphaus, *John Updike*, p. 6.
45. See George W. Hunt, *John Updike and the Three Great Secrets: Sex, Religion, and Art* (Grand Rapids, MI: William B. Eerdmans Publishing Company, 1980), pp. 129–30.
46. John Updike, *Bech: A Book* (New York: Alfred A. Knopf, 1970), p. 130.
47. John Updike, *Couples* (New York: Alfred A. Knopf, 1968), p. 336.
48. *Ibid.*, p. 346.
49. Edward Vargo, *Rainstorms and Fire: Ritual in the Novels of John Updike* (Port Washington and London: National University Publishers, Kennikat Press, 1973), p. 139.
50. Updike, *Couples*, p. 428.
51. Updike, *Self-Consciousness: A Memoir*, p. 244.
52. *Ibid.*, p. 261.
53. *Ibid.*, p. 245.
54. Also reflecting Updike's reckoning with human mortality, this time as a cultural question, is his response in a Sydney newspaper to the extraordinary new book on American memorial photography, which highlights society's changing view of death. The book is Stanley B. Burns, *Sleeping Beauty: Memorial Photography in America* (Altadena, CA: Twelvetrees Press, 1992). The book presents more than seventy photographs of the dead or dying from 1842 to 1925, with a few

black-clad live mourners included. Writes Updike, 'the body is person, with a holy value even when animation ceases. This faith, embodied in memorial images, tells us more than we want to know about corporeality and challenges our modern mysticism, the worship of disembodied energy' (John Updike, 'Images in memoriam,' *Good Weekend, Sydney Morning Herald*, 19 September 1992, pp. 56–8).

55. Both Updike's daughter and son married Africans and are now parents of children of mixed race. This outcropping of their father's liberalism is compellingly described by David Updike, 'The colorings of childhood: on the burdens, and privileges, facing my multi-racial son,' *Harper's Magazine* (January, 1992), pp. 63–7.

8   The horror of becoming saints

1. William James, *The Varieties of Religious Experience: A Study in Human Nature*, Introduction by Reinhold Neibuhr (London: Collier-Macmillan, 1961; originally published 1902), p. 264. Hereafter referred to as James, *VRE*.

2. *Ibid.*

3. *Ibid.*

4. On the significance of the body in the study of lives and for life-writing, see Richard A. Hutch, 'Reading lives to live: mortality, introspection, and the soteriological impulse,' *Biography: An Interdisciplinary Quarterly*, **17** (1994): 121–39; and 'Biography as a reliquary,' *Soundings: An Interdisciplinary Journal*, **76** (1993): 467–85.

5. Ralph Barton Perry, *The Thought and Character of William James: Briefer Version* (New York: George Braziller, 1954), p. 361.

6. Gay Wilson Allen, *William James: A Biography* (New York: Viking Press, 1967), p. 360.

7. *Ibid.*, p. 161.

8. See *Holographs* in the James Papers, Houghton Library, Harvard University.

9. Leon Edel, *Stuff of Sleep and Dreams: Experiments in Literary Psychology* (London: Chatto & Windus, 1982), p. 301.

10. Letter of 6 January 1883; quoted in Perry, *The Thought and Character of William James*, p. 253.

11. *Ibid.*, pp. 253–4.

12. Allen, *William James*, p. 406.

13. Letter of 14 November 1899; quoted in Allen, p. 406.

14. For this popular line of thought, see Cushing Strout, 'The pluralistic identity of William James: a psychohistorical reading of *The Varieties of Religious Experience*,' *American Quarterly*, **23** (1971): 135–52.

15. Mark Johnson, 'Conceptual metaphor and embodied structures of

meaning: a reply to Kennedy and Vervace,' *Philosophical Psychology*, **6** (1993): 413–22, 413; and 'Knowing through the body,' *Philosophical Psychology*, **4** (1991): 13–18. James's description of the famous 'panic fear' vision is found in James, *VRE*, pp. 138–9.

16. See Strout on this in particular.
17. John J. McDermott (ed.), *The Writings of William James: A Comprehensive Edition* (New York: Random House, 1967), pp. 3, 6–8.
18. Allen, *William James*, pp. 165–6.
19. James, *VRE*, p. 220.
20. *Ibid.*, p. 256.
21. *Ibid.*, pp. 116–17.
22. *Ibid.*, p. 119.
23. See Fyodor Vasilyuk, *The Psychology of Experiencing* (New York: New York University Press, 1992).
24. Perry, *The Thought and Character of William James*, p. 359.
25. James, *VRE*, p. 288.
26. *Ibid.*
27. *Ibid.*, p. 119.
28. Ross Aden, 'Justification and sanctification: a conversation between Lutheranism and orthodoxy,' *St. Vladimir's Theological Quarterly*, **38** (1994): 87–109, 92–6.
29. Edith Wyschogrod, *Saints and Postmodernism: Revisioning Moral Philosophy* (Chicago: University of Chicago Press, 1990), p. 17; Maurice Merleau-Ponty, *Phenomenology of Perception*, trans. Colin Smith (London: Routledge & Kegan Paul, 1962).
30. William James, *Essays in Radical Empiricism* (Cambridge, MA: Harvard University Press, 1976), p. 86.
31. Wyschogrod, *Saints and Postmodernism*, p. 17.
32. *Ibid.*, pp. 18–19. See also P. Falk, 'Corporeality and its fates in history,' *Acta Sociologica*, **28** (1985): 115–36; M. Feher, R. Naddaff, and N. Tazi (eds), *Fragments for a History of the Human Body* (New York: Zone, 1990); Johnson, 'Knowing through the body'; L.E. Sullivan, 'Body works: knowledge of the body in the study of religion,' *History of Religions*, **30** (1990): 86–99.
33. James, *VRE*, p. 200.
34. Henry James, Jr (ed.), *The Letters of William James*, 2 vols (Boston: Atlantic Monthly Press; London: Longmans, Green & Co., 1920), I, p. 220.
35. See Lawrence Cunningham, *The Meaning of Saints* (New York: Harper and Row, 1980); Richard Kieckhefer and George Bond (eds), *Sainthood: Its Manifestations in World Religions* (Berkeley and London: University of California Press, 1988).

36. Benjamin Franklin, *The Autobiography of Benjamin Franklin* (New York: Washington Square Press, 1940), pp. 103–6.
37. James Dittes, 'Beyond William James,' in *Beyond the Classics?: Essays in the Scientific Study of Religion*, ed. Charles Y. Glock and Phillip E. Hammond (New York and London: Harper and Row, Publishers, 1973), p. 310.
38. J. Kotarba and A. Fontana (eds), *The Existential Self in Society* (Chicago: University of Chicago Press, 1984).
39. James, *VRE*, p. 221.
40. *Ibid.*, p. 220.
41. *Ibid.*, p. 221.
42. *Ibid.*
43. *Ibid.*
44. *Ibid.*, p. 256.
45. *Ibid.*, p. 42.
46. *Ibid.*, p. 221.
47. *Ibid.*
48. *Ibid.*
49. *Ibid.*
50. Dittes, 'Beyond William James,' p. 310.
51. William James, *The Principles of Psychology*, 2 vols (London: Macmillan & Co., 1890), vol. I, p. 315.
52. *Ibid.*, p. 316.
53. Ernest Jones, *The Life and Works of Sigmund Freud*, edited and abridged by Lionel Trilling and Steven Marmo, with an introduction by Lionel Trilling (New York: Basic Books, 1961), pp. 267–8. From the authorized translation by James Strachey of Freud's *An Autobiographical Study* (2nd edn) (London: Hogarth Press, 1946).
54. Quoted in Perry, *The Thought and Character of William James*, p. 360.
55. James, *VRE*, p. 81.
56. Wyschogrod, *Saints and Postmodernism*, p. xiv.
57. James, *VRE*, p. 138.
58. *Ibid.*, pp. 138–9.
59. *Ibid.*, p. 139.
60. *Ibid.*, p. 141.
61. Mircea Eliade, *Patterns in Comparative Religion*, trans. Rosemary Sheed (London: Sheed & Ward, 1958); David Cave, *Mircea Eliade's Vision for a New Humanism* (Oxford: Oxford University Press, 1993).
62. James, *VRE*, p. 264.
63. *Ibid.*
64. Letter to F.C.S. Schiller, 8 April 1903; quoted in Allen, *William James*, p. 436.
65. Letter to H. Bergson, 14 December 1902; quoted in Allen, p. 435.

66. Letter to Mrs. H. Whitman, 2 August 1903; quoted in Allen, p. 437.
67. Letter to Carl Stumpf, 17 July 1904; quoted in Perry, *The Thought and Character of William James*, p. 268.
68. Henry James, *The Notebooks of Henry James*, ed. F.O. Mathiessen and K.B. Murdock (New York: Oxford University Press, 1947), p. 321.
69. James, *VRE*, pp. 136–7, and p. 138, fn. 18.
70. *Ibid.*, pp. 146–7; see fn. 6, citation about the research of Louis Gourdon on Augustine's 'premature' account of conversion.
71. Ralph Waldo Emerson, 'Self-reliance,' in *The Selected Writings of Ralph Waldo Emerson*, ed. B. Atkinson (New York: The Modern Library, 1964), p. 165.
72. James, *VRE*, pp. 140–1.
73. Emile Durkheim, *The Elementary Forms of the Religious Life*, trans. Joseph Ward Swain (London: George Allen & Unwin, Ltd., 1915); Marcel Mauss, *The Gift: Forms and Functions of Exchange in Archaic Societies*, trans. Ian Cunnison (New York and London: W.W. Norton, 1967).
74. Mauss, *The Gift*, p. 69.
75. Georges Bataille, *Théorie de le Religion* (Paris: Gallimard, 1973), p. 23.
76. *Ibid.*, p. 23, author's emphasis.
77. See Philip A. Mellor, 'Self and suffering: deconstruction and reflexive definition in Buddhism and Christianity,' *Religious Studies*, **27** (1991): 51–63.
78. Suffering is a readily available idiom of human mortality. It is an experiential point of embarkation to understanding systems of soteriology (transformation of the self) evident in the history of religions.
79. See Georges Bataille, *The Story of the Eye* (Paris: Gallimard, 1928); *Théorie de le Religion* (Paris: Gallimard, 1973); *Visions of Excess: Selected Writings, 1927–1939*, Theory and History of Literature, Vol. 14, ed. and trans. Allan Stoekl (Minneapolis: University of Minnesota Press, 1985). For commentary on Bataille's work, see Alexander Irwin, 'Ecstacy, sacrifice, communication: Bataille on religion and inner experience,' *Soundings: An Interdisciplinary Journal*, **76** (1993): 105–28; Alexander Nehamas, 'The attraction of repulsion: the deep and ugly thought of Georges Bataille,' *The New Republic* (23 October 1989): 31–6.
80. For example, the 'monastic community' implies neither a primary nor an exclusive form of religious vocational commitment amongst many Christian groups. That a 'nuptial community' predominates in historical Christianity suggests that gender complementarity, especially the biology inherent in it, forms the basis of a religious vocational commitment that is at least on a par with taking monastic vows. See C. Stevens, 'The Trinitarian roots of the nuptial community,' *St. Vladimir's Theological Quarterly*, **4** (1991): 351–8.
81. James, *VRE*, p. 57.

82. *Ibid.*
83. *Ibid.*, author's emphasis.
84. *Ibid.*, pp. 141–2.
85. There are instructive case studies of how exemplary individuals comply with the 'god of destruction' and begin to engender 'saintliness': Samuel Beckett, *Murphy* (New York: Grove Press, 1957); Georges Bernanos, *The Diary of a Country Priest*, trans. Pamela Morris (New York: The Macmillan Co., 1937); Arthur Frank, *At the Will of the Body* (New York: Houghton Mifflin, 1992); Joseph Heller, *Catch-22* (London: Corgi Books, 1964); Brian Keenan, *An Evil Cradling* (London: Hutchinson, 1993); Paul Monette, *Borrowed Time: An AIDS Memoir* (New York: Avon, 1988); Robert Murphy, *The Body Silent* (New York: W.W. Norton, 1990); Elaine Scarry, *The Body in Pain: The Making and Unmaking of the World* (New York: Oxford University Press, 1985); John Updike, *Self-Consciousness: Memoirs* (New York: Fawcett Crest, 1989). The cases of Murphy and Updike were taken up in Chapter 7, and that of Keenan contributes most to Chapter 9.

9 Magical deification of a convulsing body

1. Peter Donovan, 'Maori rituals add magic to contemporary civic life,' *British Association for the Study of Religions*, Occasional Papers, **10** (1994): 11.
2. See in general Mary Douglas, *Purity and Danger* (London: Routledge & Kegan Paul, 1966), pp. 69–71.
3. Daniel O'Keefe, *Stolen Lightning: The Social Theory of Magic* (Oxford: Martin Robertson, 1982), p. 100.
4. Other sources for contemporary discussions of magic and the associated 'crisis' psychology of narcissistic self-inflation are Fritz Staal, *Rules without Meaning: Rituals, Mantras and the Human Sciences*, Toronto Studies in Religion Series, **4** (New York: Peter Lang Publishers, Inc., 1989); Stanley Tambiah, 'A performative approach to ritual,' *Proceedings of the British Academy*, **65** (1979) (Oxford: Oxford University Press, 1981), p. 129.
5. See, Richard A. Hutch, 'Reading lives to live: mortality, introspection, and the soteriological impulse,' *Biography: An Interdisciplinary Quarterly*, **17** (2) (Spring 1994), 125–43; and 'Biography as a reliquary,' *Soundings: An Interdisciplinary Journal*, **76** (4) (Winter 1993), 467–85.
6. See Meredith McGuire, 'Religion and the body: rematerializing the human body in the social sciences,' *Journal for the Scientific Study of Religion*, **29** (1990): 283–96; Lawrence E. Sullivan, 'Bodyworks: knowledge of the body in the study of religion,' *History of Religions*, **30** (1990): 86–99.

7. For an understanding of Bataille's thought, a number of secondary sources are useful. An article that investigates the writings of Bataille which relate to spiritual and religious matters is Alexander C. Irwin, 'Ecstasy, sacrifice, communication: Bataille on religion and inner experience,' *Soundings: An Interdisciplinary Journal*, **76** (1) (1993): 105–28. An easily read exploration of Bataille on inner experience is presented by Steven Shaviro, *Passion and Excess: Blanchot, Bataille, and Literary Theory* (Tallahassee, FL: Florida State University Press, 1990), Chapter 4. A treatment that partly aims at specifying Bataille's contribution to postmodernism, and one that provides a summary of Bataille's conceptualization concerning the body, is Julian Pefanis, *Heterology and the Postmodern: Bataille, Baudrillard, and Lyotard* (Durham, NC, and London: Duke University Press, 1991). For a selection of Bataille's most important writings, see Georges Bataille, *Visions of Excess: Selected Writings, 1927–1939, Theory and History of Literature*, Vol. 14, trans. and ed. Allan Stoekl (Minneapolis: University of Minnesota Press, 1985); and, more to the point, Georges Bataille, *Eroticism, Death and Sensuality* (San Francisco: City Lights Books, 1957, 1962, 1986).

8. Shaviro, *Passion and Excess*, p. 85.

9. *Ibid.*, p. 87.

10. Irwin, 'Ecstasy, sacrifice, communication,' p. 108.

11. *Ibid.*, p. 110.

12. Quoted in R.V. Norman, 'Where's Salman?', *Soundings: An Interdisciplinary Journal*, **76** (1) (1993): 1–16, 5. Norman's article provides a brief overview of Irwin's assessment of Bataille.

13. Pefanis, *Heterology and the Postmodern*, p. 49.

14. Irwin, 'Ecstasy, sacrifice, communication,' p. 112.

15. Pefanis, *Heterology and the Postmodern*, pp. 46-7.

16. Carolyn J. Dean, *The Self and Its Pleasures: Bataille, Lacan, and the History of the Decentred Subject* (Ithaca, NY: Cornell University Press, 1992), p. 244.

17. See Mark Johnson and George Lakoff, *Metaphors We Live By* (Chicago: University of Chicago Press, 1980); Mark Johnson, *The Body in the Mind: The Bodily Basis of Meaning, Imagination, and Reason* (Chicago and London: University of Chicago Press, 1987); Mark Johnson, *Moral Imagination: Implications of Cognitive Science for Ethics* (Chicago: University of Chicago Press, 1993).

18. Brian Keenan, *An Evil Cradling* (London: Hutchinson, 1993), p. 1. A case that parallels Keenan's in its emphasis on the body as a locus of meaning in the face of life-threatening circumstances (in her case, being hit by lightning), and how spiritual empowerment is achieved as one finally faces oneself as a changed person, is Gretel Ehrlich, *A Match to the Heart* (London: Fourth Estate, 1995).

19. Keenan, *An Evil Cradling*, p. xi.
20. *Ibid.*, p. 2.
21. *Ibid.*, p. 11.
22. *Ibid.*
23. *Ibid.*
24. *Ibid.*, p. 9.
25. *Ibid.*, p. 10.
26. *Ibid.*, p. 30.
27. *Ibid.*, p. 35.
28. *Ibid.*, p. 36.
29. *Ibid.*, p. 43.
30. *Ibid.*, pp. 44–5.
31. See Anthony Giddens, *Modernity and Self-Identity: Self and Society in the Late Modern Age* (Stanford, CA: Stanford University Press, 1991), pp. 57–8. Following Goffman, Giddens notes that bodily control is crucial to being seen in the eyes of others as a 'competent agent' in daily activities.
32. Keenan, *An Evil Cradling*, p. 55.
33. *Ibid.*
34. *Ibid.*, p. 57.
35. *Ibid.*
36. *Ibid.*, p. 58.
37. *Ibid.*, p. 62.
38. *Ibid.*, p. 63.
39. *Ibid.*, p. 64.
40. *Ibid.*, p. 65.
41. *Ibid.*, pp. 66–7.
42. Pefanis, *Heterology and the Postmodern*, p. 44.
43. See Georges Bataille, 'The college of sociology,' in Georges Bataille, *Vision of Excess: Selected Writings, 1927–1939*.
44. See Marcel Mauss, *The Gift* (New York and London: W.W. Norton, 1967).
45. Bataille, *Vision of Excess*, p. 250.
46. Keenan, *An Evil Cradling*, p. 69.
47. *Ibid.*
48. *Ibid.*, p. 70.
49. *Ibid.*, p. 99.
50. *Ibid.*, p. 93.
51. *Ibid.*, p. xiii.
52. Elaine Scarry, *The Body in Pain: The Making and Unmaking of the World* (New York and Oxford: Oxford University Press, 1985), p. 35.
53. Quoted in Pasi Falk, 'Corporeality and its fates in history,' *Acta Sociologica*, **28** (2) (1985): 115–36, 130.

54. Keenan, *An Evil Cradling*, p. 1.

55. *Ibid.*, p. xi.

56. See Philip A. Mellor and Chris Shilling, 'Reflexive modernity and the religious body,' *Religion*, **24** (1994): 23–42; 'Modernity, self-identity and the sequestration of death,' *Sociology*, **27** (3) (1993): 411–31; Chris Shilling, *The Body and Social Theory* (London: Sage/Theory, Culture and Society, 1993).

10   A foretaste of the world to come

1. For example, the mortality in the United States, like Australia, has decreased in recent years. The overall death rate has decreased by about 8 percent in the most recent seven-year period available for analysis. See E. Gee, 'Mortality rate,' in Robert Kastenbaum and B. Kastenbaum (eds), *Encyclopedia of Death* (Phoenix: The Oryx Press, 1989), pp. 183–5.

2. See Gerald C. Hyner and Christopher L. Melby, *Priorities for Health Promotion and Disease Prevention* (Dubuque, IA: Eddie Bowers, 1987).

3. A critique of contemporary culture in the West in which such a social psychology of amnesia is a chronic problem is Russell Jacoby, *Social Amnesia: A Critique of Conformist Psychology from Adler to Laing* (Boston: Beacon Press, 1975). What is interesting is that the book is introduced by Christopher Lasch, whose book, *The Culture of Narcissism: American Life in An Age of Diminishing Expectations* (New York: W.W. Norton, 1979), carried forward Jacoby's argument and focused it on the psychology of the self, and the self's persistence, as the major problematic of our times, one that is based on the psychology of narcissism which itself implies an illusion of human 'immortality.'

4. On the history of Western attitudes toward death and their lessening links to the body, see Philippe Ariès, *Western Attitudes Toward Death, from the Middle Ages to the Present*, trans. Patricia M. Ranum (Baltimore and London: The Johns Hopkins University Press, 1974).

5. The Australian community suddenly realized this in the aftermath of the murders of thirty-five innocent tourists and bystanders by a gunman on Sunday, 28 April 1996, at the Port Arthur Historical Site in the State of Tasmania. One is naturally shocked by such a tragedy. However, reflecting on the event one could well wonder, 'Why were the victims unprepared to die that day?' Or, more to the point, 'Why did the public assume such "innocence" that the massacre was thought to be "unthinkable" in Australia?' In spite of the horror of the day and the wave of public sentiment elicited since, the entire occasion serves to raise the issue of how to engender responsibility to live today as if it

were our last. Moral responsibility for living can be highlighted by such occasions.

6. 'Embodied living,' or life (*bios*) and the story of a life (*graphos*) joined together, is elaborated in Richard A. Hutch, 'Biography as a reliquary,' *Soundings: An Interdisciplinary Journal*, **76** (4) (1993): 467–85. The argument of the article is that bodily continuity after a person's death is sustained by biographical accounts of his or her life, which themselves are taken as intimations of bodily resurrection on the basis of a necessary sexual appreciation of the embodied, ethological turnover of human generations. On the 'spiritual operation' of life simulation, see Paul Murray Kendall, *The Art of Biography* (New York: W.W. Norton, 1985), pp. 147–8.

7. On how flesh may be potent with 'resurrection,' see the insightful, though perhaps neglected work of Norman O. Brown, *Life Against Death: The Psychoanalytical Meaning of History* (Middletown, CT: Wesleyan University Press, 1959; by arrangement with New York: Vintage/Random House Inc., 1959). The chapter 'The resurrection of the body' (pp. 307–22) is specifically to the point.

8. On the Eastern Orthodox emphasis, see Father Kallistos Ware, *The Orthodox Way* (Crestwood, NY: St Vladimir's Seminary Press, 1979), p. 28. The spirit of such an emphasis is articulated throughout Alexander Schmemman's *For the Life of the World: Sacraments and Orthodoxy* (Crestwood, NY: St Vladimir's Seminary Press, 1973).

9. An audacious, if not outrageous, argument for the end of the universe, that is, the end of time, that incorporates the reconstruction of every person who has ever lived, along with every person who might ever have lived, based on sound principles of physics, is put by Frank Tippler, *The Physics of Immortality: Modern Cosmology, God, and the Resurrection of the Dead* (New York: Doubleday, 1994).

10. See Caroline Walker Bynum, *The Resurrection of the Body in Western Christianity, 200–1336* (New York: Columbia University Press, 1995).

11. Anthony Giddens, *Modernity and Self-Identity: Self and Society in the Late Modern Age* (Stanford, CA: Stanford University Press, 1991), p. 54.

12. This is pointed out in Lawrence E. Sullivan, 'Bodyworks: knowledge of the body in the study of religion,' *History of Religions*, **30** (1990): 86–99. I am grateful to Sullivan for putting me on to the intriguing work of Piero Camporesi.

13. Piero Camporesi, *The Incorruptible Flesh: Bodily Mutation and Mortification in Religion and Folklore*, trans. Tania Croft-Murray and Jelen Elsom (Cambridge and New York: Cambridge University Press, 1988), p. 269.

14. *Ibid.*, p. 186.

15. *Ibid.*, p. 155.

16. *Ibid.*, p. 3.
17. Valuable for the way it scours such sources is Aline Rousselle, *Porneia: On Desire and the Body in Antiquity*, trans. Felicia Pheasant (New York: Basil Blackwell, 1988), which is an important complement to Peter Brown, *The Body and Society: Men, Women, and Sexual Renunciation in Early Christianity* (New York: Columbia University Press, 1988).
18. Camporesi, *The Incorruptible Flesh*, p. 251.
19. *Ibid.*
20. *Ibid.*, p. 275.
21. *Ibid.*, quoting Tommaso Campanella without citing the work quoted.
22. *Ibid.*
23. *Ibid.*
24. Implied in addressing 'mythic reverie' as undergirding all thought is the exemplary methodological bulwark articulated by Gaston Bachelard, *The Poetics of Reverie: Childhood, Language, and the Cosmos*, trans. Daniel Russell (Paris: Presses Universitaires de France, 1960; Boston: Beacon Press, 1971). A specific study of the mythic reverie beneath human imagination is Gaston Bachelard, *The Psychoanalysis of Fire*, trans. Alan C.M. Ross (Paris: Librairie Gallimard, 1938; Boston: Beacon, 1964).

Select bibliography

Aaron, Daniel (ed.). *Studies in Biography*. Harvard English Series 8. Cambridge, MA: Harvard University Press, 1978.

Abel, Theodore. 'The operation called Verstehen.' *American Journal of Sociology*, **54** (1948): 211–18.

Adams, W.H. Davenport. *Wrecked Lives; or, Men Who Have Failed*. Second Series. London: Society for Promoting Christian Knowledge, 1880.

Allen, Gay Wilson. *Waldo Emerson: A Biography*. New York: Viking Press, 1981.

Allen, Gay Wilson. *William James: A Biography*. New York: Viking Press, 1967.

Allport, Gordon. *The Individual and His Religion*. New York: Macmillan, 1950.

Alter, Robert. *Motives for Fiction*. Cambridge, MA: Harvard University Press, 1984.

Altick, Richard D. *Lives and Letters: A History of Literary Biography in England and America* (1st edn). New York: Alfred Knopf, 1965.

Anderson, Graham. *Philostratus: Biography and Belles Lettres in the Third Century A.D.* London and Dover, NH: Croom Helm, 1986.

Anderson, James W. 'The methodology of psychological biography,' *Journal of Interdisciplinary History*, **11** (3) (Winter 1981): 455–75.

Anderson, James W. 'Psychobiographical methodology: the case of William James,' in L. Wheeler (ed.), *Review of Personality and Social Psychology*, Vol. 2. Beverly Hills, CA: Sage, 1981.

Apel, Karl-Otto. *Archiv für Begriffsgeschichte*, **1** (1955): 142–99.

Arendt, Hannah. *Men in Dark Times* (1st edn). New York: Harcourt, Brace & World, 1968.

Ariès, Philippe. *Western Attitudes Toward Death, from the Middle Ages to the Present*, trans. Patricia M. Ranum. Baltimore and London: The Johns Hopkins University Press, 1974.

Arnheim, Rudolph. *Art and Visual Perception*. Berkeley: University of California Press, 1971.

Arnheim, Rudolph. 'Psychological notes on the poetical process,' in *Poets at Work*, Introduction by Charles D. Abbott. New York: Harcourt, Brace & World, 1948, pp. 123–62.

Arnheim, Rudolph. *Visual Thinking*. Berkeley: University of California Press, 1969.

Arzt, Donna. 'Psychohistory and its discontents,' *Biography: An Interdisciplinary Quarterly*, **1** (3) (1978): 1–36.

Asch, Solomon E. 'Gestalt theory,' in David L. Sills (ed.), *International Encyclopedia of the Social Sciences*, Vol. 6. New York: Macmillan/The Free Press, 1968, pp. 158–75.

Atlas, James. 'Literary biography,' *American Scholar*, **46** (Summer 1976): 448–60.

Bachelard, Gaston. *The Poetics of Reverie: Childhood, Language, and the Cosmos*, trans. Daniel Russell. Paris: Presses Universitaires de France, 1960; Boston: Beacon Press, 1971.

Bainton, Roland. 'Psychiatry and history: an examination of Erikson's *Young Man Luther*,' *Religion and Life* (Winter 1971): 450–78.

Baker, Carlos. 'From Genesis to revelation,' *Virginia Quarterly Review*, **50** (Summer 1974): 438–40.

Barbato, Joseph. 'Author of a new life of Martin Luther King sounds the trumpet for narrative history.' *Chronicle of Higher Education*, 3 November 1982: 23, 25.

Barbu, Zevedei. *Problems of Historical Psychology*. New York: Grove Press, 1960.

Barish, Evelyn. *Emerson: The Roots of Prophecy*. Princeton: Princeton University Press, 1989.

Baron, Samuel H. and Pletsch, Carl (eds). *Introspection in Biography: The Biographer's Quest for Self-Awareness*. Hillsdale, NJ: Analytic Press; distributed solely by Lawrence Erlbaum Associates, 1985.

Barthes, Roland. *S/A*, trans. Richard Miller. New York: Hill & Wang, 1974.

Barzun, Jacques. 'Biography and criticism – a misalliance disputed', *Critical Inquiry*, **1** (March 1975): 479–96.

Barzun, Jacques. 'History: her muse and her doctors,' *Journal of History*, **77** (1972): 36–64.

Bataille, Georges. *Eroticism, Death and Sensuality*. San Francisco: City Lights Books, 1957, 1962, 1986.

Bataille, Georges. *Théorie de Religion*. Paris: Gallimard, 1973.

Bataille, Georges. *Visions of Excess: Selected Writings, 1927–1939*. Theory and History of Literature, Vol. 14, ed. Allan Stoekl. Minneapolis: University of Minnesota Press, 1985.

Batson, C. Daniel, Schoenrade, Patricia, and Ventis, W. Larry. *Religion and the Individual: A Social-Psychological Perspective*. New York and Oxford: Oxford University Press, 1993.

Bennett, E.A. *C.G. Jung*. London: Barrie & Rockliff, 1961.

Bergan, Helen. *Where the Money Is: A Fund Raiser's Guide to the Rich*. Alexandria, VA: BioGuide Press, 1985.

Berger, Peter and Luckmann, Thomas. *The Social Construction of Reality*. New York: Anchor Books, 1966.

Berry, Thomas E. (ed.). *The Biographer's Craft*. New York: Odyssey Press, 1967.

Bertaux, Daniel (ed.). *Biography and Society: The Life History Approach in the Social Sciences*. Beverly Hills, CA: Sage Publications, 1981.

Bettelheim, Bruno. *Freud and Man's Soul*. London: Fontana/Flamingo, 1985; first published 1982.

Black, Max. *Models and Metaphors*. Ithaca, NY: Cornell University Press, 1962.

Bloch, Mare. *The Historian's Craft*, trans. Peter Putnam. New York: Princeton University Press, 1953.

Bloom, Harold *Agon: Towards a Theory of Revisionism*. Oxford: Oxford University Press, 1982.

Bloom, Harold (ed.). *Deconstruction and Criticism*. New York: Seabury Press, 1979.

Booth, Wayne. *A Rhetoric of Irony*. Chicago: University of Chicago Press, 1974.

Boswell, James. *Life of Johnson*, ed. George Birkbeck Hill and revised L.F. Powell, Vols I–VI. Oxford: The Clarendon Press, 1934–50.

Bouson, J. Brooks. *The Empathic Reader: A Study of the Narcissistic Character and the Drama of the Self*. Amherst: University of Massachusetts Press, 1989.

Bowen, Catherine Drinker. *Adventures of a Biographer* (1st edn). Boston: Little, Brown, 1959.

Bowen, Catherine Drinker. *Biography: The Craft and the Calling*. Boston: Little, Brown, 1969.

Bowker (R.R.) Company, New York. *Biographical Books, 1876–1949: Vocation Index, Name/Subject Index, Author Index, Title Index*. New York: R.R. Bowker Co., 1983.

Bowker (R.R.) Company, New York. *Biographical Books, 1950–1980*. New York: R.R. Bowker Co., 1980.

Bradford, Gamaliel. *A Naturalist of Souls*. New York: Dodd, Mead & Co, 1917.

Bradford, Gamaliel. *American Portraits*. Boston: Houghton Mifflin, 1922.

Bradford, Gamaliel. *Biography and the Human Heart*. Boston: Houghton Mifflin, 1932.

Bradford, Gamaliel. *The Journal of Gamaliel Bradford, 1883–1932*, ed. Van Wyck Brooks. Boston: Houghton Mifflin, 1933.

Bradford, Gamaliel. *Types of American Character*. New York: Macmillan, 1895.

Bregman, Lucy and Thiermann, Sara. *First Person Mortal: Personal Narratives of Illness, Dying and Grief*. New York: Paragon House, 1995.

Britt, Albert. *The Great Biographers*. Freeport, NY: Books for Libraries Press, 1969.

Brome, Vincent. *Jung: Man and Myth*. New York: Atheneum, 1981.

Bromwich, David. 'The uses of biography,' *The Yale Review*, **73** (2) (1984): 161–76.

Brown, Norman O. *Life Against Death: The Psychoanalytic Meaning of History*. Middletown, CT: Wesleyan University Press, 1959; by arrangement with New York: Vintage/Random House Inc., 1959.

Brown, Peter. *The Body and Society: Men, Women, and Sexual Renunciation in Early Christianity*. New York: Columbia University Press, 1988.

Brown, Peter. *The Cult of the Saints: Its Rise and Function in Latin Christianity*. Chicago: University of Chicago Press, 1981.

Brown, Peter. 'The rise and function of the holy man in late antiquity,' *Journal of Roman Studies*, **61** (1971): 81–101.

Brown, Peter. 'The saint as exemplar in late antiquity,' *Representations*, **1** (1983): 1–25.

Buber, Martin. *I and Thou*. Edinburgh: T. & T. Clark, 1970.

Buckle, Henry T. *History of Civilization in England*. London, 1891.

Bugental, James F.T. *The Art of the Psychotherapist*. New York: W.W. Norton, 1987.

Bunyan, John. *Grace Abounding to the Chief of Sinners*, ed. James Thorpe. Boston: Houghton Mifflin, 1969.

Burns, Stanley B. *Sleeping Beauty: Memorial Photography in America*. Altadena, CA: Twelvetrees Press, 1992.

Bushman, Richard L. 'On the uses of psychology: conflict and conciliation in Benjamin Franklin,' *History and Theory*, **5** (3) (1966): 225–40.

Bynum, Caroline Walker. *The Resurrection of the Body in Western Christianity, 200–1336*. New York: Columbia University Press, 1995.

Camporesi, Piero. *The Incorruptible Flesh: Bodily Mutation and Mortification in Religion and Folklore*, trans. Tania Croft-Murray and Jelen Elsom. Cambridge and New York: Cambridge University Press, 1988.

Capps, Donald E. 'Erikson's life-cycle theory: religious dimensions,' *Religious Studies Review*, **10** (2) (April 1984): 120–7.

Capps, Donald E. 'Psychohistory and historical genres: the plight and promise of Eriksonian biography,' in Peter Homans (ed.), *Childhood and Selfhood: Essays on Tradition, Religion and Modernity in the Psychology of Erik H. Erikson*. Lewisburg, PA: Bucknell University Press; London: Associated University Presses, 1978, pp. 189–228.

Capps, Donald E. 'Some interpretive uses of psych-history,' *Criterion* (Autumn 1969): 3–4.

Capps, Donald E., Capps, Walter and Bradford, M. Gerald (eds). *Encounter with Erikson: Historical Interpretation and Religious Biography*. Missoula, MT: Scholars Press, 1977.

Capps, Walter and Capps, Donald E. *The Religious Personality*. Belmont, CA: Wadsworth, 1970.

Cave, David. *Mircea Eliade's Vision for a New Humanism*. Oxford: Oxford University Press, 1993.

Chapman, Hester W. 'Notes on historical biography,' *Times Literary Supplement* (8 August 1959).

Charmley, John and Homberger, Eric (eds). *The Troubled Face of Biography*. New York: St. Martin's Press, 1988.

Chevigny, Bell Gale. *Twentieth Century Interpretations of Endgame: A Collection of Critical Essays*. Englewood Cliffs, NJ: Prentice-Hall, 1969.

Chicorel, Marietta (ed.). *Chicorel Index to Biographies* (1st edn). New York: Chicorel Library Pub. Corp., 1974.

Chomsky, Noam. *Language and Mind*. New York: Harcourt, Brace & World, 1968.

Christ, Carol P. *Diving Deep and Surfacing: Women Writers on Spiritual Quest* (2nd edn). Boston: Beacon, 1986.

Cimbala, Diane J., Cargill, J., and Alley, Brian. *Biographical Sources: A Guide to Dictionaries and Reference Works*. Phoenix, AZ: Oryx Press, 1986.

Clanchy, M.T. *From Memory to Written Record* (2nd edn). Oxford: Blackwell, 1993.

Clifford, James Lowry. *Biography as an Art: Selected Criticism, 1560–1960*. New York: Oxford University Press, 1962.

Clifford, James Lowry. *From Puzzles to Portraits: Problems of a Literary Biographer*. Chapel Hill: University of North Carolina Press, 1970.

Cockshut, A.O.J. *Truth to Life: The Art of Biography in the Nineteenth Century*. London: Collins, 1974.

Cohler, B.J. 'Persona narrative and life-course,' in P. Baltes and O.G. Brim, Jr (eds), *Life-Span Development and Behavior*, Vol. 4. New York: Academic Press, 1982.

Cole, John Y. (ed.). *Biography and Books*. Washington: Library of Congress, 1986.

Coles, Robert. *Erik H. Erikson: The Growth of His Work*. Boston: Little, Brown & Co., 1970.

Cowper, William. 'Memoir of the early life of William Cowper,' ed. Maurice J. Quinlan, *Proceedings of the American Philosophical Society*, **97** (4) (1953): 366–82.

Cox, Patricia. *Biography in Late Antiquity: A Quest for the Holy Man*. Berkeley: University of California Press, 1983.

Craven, Paul R. *Biography*. Belmont, CA: Dickenson Pub. Co., 1968.

Cross, Wilbur. *An Outline of Biography: From Plutarch to Strachey*. New York: H. Holt & Co., 1924.

Culler, Jonathan. *On Deconstruction: Theory and Criticism after Structuralism*. Ithaca, NY: Cornell University Press, 1982.

Cunningham, Lawrence. *The Meaning of Saints*. New York: Harper & Row, 1980.

Davenport, William H. and Seigel, Ben (eds). *Biography Past and Present: Selections and Critical Essays*. New York: Scribner, 1965.

Denzin, Norman K. *Interpretive Biography*. Newbury Park, CA: Sage, 1989.

Dilthey, Wilhelm. *The Essence of Philosophy*, trans. Stephen A. and William T. Emery. Chapel Hill: University of North Carolina Press, 1954.

Dilthey, Wilhelm. *Introduction to the Human Sciences: An Attempt to Lay a Foundation for the Study of Society and History*, trans. Ramon J. Betanzos. London: Harvester Wheatsheaf, 1988.

Dilthey, Wilhelm. *Pattern and Meaning in History*, ed. H.P. Rickman. New York: Harper & Row, 1961.

Dodds, E.R. *Pagan and Christian in an Age of Anxiety*. New York: W.W. Norton, 1965.

Donaldson, Norman and Donaldson, Betty. *How Did They Die?* New York: St Martin's Press, 1980.

Donn, Linda. *Freud and Jung: Years of Friendship, Years of Loss*. New York: Charles Scribner's, 1988.

Douglas, Mary. 'Judgments on James Frazer,' *Daedalus*, **4** (1978): 151–64.

Dunaway, Philip (ed.). *Turning Point: Fateful Moments that Revealed Men and Made History*. New York: Random House, 1958.

Durling, Dwight L. and Watt, William (eds). *Biography: Varieties and Parallels*. New York: The Dryden Press, 1941.

Eakin, John Paul. *Fictions in Autobiography: Studies in the Art of Self-Invention*. Princeton: Princeton University Press, 1985.

Edel, Leon. 'Biographer and subject: Lytton Strachey and Van Wyck Brooks,' in *Prose Studies*. Special Issue on Biography, 1983.

Edel, Leon. 'Biography: a manifesto,' *Biography: An Interdisciplinary Quarterly*, **1** (Winter 1978): 1–3.

Edel, Leon. *Bloomsbury: A House of Lions*. Philadelphia: J.B. Lippincott, 1979.

Edel, Leon. *Literary Biography*. London: Rupert Hart-Davis, 1957.

Edel, Leon. 'The poetics of biography,' in Hilda Schiff (ed.), *Contemporary Approaches to English Studies*. London: Heinemann, 1977.

Edel, Leon. *Stuff of Sleep and Dreams: Experiments in Literary Psychology*. London: Chatto and Windus, 1982.

Edel, Leon. *Writing Lives: Principia Biographica* (1st edn). New York and London: W.W. Norton, 1984.

Ehrenzweig, Anton. *The Psychoanalysis of Artistic Vision and Hearing*. New York: George Braziller, 1956.

Ehrlich, Gretel. *A Match to the Heart*. London: Fourth Estate, 1995.

Eliade, Mircea. *Cosmos and History: The Myth of the Eternal Return*, trans. Willard R. Trask. New York: Harper & Row, 1959.

Eliade, Mircea. *Patterns in Comparative Religion*, trans. Rosemary Sheed. Cleveland: World Publishing Co., 1958; London: Sheed & Ward, 1958.

Eliade, Mircea. *The Quest: History and Meaning in Religion*. Chicago:

University of Chicago Press, 1969.

Eliade, Mircea. *The Sacred and the Profane: The Nature of Religion,* trans. Willard R. Trask. New York: Harcourt, Brace & World, 1959.

Ellis, Julian. *Fame and Failure: The Story of Certain Celebrities Who Rose Only to Fall.* Philadelphia: J.B. Lippincott Co., n.d.

Ellman, Richard. 'Freud as biographer,' *The American Scholar,* **53** (4) (1984): 465–78.

Ellman, Richard. *Golden Codgers: Biographical Speculations.* New York and London: Oxford University Press, 1973.

Ellman, Richard. *Literary Biography.* Oxford: Clarendon Press, 1971.

Emerson, Ralph Waldo. 'Self-reliance,' in Brooks Atkinson (ed.), *The Selected Writings of Ralph Waldo Emerson.* New York: The Modern Library, 1964, pp. 145–69.

Epstein, William H. *Recognizing Biography.* Philadelphia: University of Pennsylvania Press, 1987.

Erikson, Erik H. *Childhood and Society.* New York: W.W. Norton, 1963.

Erikson, Erik H. *Dimensions of a New Identity.* New York: W.W. Norton, 1974.

Erikson, Erik H. 'The Galilean sayings and the sense of "I",' *Yale Review,* **70** (3) (1981): 321–62.

Erikson, Erik H. *Gandhi's Truth: On the Origins of Militant Nonviolence.* New York: W.W. Norton, 1969.

Erikson, Erik H. 'Identity and the life cycle,' *Psychological Issues,* Vol. 1, No. 1. New York: International Universities Press, 1959.

Erikson, Erik H. *Identity, Youth and Crisis.* New York: W.W. Norton, 1968.

Erikson, Erik H. *Insight and Responsibility: Lectures on the Ethical Implications of Psychoanalytic Thought.* New York: W.W. Norton, 1964.

Erikson, Erik H. 'Jefferson Lectures, 1973,' in *The Congressional Record,* 2 May 1973: S8122.

Erikson, Erik H. *The Life Cycle Completed.* New York: W.W. Norton, 1982.

Erikson, Erik H. *Life History and the Historical Moment.* New York: W.W. Norton, 1975.

Erikson, Erik H. 'The ontogeny of ritualization in man,' in Rudolph M. Lowenstein (ed.), *Psychoanalysis: A General Psychology.* New York: International Universities Press, 1966.

Erikson, Erik H. 'Pseudospeciation and the nuclear age,' *Political Psychology,* **6** (2) (June 1985): 213–17.

Erikson, Erik H. 'Reflections on ethics and war,' *Yale Review* (Summer 1984): 481–6.

Erikson, Erik H. *Toys and Reasons: Stages in the Ritualization of Experience.* New York: W.W. Norton, 1977.

Erikson, Erik H. *Young Man Luther: A Study in Psychoanalysis and History.* New York: W.W. Norton, 1958.

Erikson, Erik H., Erikson, Joan M., and Kivnick, Helen Q. *Vital Involvement in Old Age: An Experience of Old Age in Our Time*. New York and London: W.W. Norton, 1986.

Fallaci, Oriana. *The Egotists: Sixteen Surprising Interviews*. Chicago: H. Regency Co., 1968.

Fish, Stanley. *Is There a Text in this Class? The Authority of Interpretive Communities*. Cambridge, MA: Harvard University Press, 1980.

Flanagan, Thomas. 'Problems of psychobiography,' *Queen's Quarterly*, **89** (3) (Autumn 1982): 576–610.

Focht, Mildred. *What Is Gestalt Theory?* New York: Columbia University Press, 1935.

Forbes, Malcolm S. (with Jeff Bloch). *They Went That-A-Way*. New York: Simon & Schuster, 1988.

Forster, E.M. *Two Cheers for Democracy* (1st US edn). New York: Harcourt, Brace, 1959.

Forster, E.M. 'English prose between 1918 and 1939,' in *Two Cheers for Democracy* (1st US edn). New York: Harcourt, Brace, 1959.

Foucault, Michel. 'Afterword: the subject and power,' in Hubert L. Dreyfus and Paul Rabinow (eds), *Michel Foucault: Beyond Structuralism and Hermeneutics* (2nd edn). Chicago: University of Chicago Press, 1983, pp. 208–26.

Fowler, Henry. *A Dictionary of Modern English Usage*. London: Oxford, 1954.

Frank, Arthur. *At the Will of the Body*. New York: Houghton Mifflin, 1992.

Frank, Gelya. 'Becoming the Other: empathy and biographical interpretation,' *Biography: An Interdisciplinary Quarterly*, **8** (3) (Summer 1985): 189–210.

Frank, Katherine. 'Writing lives: theory and practice in literary biography,' *Genre*, **13** (4) (Winter 1980): 499–516.

Franklin, Benjamin. *The Autobiography of Benjamin Franklin*. New York: Washington Square Press, 1940.

Freud, Sigmund. *Jokes and Their Relation to the Unconscious*, trans. and ed. James Strachey. New York: W.W. Norton, 1963.

Freud, Sigmund. *Leonardo da Vinci: A Study in Psychosexuality*, trans. A.A. Brill. New York: Random House, Vintage Books, 1947.

Friedman, Maurice. *Martin Buber's Life and Work: The Early Years, 1878–1923*. London: Search Press, 1982.

Friedson, Anthony M. (ed.). *New Directions in Biography: Essays*. Honolulu: published for the Biographical Research Center by the University of Hawaii Press, 1981.

Fromm, Gloria G. (ed.). *Essaying Biography: A Celebration for Leon Edel*. Honolulu: Published for the Biographical Research Center by the University of Hawaii Press, 1986.

Frye, Northrup. *Fables of Identity: Studies in Poetic Mythology*. New York: Harcourt, Brace & World, 1963.

Garis, Robert. 'Anti-literary biography,' *The Hudson Review*, **23** (1970): 143–53.

Garraty, John Arthur. 'The interrelations of psychology and biography,' *Psychological Bulletin*, **51** (1954): 569–82.

Garraty, John Arthur. *The Nature of Biography*. London: Jonathan Cape, 1958.

Gay, Peter. *Freud for Historians*. New York: Oxford University Press, 1985.

Geertz, Clifford. *Works and Lives: The Anthropologist as Author*. Stanford, CA: Stanford University Press, 1988.

George, Alexander L. and George, Julliete L. *Woodrow Wilson and Colonel House: A Personality Study*. New York: Dover Publications, 1956 and 1964.

Giddens, Anthony. *Modernity and Self-Identity: Self and Society in the Late Modern Age*. Stanford, CA: Stanford University Press, 1991.

Gifford, Edward S., Jr. *The Evil Eye: Studies in the Folklore of Vision*. New York: Macmillan, 1958.

Gilbert, Judson B. *Disease and Destiny: A Bibliography of Medical References to the Famous*. London: Dawsons of Pall Mall, 1962.

Gilmore, W. 'The method of psychohistory: an annotated bibliography,' *Psychohistory Review*, **5**(2) (1976): 4–33.

Gilmore, W. 'Paths recently crossed: alternatives to psychoanalytic psychohistory,' *Psychohistory Review*, **7** (3) (1979): 43–9; and **7** (4) (1979): 26–42.

Gittings, Robert. *The Nature of Biography*. Seattle: University of Washington Press, 1978.

Gobar, Ash. *Philosophic Foundations of Genetic Psychology and Gestalt Psychology*. The Hague: Martinus Nijhoff, 1968.

Golson, G. Barry (ed.). *The Playboy Interview* (1st edn). New York: Playboy Press, 1981.

Gombrich, E.H. *Art and Illusion*. Princeton: Bollingen Series, Princeton University Press, 1969.

Goodman, Jonathan. *Who He? Goodman's Dictionary of the Unknown Famous*. London: Buchan & Enright, 1984.

Gorman, Herbert. *A Victorian American: Henry Wadsworth Longfellow*. New York: George Doran, 1926.

Gould, Stephen Jay. 'A biological comment on Erikson's notion of pseudospeciation,' *Yale Review* (Summer 1984): 487–90.

Gransden, Antonia. 'Anglo Saxon sacred biography,' in *Historical Writing in England*. London: n.p., 1974.

Greenacre, Phyllis. 'The eye motif in delusion and fantasy,' *American Journal of Psychiatry*, **25** (1938): 297–334.

Habermas, Jurgen. *Knowledge and Human Interests*, trans. J. Shapiro. Boston: Beacon Press, 1971.

Hadas, Moses and Smith, Morton. *Heroes and Gods: Spiritual Biographies in Antiquity*. New York: Harper & Row, 1965.

Hannah, Barbara. *Jung: His Life and Work: A Biographical Memoir*. New

York: G.P. Putnam's Sons, 1976.

Harris, Thomas. *I'm OK – You're OK*. New York: Avon, 1969.

Hart, Henry. 'The eye in symbol and symptom,' *The Psychoanalytic Review*, **36** (1949): 1–21.

Havelock, Ellis. *Views and Reasons*. London: Harnsworth, 1932.

Hayman, Ronald. *Nietzsche: A Critical Life*. Harmondsworth: Penguin, 1982.

Heffernan, Thomas J. *Sacred Biography: Saints and Their Biographers in the Middle Ages*. New York: Oxford University Press, 1988.

Heilbrun, Carolyn. *Writing a Woman's Life* (1st edn). New York: Norton, 1988.

Henle, Mary (ed.). *The Selected Papers of Wolfgang Kohler*. New York: Liveright, 1971.

Hermansen, Marcia K. 'Survey article: interdisciplinary approaches to Islamic biographical materials,' *Religion*, **18** (1988): 163–82.

Hillman, James. *The Myth of Analysis: Three Essays on Archetypal Analysis*. New York: Harper & Row, 1972.

Hodges, H.A. *The Philosophy of Wilhelm Dilthey*. London: Routledge & Kegan Paul, 1952.

Hodges, H.A. *Wilhelm Dilthey: An Introduction*. London: Routledge & Kegan Paul, 1944.

Hoffman, Louise E. 'Psychobiography, 1900–1930: some reconsiderations,' *Biography: An Interdisciplinary Quarterly*, **7** (4) (1984): 341–51.

Holland, Norman H. *The Dynamic of Literary Response*. New York: Oxford University Press, 1964.

Holmes, Richard. *Footsteps: Adventures of a Romantic Biographer*. London: Hodder & Stoughton, 1985; 1st US edn, New York: Viking, 1985.

Holroyd, Michael. *Lytton Strachey: A Biography*. Baltimore: Penguin, 1971.

Holroyd, Michael (ed.). *Lytton Strachey by Himself: A Self-Portrait*. New York: Holt, Rinehart and Winston, 1971.

Homans, Peter. *The Ability to Mourn: Disillusionment and the Social Origins of Psychoanalysis*. Chicago: University of Chicago Press, 1989.

Homans, Peter (ed.). *Childhood and Selfhood: Essays on Tradition, Religion and Modernity in the Psychology of Erik H. Erikson*. Lewisburg, PA: Bucknell University Press; London: Associated University Presses, 1978.

Homans, Peter. *Theology after Freud*. Indianapolis: Bobbs-Merrill, 1970.

Honan, Park. 'The theory of biography,' *Novel*, **13** (1) (1979): 109–20.

Hood, Edwin Paxton. *The Uses of Biography: Romantic, Philosophic and Didactic*. London: Partridge and Oakley, 1852.

Hood, Lynley. *Who Is Sylvia?: The Diary of a Biography*. Dunedin: John McIndoe Ltd, 1990.

Hoover, Dwight W. and Koumoulides, John T.A. (eds). *Focus on Biography*. Muncie, IN: Department of History, Ball State University, 1975.

Hughes, H. Stuart. *History as Art and as Science.* New York: Harper & Row, 1964.

Hutch, Richard A. 'Biographies of the Buddha,' *Asia Journal of Theology,* **2** (1988): 440–9.

Hutch, Richard A. 'Biography as a reliquary,' *Soundings: An Interdisciplinary Journal,* **76** (4) (Winter 1993): 467–85.

Hutch, Richard A. 'Biography, individuality and the study of religion,' *Religious Studies,* **23** (1987): 509–22.

Hutch, Richard A. 'Called home: the creation of family life,' *Journal of Religion and Health,* **3** (1992): 221–36.

Hutch, Richard A. *Emerson's Optics: Biographical Process and the Dawn of Religious Leadership.* Washington, DC: University Press of America, 1983.

Hutch, Richard A. 'Explorations in character: Gamaliel Bradford and Henry Murray as psychobiographers,' *Biography: An Interdisciplinary Quarterly,* **4** (4) (1981): 312–25.

Hutch, Richard A. 'Helena Blavatsky unveiled,' *Journal of Religious History,* **11** (1980): 320–41.

Hutch, Richard A. 'Mircea Eliade and orthodoxy,' *Phronema,* **2** (1987): 55–67.

Hutch, Richard A. 'Over my dead body: a "common sense" test of saintliness,' in Donald Capps and Janet L. Jacobs (eds), *The Struggle for Life: A Companion to William James's The Varieties of Religious Experience.* West Lafayette, IN: Society for the Scientific Study of Religion Monograph Series No. 9, 1995, pp. 147–62.

Hutch, Richard A. 'Reading lives to live: mortality, introspection and the soteriological impulse,' *Biography: An Interdisciplinary Quarterly,* **17** (2) (Spring 1994): 125–43.

Hutch, Richard A. *Religious Leadership: Personality, History and Sacred Authority.* Vol. 10. Toronto Studies in Religion Series. Donald Wiebe, General Editor. New York: Peter Lang, 1991.

Hutch, Richard A. 'Strategic irony and Lytton Strachey's contribution to biography,' *Biography: An Interdisciplinary Quarterly,* **11** (1) (1988): 1–15.

Hutch, Richard A. 'Types of women religious leaders,' *Religion,* **14** (1984): 155–73.

Hutch, Richard A. 'Writing lives in psychoanalytic silence,' *Religious Studies Review,* **22** (2) (April 1996): 114–18.

Jaffé, Aneila. *From the Life and Work of C.G. Jung,* trans. R.F.C. Hull. New York and London: Harper & Row, 1971.

Jaffe, Daniel S. 'Empathy, counteridentification, countertransference: a review, with some personal perspectives on the "Analytic Instrument",' *Psychoanalytic Quarterly,* **55** (1986): 215–43.

James, William. *The Varieties of Religious Experience: A Study in Human Nature.* London: Crowell-Collier, 1961.

Johnson, Allen and Malone, Dumas (eds). *Dictionary of American Biography*, 20 vols. New York: Charles Scribner's, 1930.

Johnson, Dorothy and Turner, R.T. *The Bedside Book of Bastards*. New York: McGraw-Hill, 1973.

Johnson, Mark. *The Body in the Mind: The Bodily Basis of Meaning, Imagination, and Reason.* Chicago and London: University of Chicago Press, 1987.

Johnson, Mark. *Moral Imagination: Implications of Cognitive Science for Ethics.* Chicago: University of Chicago Press, 1993.

Johnson, Samuel. *Idler*, **84** (24 November 1795).

Johnston, James C. *Biography: The Literature of Personality*. Introduction by Gamaliel Bradford. New York and London: The Century Co., 1927.

Jones, Percy Mansell. *French Introspectives: From Montaigne to Andre Gide.* Port Washington, NY: Kennikat Press, 1970.

Kallich, Martin. 'Psychoanalysis, sexuality, and Lytton Strachey's theory of biography,' *American Imago*, **15** (4) (1958): 331–70.

Kallich, Martin. *The Psychological Milieu of Lytton Strachey*. New York: Bookman Associates, 1961.

Keenan, Brian. *An Evil Cradling*. London: Hutchinson, 1993.

Kendall, Paul Murray. *The Art of Biography*. London: G. Allen & Unwin, 1965; (1st edn) New York: W.W. Norton, 1965.

Kendall, Paul Murray. *The Art of Biography*. New Prologue by Stephen B. Oates. New York: W.W. Norton, 1985.

Keyes, C. 'Charisma: from social life to sacred biography,' *Journal of the American Academy of Religion*, **48** (1982): 1–22.

Kieckhefer, Richard and Bond, George (eds). *Sainthood: Its Manifestations in World Religions*. Berkeley and London: University of California Press, 1988.

Kierkegaard, Søren. *Repetition: An Essay in Experimental Psychology*, trans. Walter Lowrie. New York: Harper Torchbook, 1964.

Kleinman, A. *The Illness Narratives: Suffering, Healing and the Human Condition*. New York: Basic Books, 1988.

Knox, Norman. *The Word Irony and Its Context*. Durham, NC: Duke University Press, 1961.

Koffka, Kurt. 'Beiträge zur Psychologie der Gestalt und Bewegungs-erlebnisse,' *Zeitschrift für Psychologie*, **72** (1915): 193–296.

Koffka, Kurt. 'Experimental Untersuchunger zur Lehre von Rhythmus,' *Zeitschrift für Psychologie*, **52** (1909): 4–109.

Koffka, Kurt. *Principles of Gestalt Psychology*. New York: Harcourt, 1935.

Koffka, Kurt. 'Psychologie der Wahrnehmung,' *Geisteswiss*, **1** (1914).

Kohler, Wolfgang. 'Akustiche Untersuchungen,' *Zeitschrift für Psychologie* (1910–15): **54**: 241–89, **58**: 59–140, **64**: 92–105, **72**: 1–192.

Kohler, Wolfgang. 'Uberunbemerkte Empfindungen und Urteilstäuschun-gen,' *Zeitschrift für Psychologie*, **66** (1913): 51–80.

Kohut, Heinz. 'The future of psychoanalysis,' *Search*, **2** (n.d.): 663–84.

Kohut, Heinz. *How Does Analysis Cure?* Chicago: University of Chicago Press, 1984.

Kohut, Heinz. 'Introspection, empathy, and the semicircle of mental health,' *International Journal of Psychoanalysis*, **63** (1982): 395–408.

Kohut, Heinz. 'The psychoanalyst in the community of scholars,' *Search*, **2** (n.d.): 685–724.

Kramer, Hilton. 'The lesson of the master,' *Time*, 22 August 1977.

Kramer, Hilton. 'Raw bones, fire and patience,' *Time*, 21 February 1983.

Kramer, Hilton. 'Writing writers' lives,' *New York Times Book Review*, 8 May 1977.

Kris, Ernst. 'The image of the artist,' in *Psychoanalytic Explorations in Art*. New York: International Universities Press, 1952, pp. 64–8.

Lakoff, George and Johnson, Mark. *Metaphors We Live By*. Chicago: University of Chicago Press, 1980.

Lane, Michael. *Structuralism*. London: Jonathan Cape, 1970.

Langness, Lewis L. and Frank, Gelya. *Lives: An Anthropological Approach to Biography*. Novato, CA: Chandler & Sharp, 1981.

Lasswell, Harold. *Power and Personality*. New York: W.W. Norton, 1948.

Leibowitz, Herbert A. *Fabricating Lives: Explorations in American Autobiography* (1st edn). New York: Knopf Random House, 1989.

Lerner, Daniel (ed.). *Evidence and Inference*. Glencoe, IL: Free Press, 1959.

Levin, David. *Exemplary Elders*. Athens and London: University of Georgia Press, 1990.

Levin, David. *History as Romantic Art*. New York: Harcourt, Brace, & World, 1959.

Levin, David. *In Defense of Historical Literature*. New York: Hill & Wang, 1967.

Lionnet, Francoise. *Autobiographical Voices: Race, Gender, Self-Portraiture*. Ithaca, NY: Cornell University Press, 1989.

Lomask, Milton. *The Biographer's Craft* (1st edn). New York: Harper & Row, 1986.

Lowrie, Walter. *A Short Life of Kierkegaard*. Princeton: Princeton University Press, 1946.

Lucas, Eric (ed.). *What Is Greatness?* London: Oxford University Press, 1967.

Lyons, Joseph. *Ecology of the Body: Styles of Behavior in Human Life*. Durham, NC: Duke University Press, 1987.

McAdams, Dan P. and Ochberg, Richard L. (eds). *Psychobiography and Life Narratives*. Durham, NC, and London: Duke University Press, 1988.

MacCarthy, Mary. *Handicaps: Six Studies*. Freeport, NY: Books for Libraries Press Inc., 1936; reprinted 1967.

MacDougall, Curtis, D. *Greater Dead than Alive*. Washington, DC: Public Affairs Press, 1963.

MacIntyre, Alasdair. *After Virtue: A Study in Moral Philosophy*. South Bend, IN: University of Notre Dame Press, 1981.

MacIntyre, Alasdair. *Three Rival Versions of Moral Philosophy*. South Bend, IN: University of Notre Dame Press, 1990.

McGuire, William and Hull, R.F.C. *C.G. Jung Speaking: Interviews and Encounters*. Princeton: Princeton University Press, 1977. Bollingen Series XCVII.

McKnight, Edgar. *Postmodern Use of the Bible: The Emergence of Reader-oriented Criticism*. Nashville, TN: Abingdon, 1988.

McLaurin, Charles. *Post-mortems of Mere Mortals: Essays Historical and Medical*. Garden City, NY: Doubleday Doran & Co., 1930.

Mailer, Norman. *Marilyn: A Biography*. New York: Grosset & Dunlap, 1973.

Martinello, Marian L. *The Search for Emma's Story: A Model for Humanities Detective Work*. Fort Worth, TX: Texas Christian University Press, 1987.

Maurois, Andre. *Aspects of Biography*, trans. S.C. Roberts. New York: Ungar, 1966.

Mauss, Marcel. *The Gift: Forms and Functions of Exchange in Archaic Societies*, trans. Ian Cunnison. New York and London: W.W. Norton, 1967.

Mazlish, Bruce (ed.). *Psychoanalysis and History*. New York: Grosset & Dunlap, 1971.

Merrill, Dana K. *American Biography: Its Theory and Practice*. Portland, ME: Bowker Press, 1957.

Meyer, Leonard. *Emotion and Meaning in Music*. Chicago: University of Chicago Press, 1956.

Meyers, Jeffrey. *The Craft of Literary Biography* (1st US edn). New York: Schocken Books, 1985.

Momigliano, Arnaldo. *The Development of Greek Biography*. Cambridge, MA: Harvard University Press, 1971.

Moraitis, George and Pollock, George H. (eds). *Psychoanalytic Studies of Biography*. Madison, CT: International Universities Press, 1987. (Emotions and Behavior Monographs, no. 4).

Moynihan, Berkeley G.A. *Truants: The Story of Some Who Deserted Medicine But Triumphed*. Cambridge: Cambridge University Press, 1937.

Mucchielli, Roger. *An Introduction to Structural Psychology*, trans. Charles Lam Markmann. New York: Funk & Wagnalls, 1970.

Mudrick, Marvin. *Nobody Here But Us Chickens*. New Haven: Ticknor & Fields, 1981.

Muecke, Douglas. *The Compass of Irony*. London: Methuen, 1969.

Muecke, Douglas. *Irony: The Critical Idiom*. London: Methuen, 1970.

Muecke, Douglas. *Irony and the Ironic: The Critical Idiom*. London: Methuen, 1982.

Muller-Volmer, Kurt. *Towards a Phenomenological Theory of Literature: A Study of Wilhelm Dilthey's 'Poetik'*. The Hague: Mouton Press, 1963.

Murphy, Robert. *The Body Silent.* New York: W.W. Norton, 1990.

Murray, Henry A. *Explorations in Personality.* New York: Oxford University Press, 1938.

Murray, Henry A. *Manual of the Thematic Apperception Test.* Cambridge, MA: Harvard University Press, 1943.

Murray, Henry A. 'What should psychologists do about psychoanalysis?,' *Journal of Abnormal and Social Psychology,* **35** (1940): 152–3.

Murray, Henry A. and Kluckhohn, C. 'Outline of a conception of personality,' in H.A. Murray, D. Schneider, and C. Kluckhohn (eds), *Personality in Nature, Society, and Culture.* New York: Alfred Knopf, 1953.

Myers, Jay Arthur. *Fighters of Fate: A Story of Men and Women Who Have Achieved Greatly Despite the Handicaps of the Great White Plague,* Introduction by Charles H. Mayo. Freeport, NY: Books for Libraries Press, 1927; reprinted 1969.

Nadel, Ira Bruce. *Biography: Fiction, Fact, and Form.* New York: St Martin's Press, 1984.

Nadel, Ira Bruce. 'Lytton Strachey's "subtler strategy": metaphor in *Eminent Victorians,*' *Prose Studies,* **4** (2) (1981): 146–52.

Nagourney, Peter. 'The basic assumptions of literary biography,' *Biography: An Interdisciplinary Quarterly,* **1** (Spring 1978): 86–104.

Newman, John Henry. *Apologia Pro Vita Sua,* ed. Charles F. Harrold. New York: Longmans, Green & Co., 1947.

Newman, John Henry. *Letters and Correspondence of John Henry Newman,* Vol. I, ed. Anne Mozley. London: Longmans, Green & Co., 1890.

Nicholson, Margaret E. *People in Books: A Selective Guide to Biographical Literature Arranged by Vocations and Other Fields of Reader Interest.* New York: H.W. Wilson, 1969.

Nicolson, Harold. *The Development of English Biography* (1928). Reprinted London: Hogarth Press, 1968.

Nicolson, Harold. 'The practice of biography,' *American Scholar,* **23** (Spring 1954): 153–61.

Norris, Christopher. *Deconstruction: Theory and Practice.* London: Methuen, 1982.

Norton, David L. *Personal Destinies: A Philosophy of Ethical Individualism.* Princeton: Princeton University Press, 1976.

Novak, Michael. *Ascent of the Mountain, Flight of the Dove: An Invitation to Religious Studies.* New York: Harper & Row, 1971.

Novarr, David. *The Lines of Life: Theories of Biography, 1880–1970.* West Lafayette, IN: Purdue University Press, 1986.

Oates, Stephen B. (ed.). *Biography as High Adventure: Life-Writers Speak on Their Art.* Amherst, MA: University of Massachusetts Press, 1986.

O'Keefe, Daniel. *Stolen Lightning: The Social Theory of Magic.* Oxford: Martin Robertson, 1982.

O'Neill, Edward H. *A History of American Biography, 1800–1935*. New York: Russell, 1968.

Olney, James. *Metaphors of Self: The Meaning of Autobiography*. Princeton: Princeton University Press, 1972.

Olney, James (ed.). *Studies in Autobiography*. New York and Oxford: Oxford University Press, 1988.

Otto, Rudolf. *The Idea of the Holy*, trans. John W. Harvey. New York: Oxford University Press, 1923.

Overend, Eileen. 'Attitude, drama, and role in Strachey's Elizabeth and Essex,' *Biography: An Interdisciplinary Quarterly*, 7 (2) (Spring 1984), 158–68.

Pachter, Marc (ed.). *Telling Lives: The Biographer's Art* (by Leon Edel). Philadelphia: University of Pennsylvania Press, 1981.

Pastore, Nicholas. *Selective History of Theories of Visual Perception: 1650–1950*. New York: Oxford University Press, 1971.

Paul, Angus. 'Biography is one sign of what may be new life in the art of recounting lives,' *Chronicle of Higher Education*, 24 March 1982.

Petermann, Bruno. *The Gestalt Theory and the Problem of Configuration*. London: Routledge & Kegan Paul, 1932.

Petrie, Dennis. *Ultimately Fiction: Design in Modern American Literary Biography*. West Lafayette, IN: Purdue University Press, 1981.

Pickering George White. *Creative Malady: Illness in the Lives and Minds of Charles Darwin*. London: Allen & Unwin, 1974.

Playboy Interviews. Selected by the Editors of *Playboy* (1st edn). Chicago: Playboy Press, 1967.

Pommer, Henry. *Emerson's First Marriage*. Carbondale, IL: Southern Illinois University Press, 1967.

Porte, Joel. *Representative Man: Ralph Waldo Emerson in His Time*. New York: Oxford University Press, 1979.

Post, Stephen L. and Miller, Jule P., Jr. 'Apprehensions of empathy,' in Joseph Lichtenberg, Melvin Bornstein, and Donald Silver (eds), *Empathy* (2 vols). Hillsdale, NJ: Analytic Press, 1984.

Postman, Neil. *The Disappearance of Childhood*. New York: Vintage Books, 1982; 1994.

Postman, Neil. *Technopoly: The Surrender of Culture to Technology*. New York: Vintage Books, 1992.

Powers, Lyall (ed.). *Leon Edel and Literary Art*. Ann Arbor, MI: UMI Research Press, 1988.

Prochnick, Leon. *Endings: Death, Glorious and Otherwise, as Faced by Ten Outstanding Figures of Our Times*. New York: Crown Publishers, 1980.

Rank, Otto. *The Myth of the Birth of the Hero and Other Essays*, ed. Philip Freund. New York: Vintage, 1964.

Reat, N. Ross and Perry, Edmund. *A World Theology: The Central Spiritual Reality of Humankind*. New York: Cambridge University Press, 1991.

Reid, B.L. *Necessary Lives: Biographical Reflections*. Columbia: University of Missouri Press, 1990.

Rewa, Michael. *Reborn as Meaning: Panegyrical Biography from Isocrates to Walton*. Washington, DC: University Press of America, 1983.

Reynolds, Frank E. and Capps, Donald E. (eds). *The Biographical Process: Studies in the History and Psychology of Religion*. The Hague: Mouton, 1976.

Richards, I.A. *The Philosophy of Rhetoric*. New York: Oxford University Press, 1936.

Rickards, Maurice. *Where They Lived in London*. London: David & Charles, 1972.

Rousselle, Aline. *Porneia: On Desire and the Body in Antiquity*, trans. Felicia Pheasant. New York: Basil Blackwell, 1988.

Ruddick, Sarah. *Maternal Thinking: Toward a Politics of Peace*. Boston: Beacon Press, 1989.

Runyan, William McKinley. 'Alternative accounts of lives: an argument for epistemological relativism,' *Biography: An Interdisciplinary Quarterly*, 3 (3) (Summer 1980): 209–24.

Runyan, William McKinley. *Life Histories and Psychobiography: Explorations in Theory and Method*. New York: Oxford University Press, 1982.

Runyan, William McKinley. 'The psychobiography debate: an analytical review,' in L. Wheeler (ed.), *Review of Personality and Social Psychology*, Vol. 3. Beverly Hills, CA: Sage, 1982.

Rusk, Ralph L. *The Life of Ralph Waldo Emerson*. New York: Columbia University Press, 1949.

Rustow, Dankwart (ed.). *Philosophers and Kings: Studies in Leadership*. New York: George Braziller, 1970.

Said, Edward W. *Beginnings: Intention and Method*. New York: Basic Books, 1975.

Sainte-Beuve, Charles Augustin. *Portraits of the Eighteenth Century: Historic and Literary*, Introduction by Edmond Scherer. New York and London: G.P. Putnam's Sons, 1905.

Scarry, Elaine. *The Body in Pain: The Making and Unmaking of the World*. New York and Oxford: Oxford University Press, 1985.

Schabert, Ina. 'Fictional biography, factual biography, and their contaminations,' *Biography: An Interdisciplinary Quarterly*, 5 (1) (Winter 1982): 1–16.

Schachtel, Ernest G. *Experiential Foundations of Rorschach's Test*. New York: Basic Books, 1966.

Schachtel, Ernest G. *Metamorphosis*. New York: Basic Books, 1959.

Schwartz, Murray. 'The literary use of transference,' *Psychoanalysis and Contemporary Culture*, 5 (1982): 35–44.

Seldes, George. *Witness to a Century: Encounters with the Noted, the Notorious, and the Three SOB's* (1st edn). New York: Ballantine Books, 1987.

Shaner, Edward. 'Biographies of the Buddha,' *Philosophy East and West*, **37** (3) (1987): 306–22.

Shelston, Alan. *Biography*. The Critical Idiom Series, 34. London: Methuen, 1977.

Shilling, Chris. *The Body and Social Theory*. London: Sage/Theory, Culture and Society, 1993.

Siebenschuh, William R. *Fictional Techniques and Factual Works*. Athens, GA: University of Georgia Press, 1983.

Sigourney, Lydia H. *Examples of Life and Death*. New York: Scribner, 1852.

Simpson, Donald H. *Biography Catalogue of the Library of the Royal Commonwealth Society*. London: Royal Commonwealth Society, 1961.

Slocum, Robert B. (ed.). *Biographical Dictionaries and Related Works: An International Bibliography of Approximately 16,000 Collective Biographies*. Detroit: Gale Research Co., 1986.

Smith, Barbara H. *On the Margins of Discourses: The Relation of Literature to Language*. Chicago: University of Chicago Press, 1978.

Smith, David L. 'Emerson and deconstruction: the end(s) of scholarship,' *Soundings*, **67** (4) (Winter 1984): 379–98.

Smith, Edward H. *Mysteries of the Missing*. New York: L. McVeagh/The Dial Press, 1927.

Smith, Page. *The Historian and History*. New York: Vintage Random, 1964.

'Special Issue: Erik H. Erikson,' *The Psychohistory Review: Studies of Motivation in History and Culture*, **22** (1) (Fall 1993).

Spelman, Elizabeth V. *Inessential Woman: Problems of Exclusion in Feminist Thought*. Boston: Beacon Press, 1988.

Stanfield, James Field. *An Essay on the Study and Composition of Biography*. Sunderland: George Garbutt, 1813.

Stern, Madaleine B. *A Phrenological Dictionary of Nineteenth-Century Americans*. Westport, CT: Greenwood Press, 1982.

Stern, Paul J. *C.G. Jung: The Haunted Prophet*. New York: George Braziller, 1976.

Stone, Lawrence. 'Prosopography,' *Daedalus*, (Winter 1971): 46–9.

Strachey, Lytton. 'Froude,' in *Biographical Essays*. New York: Harcourt, Brace, 1969.

Strachey, Lytton. *Queen Victoria*. New York: Blue Ribbon Books, 1921.

Strauss, Anselm L. *Mirrors and Masks: The Search for Identity*. Berkeley: The Sociology Press of the University of California, 1969.

Strout, Cushing. *The Veracious Imagination: Essays on American History, Literature, and Biography*. Middletown, CT: Wesleyan University Press, 1981.

Strozier, Charles B. 'Heinz Kohut and the historical imagination,' in A. Goldberg (ed.), *Advances in Self Psychology*. New York: International Universities Press, 1980.

Stumpf, Carl. *Erscheinunger und Psychische Funktionen*. Berlin: Abhdlg Preuss, 1906.

Suleiman, Susan Rubin (ed.). *The Female Body in Western Culture: Contemporary Perspectives*. Cambridge, MA, and London: Harvard University Press, 1986.

Tippler, Frank. *The Physics of Immortality: Modern Cosmology, God, and the Resurrection of the Dead*. New York: Doubleday, 1994.

Todorov, Tzvetan. *The Poetics of Prose*, trans. Richard Howard. Ithaca, NY: Cornell University Press, 1917; 1977.

Twain, Mark. *Complete Works* (Hillcrest, 5th edn). New York: Harper, 1913.

Tyrrell, R. Emmett. *Public Nuisances*. New York: Basic Books, 1979.

Updike, John. *Self-Consciousness*. New York: Fawcett Crest, 1989.

US Library of Congress. General Reference and Bibliography Division. *Biographical Sources for the United States*. Compiled by Jane Kline. Washington, DC, 1961.

Van der Post, Laurens. *Jung and the Story of Our Time*. New York: Random House, 1975.

Veninga, James F. *The Biographer's Gift: Life Histories and Humanism* (1st edn). College Station, TX: Published for the Texas Committee for the Humanities by Texas A & M University Press, 1983.

Von Laue, Theodore H. *Leopold Ranke: The Formative Years*. Princeton: Princeton University Press, 1950.

Wach, Joachim. *Das Verstehen: Grundzüge einer Geschicte der Hermeneutischen Theorie im 19. Jahrhundert* (3 Vols). Tübingen: J.C.B. Mohr Verlag, 1926–33.

Wagenknecht, Edward. *Ralph Waldo Emerson: Portrait of a Balanced Soul*. New York: Oxford University Press, 1974.

Waghorne, Joanne P. 'The case of the missing autobiography,' *Journal of the American Academy of Religion*, **49** (1981): 589–603.

Wain, John. *Dear Shadows: Portraits from Memory*. London: John Murray, 1986.

Walter, James (ed.). *Reading Life Histories: Griffith Papers on Biography*. Nathan, Queensland: Institute for Modern Biography, 1981.

Wehr, Gerhard. *Jung: A Biography*, trans. David M. Weeks. Boston: Shambhala; New York: Random House, 1987. Original edition: *Carl Gustav Jung: Leben, Werk, Wirkung*. Munich: Kösel-Verlag Gmbtt und Co., 1985.

Wehr, Gerhard. *Portrait of Jung: An Illustrated Biography*, trans. W.A. Hargreaves. New York: Herder and Herder, 1971. Original edition: *C.G. Jung in Selbstzeugnissen und Bilddokumenten*. Reinbek bei Hamburg: Rowohlt Taschenbuch Verlag GmbH, 1969.

Weintraub, Karl. 'Autobiography and historical consciousness,' *Critical Inquiry*, **1** (4) (June 1975): 821–48.

Weintraub, Karl. *The Value of the Individual*. Chicago: University of Chicago Press, 1978.

Wellek, Rene and Warren, Austin. 'Literature and biography,' in *Theory of Literature* (3rd edn). New York: Harcourt, 1978.

Wertheimer, Max. 'Experimentelle Studien über das Sehen von Bewegung,' *Zeitschrift für Psychologie*, **11** (1925): 78–99.

Wertheimer, Max. 'Gestalt theory,' *Social Research*, **11** (1925): 78–99.

Wertheimer, Max. 'Über das Denken der Naturvölker,' *Zeitschrift für Psychologie*, **61** (1912).

Wertheimer, Max. 'Unterschungen zur Lehre von der Gestalt; I Prinzipielle Demerkungen,' *Psychologische Forschung*, **1** (1922): 47–58.

Wheeler, David. *Domestick Privacies: Samuel Johnson and the Art of Biography*. Lexington, KY: University Press of Kentucky, 1987.

Wheelwright, Philip. *Metaphor and Reality*. Bloomington: Indiana University Press, 1962.

White, Hayden. *Tropics of Discourse: Essays in Cultural Criticism*. Baltimore: Johns Hopkins University Press, 1978.

White, Robert W. *Lives in Progress*. New York: Holt, Rinehart and Winston, 1966.

White, Robert W. (ed.). *The Study of Lives: Essays on Personality in Honor of Henry A. Murray*. Chicago: Aldine Atherton Press, 1963.

Whittemore, Reed. *Pure Lives: The Early Biographers*. Baltimore: Johns Hopkins University Press, 1988.

Whittemore, Reed. *Whole Lives: Shapers of Modern Biography*. Baltimore: Johns Hopkins University Press, 1989.

Williams, Michael A. (ed.). *Charisma and Sacred Biography*. Journal of the American Academy of Religion Thematic Studies, **48** (3 and 4). Atlanta: Scholars Press, 1982.

Winnicott, Donald W. Review of Jung's *Memories, Dreams, Reflections*, *International Journal of Psychoanalysis*, **45** (1964): 450–5.

Winslow, Donald J. *Life-Writing: A Glossary of Terms in Biography, Autobiography, and Related Forms*. Honolulu: Published for the Biographical Research Center by the University Press of Hawaii, 1980.

Woolf, Virginia. 'The art of biography,' *Granite and Rainbow*, Part Two. New York: Harcourt, 1958.

Wyschogrod, Edith. *Saints and Postmodernism: Revisioning Moral Philosophy*. Chicago: University of Chicago Press, 1990.

Yelton, Donald C. *Brief American Lives: Four Studies in Collective Biography*. Metuchen, NJ: Sacrecrow Press, 1978.

Zinsser, William (ed.). *Extraordinary Lives: The Art and Craft of American Biography*. New York: American Heritage, 1986.

Zinsser, William (ed.). *Spiritual Quests: The Art and Craft of Religious Writing*. Boston: Houghton Mifflin, 1988.

Zipf, George K. *The Psycho-biology of Language: An Introduction to Dynamic Philology*. Cambridge, MA: MIT Press, 1965.

Index